AAT

Financial Statements of Limited Companies

Level 4

Professional Diploma in Accounting

Question Bank

Third edition 2018

ISBN 9781 5097 1877 1

British Library Cataloguing-in-Publication Data

A catalogue record for this book is available from the British Library

Published by

BPP Learning Media Ltd
BPP House, Aldine Place
142-144 Uxbridge Road
London W12 8AA

www.bpp.com/learningmedia

Printed in the United Kingdom

Your learning materials, published by BPP Learning Media Ltd, are printed on paper obtained from traceable sustainable sources.

BPP
LEARNING MEDIA

Contents

*Note. This chapter provides tasks on the material in Chapter 3 *The statement of financial position*, Chapter 4 *The statements of financial performance* and Chapter 5 *The statement of cash flows*. These topics are highly integrated and tested together, so the tasks are combined in one chapter.

Introduction

This is BPP Learning Media's AAT Question Bank for *Financial Statements of Limited Companies*. It is part of a suite of ground-breaking resources produced by BPP Learning Media for AAT assessments.

This Question Bank has been written in conjunction with the BPP Course Book, and has been carefully designed to enable students to practise all of the learning outcomes and assessment criteria for the units that make up *Financial Statements of Limited Companies*. It is fully up to date as at April 2018 and reflects both the AAT's qualification specification and the sample assessment provided by the AAT.

This Question Bank contains these key features:

- Tasks corresponding to each chapter of the Course Book. Some tasks are designed for learning purposes, others are of assessment standard

- AAT's AQ2016 sample assessment 1 and answers for *Financial Statements of Limited Companies* and further BPP practice assessments

The emphasis in all tasks and assessments is on the practical application of the skills acquired.

VAT

You may find tasks in this Question Bank that need you to calculate or be aware of a rate of VAT. This is stated at 20% in these examples and questions.

Approaching the assessment

When you sit the assessment it is very important that you follow the on screen instructions. This means you need to carefully read the instructions, both on the introduction screens and during specific tasks.

When you access the assessment you should be presented with an introductory screen with information similar to that shown below (taken from the introductory screen from one of the AAT's AQ2016 sample assessment for *Financial Statements of Limited Companies.*

aat | Assessment: Financial Statements of Limited Companies (... | Membership No.: Sample Candidate Ref | Finish
Introduction | Progress: 0%

We have provided this sample assessment to help you familiarise yourself with our e-assessment environment. It is designed to demonstrate as many of the question types that you may find in a live assessment as possible. It is not designed to be used on its own to determine whether you are ready for a live assessment.

At the end of this sample assessment you will receive an immediate assessment result. This will only take into account your responses to tasks 1, 2, 5, 6 and 7, as these are the elements of the assessment that are computer marked. In the live assessment, your responses to tasks 3, 4 and 8 will be human marked.

Assessment information:

You have **2 hours and 30 minutes** to complete this sample assessment.

This assessment contains 8 tasks and you should attempt to complete **every** task.
Read every task carefully to make sure you understand what is required.

In tasks 1, 2 and 6 you may be presented with tables that can be used for your workings for your proformas. You don't have to use the workings tables to achieve full marks in these tasks, but any data entered into the workings tables will be taken into consideration if you make errors in the proforma.

Tasks 3, 4 and 8 require extended writing as part of your response to the questions. You should make sure you allow adequate time to complete these tasks.

Where the date is relevant, it is given in the task data.
Both minus signs and brackets can be used to indicate negative numbers **unless** task instructions say otherwise.

You must use a full stop to indicate a decimal point. For example, write 100.57 NOT 100,57 or 100 57
You may use a comma to indicate a number in the thousands, but you don't have to. For example 10000 and 10,000 are both acceptable.

When you access the assessment you should be presented with an introductory screen with information similar to that shown below (taken from the introductory screen from one of the AAT's AQ2016 sample assessment for *Financial Statements of Limited Companies.*

We have provided the following assessment to help you familiarise yourself with AAT's e-assessment environment. It is designed to demonstrate as many as possible of the question types that you may find in a live assessment. It is not designed to be used on its own to determine whether you are ready for a live assessment.

This assessment contains 8 tasks and you should therefore attempt and aim to complete EVERY task.
Each task is independent. You will not need to refer to your answers to previous tasks.
Read every task carefully to make sure you understand what is required.

Please note that in this sample assessment only your responses to tasks 1, 2, 5, 6 and 7 will be marked.
The equivalents of tasks 3, 4 and 8 will be human marked in the live assessment.

In tasks 1, 2 and 6 you will see there are tables that can be used as workings for your proformas.
You don't have to use the workings to achieve full marks on the task, but data entered into the workings tables will be taken into consideration if you make errors in the proforma.

Where the date is relevant, it is given in the task data.

Both minus signs and brackets can be used to indicate negative numbers UNLESS task instructions say otherwise.

You must use a full stop to indicate a decimal point.
For example, write 100.57 NOT 100,57 or 100 57

You may use a comma to indicate a number in the thousands, but you don't have to.
For example, 10000 and 10,000 are both OK.

Other indicators are not compatible with the computer-marked system.

BPP
LEARNING MEDIA

The actual instructions will vary depending on the subject you are studying for. It is very important you read the instructions on the introductory screen and apply them in the assessment. You don't want to lose marks when you know the correct answer just because you have not entered it in the right format.

In general, the rules set out in the AAT sample assessments for the subject you are studying for will apply in the real assessment, but you should again read the information on this screen in the real assessment carefully just to make sure.

A full stop is needed to indicate a decimal point. We would recommend using minus signs to indicate negative numbers and leaving out the comma signs to indicate thousands, as this results in a lower number of key strokes and less margin for error when working under time pressure. Having said that, you can use whatever is easiest for you as long as you operate within the rules set out for your particular assessment.

You have to show competence throughout the assessment and you should therefore complete all of the tasks. Don't leave questions unanswered.

In the *Financial Statements of Limited Companies* assessment the written tasks are human marked. In this case you are given a blank space or table to enter your answer into. You are told in the assessments which tasks these are.

If these tasks involve calculations, it is a good idea to decide in advance how you are going to lay out your answers to such tasks by practising answering them on a word document, and certainly you should try all such tasks in this question bank and in the AAT's environment using the sample/practice assessments.

When asked to fill in tables, or gaps, never leave any blank even if you are unsure of the answer. Fill in your best estimate.

Note that for some assessments where there is a lot of scenario information or tables of data provided, you may need to access these via 'pop-ups'. Instructions will be provided on how you can bring up the necessary data during the assessment. For example, the following is taken from the introductory screen of the AAT AQ2016 sample assessment for *Financial Statements of Limited Companies*.

You have been asked to prepare the statement of cash flows and statement of changes in equity for Chicago Ltd for the year ended 31 December 20X1.

The most recent statement of profit or loss and statement of financial position (with comparatives for the previous year) of Chicago Ltd can be viewed by clicking on the buttons below.

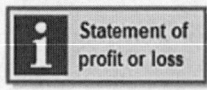 Statement of profit or loss

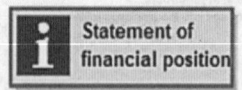 Statement of financial position

(a) Draft a reconciliation of profit before tax to net cash from operating activities for Chicago Ltd for the year ended 31 December 20X1.

(b) Draft the statement of cash flows for Chicago Ltd for the year ended 31 December 20X1.

Finally, take note of any task specific instructions once you are in the assessment. For example you may be asked to enter a date in a certain format or to enter a number to a certain number of decimal places.

Remember you can practise the BPP questions in this question bank in an online environment on our dedicated AAT Online page. On the same page is a link to the current AAT sample assessment(s) as well.

Grading

To achieve the qualification and to be awarded a grade, you must pass all the mandatory unit assessments, all optional unit assessments (where applicable) and the synoptic assessment.

The AAT Level 4 Professional Diploma in Accounting will be awarded a grade. This grade will be based on performance across the qualification. Unit assessments and synoptic assessments are not individually graded. These assessments are given a mark that is used in calculating the overall grade.

How overall grade is determined

You will be awarded an overall qualification grade (Distinction, Merit, and Pass). If you do not achieve the qualification you will not receive a qualification certificate, and the grade will be shown as unclassified.

The marks of each assessment will be converted into a percentage mark and rounded up or down to the nearest whole number. This percentage mark is then weighted according to the weighting of the unit assessment or synoptic assessment within the qualification. The resulting weighted assessment percentages are combined to arrive at a percentage mark for the whole qualification.

Grade definition	Percentage threshold
Distinction	90–100%
Merit	80–89%
Pass	70–79%
Unclassified	0–69% Or failure to pass one or more assessment/s

Re-sits

The AAT Professional Diploma In Accounting is not subject to re-sit restrictions.

You should only be entered for an assessment when you are well prepared and you expect to pass the assessment.

AAT qualifications

The material in this book may support the following AAT qualifications:

AAT Professional Diploma in Accounting Level 4 Professional Diploma in Accounting at SCQF Level 8.

Supplements

From time to time we may need to publish supplementary materials to one of our titles. This can be for a variety of reasons. From a small change in the AAT unit guidance to new legislation coming into effect between editions.

You should check our supplements page regularly for anything that may affect your learning materials. All supplements are available free of charge on our supplements page on our website at:

www.bpp.com/learning-media/about/students

Improving material and removing errors

There is a constant need to update and enhance our study materials in line with both regulatory changes and new insights into the assessments.

From our team of authors BPP appoints a subject expert to update and improve these materials for each new edition.

Their updated draft is subsequently technically checked by another author and from time to time non-technically checked by a proof reader.

We are very keen to remove as many numerical errors and narrative typos as we can but given the volume of detailed information being changed in a short space of time we know that a few errors will sometimes get through our net.

We apologise in advance for any inconvenience that an error might cause. We continue to look for new ways to improve these study materials and would welcome your suggestions. If you have any comments about this book, please email nisarahmed@bpp.com or write to Nisar Ahmed, AAT Head of Programme, BPP Learning Media Ltd, BPP House, Aldine Place, London W12 8AA.

Question Bank

Chapter 1 – Introduction to limited companies

Task 1.1

(a)   Define limited liability.

(b)   What are the advantages of operating as a limited liability company rather than as a sole trader or partnership?

(c)   Give two possible disadvantages of limited liability.

....

Task 1.2

A client of your firm has been trading successfully as a sole trader for a number of years. However, her business has grown so much that she now thinks it is time to consider converting the business into a limited liability company. She has heard that there are two types of capital: share capital and loan capital (which is sometimes known as loan stock or loan notes). However, she is unsure what the difference is.

Explain to your client the difference between share capital and loan capital.

....

Task 1.3

On 1 April 20X3 Pulsar plc issues 500,000 25p ordinary shares at their nominal value. At 31 March 20X4 the market price of one ordinary share in Pulsar plc is £1.50.

At 31 March 20X4, these shares are included in Pulsar plc's statement of financial position at:

£125,000	
£500,000	
£750,000	
£150,000	

....

Task 1.4

A company issues 50,000 £1 shares at a price of £1.25 per share.

How much should be posted to the share premium account?

£50,000	
£12,500	
£62,500	
£60,000	

Task 1.5

A company has £200,000 12% loan stock. The year end is 31 December. Interest is payable half-yearly on 31 July and 31 January.

Calculate the total interest payable for the year.

£	

State what accounting adjustment must be made at the year end.

Journal

Account name	Debit £	Credit £

Task 1.6

The accounting equation of a company is as follows:

Assets £1,200 – Liabilities £800 = Equity £400

The company subsequently makes two transactions.

- It purchases inventories costing £120 on credit
- It sells these inventories for £180 cash

(a) **Explain what is meant by 'assets', 'liabilities' and 'equity'.**

(b) **Explain the effect of each transaction on the elements in the statement of financial position.**

(c) **State the accounting equation for the company after the two transactions have taken place.**

Task 1.7

Financial performance of a company is assessed using the statement of profit or loss and other comprehensive income and/or the statement of cash flows.

A statement of profit or loss and other comprehensive income is prepared on the accruals basis, whereas the statement of cash flows is prepared on the basis of past cash flows.

Explain the following terms and their importance to the user:

(a) **Accruals basis**
(b) **Cash flow basis**

Task 1.8

Silver Ltd is a private limited company. The trial balance for the year ended 31 December 20X3 is shown below:

Trial balance as at 31 December 20X3

	Debit £000	Credit £000
Sales		31,500
Purchases	18,900	
Operating expenses	7,400	
Inventories at 1 January 20X3	3,390	
Interest paid	250	
Property, plant and equipment at cost	17,700	
Accumulated depreciation		4,250
Bank loan		4,000
Trade and other receivables	4,300	
Trade and other payables		2,900
Cash at bank	2,250	
Retained earnings at 1 January 20X3		6,540
Share capital		5,000
	54,190	54,190

The following information is also available.

(a)   Inventories were valued at £4,640,000 on 31 December 20X3.

(b)   Tax for the year has been estimated at £1,450,000.

Using the proforma below, draft Silver Ltd's statement of profit or loss for the year ended 31 December 20X3 and statement of financial position at that date.

Silver Ltd – Statement of profit or loss for the year ended 31 December 20X3

	£000
Revenue	
Cost of sales	
Gross profit	
Operating expenses	
Profit from operations	
Finance costs	
Profit before tax	
Tax	
Profit for the year	

Silver Ltd – Statement of financial position as at 31 December 20X3

	£000
ASSETS	
Non-current assets	
Property, plant and equipment	
Current assets	
Inventories	
Trade and other receivables	
Cash and cash equivalents	
Total assets	
EQUITY AND LIABILITIES	
Equity	
Share capital	
Retained earnings	
Total equity	
Non-current liabilities	
Bank loan	
Current liabilities	
Trade and other payables	
Tax payable	
Total liabilities	
Total equity and liabilities	

Chapter 2 – The frameworks and ethical principles

Task 2.1

Who issues International Financial Reporting Standards?

The IFRS Advisory Committee	
The stock exchange	
The International Accounting Standards Board	
The government	

Task 2.2

Which of the following statements is/are true?

1   The directors of a company are ultimately responsible for the preparation of financial statements, even if the majority of the work on them is performed by the finance department.

2   If financial statements are audited, then the responsibility for those financial statements instead falls on the auditors instead of the directors.

3   There are generally no laws surrounding the duties of directors in managing the affairs of a company.

1 only	
1 and 2 only	
1, 2 and 3	
2 and 3 only	

Task 2.3

Which of the following statements is/are true?

1   Directors of companies have a duty of care to show reasonable competence in their management of the affairs of a company.

2   Directors of companies must act honestly in what they consider to be the best interest of the company.

3   A Director's main aim should be to create wealth for the shareholders of the company.

1 and 2	
2 only	
1, 2 and 3	
1 and 3 only	

Task 2.4

Explain what is meant by GAAP.

Task 2.5

The purpose (objective) of financial statements is to provide financial information about the reporting entity that is useful in making decisions about providing resources to the entity. Financial statements provide, among other things, information about the equity of the company.

Prepare brief notes to answer the following questions:

(a)   According to the IASB's *Conceptual Framework for Financial Reporting*, who are the most important (primary) users of financial statements (general purpose financial reports)?

(b)   Explain how the financial statements might be used by a user who is interested in finding out how well a company has managed working capital.

(c)   What is meant by 'equity'? How is it related to other elements in the accounting equation?

Task 2.6

Your finance director is proposing that items should be omitted from the financial statements on the grounds that they are not material.

Explain what is meant by 'material'. Your answer should make no more than three brief points.

Task 2.7

The accounting equation is:

Assets – Liabilities = Equity

(a)   Define the following elements of financial statements:

   (i)   Assets
   (ii)   Liabilities
   (iii) Equity

(b)   Explain why inventories are an asset of a company.

Task 2.8

The IASB's *Conceptual Framework for Financial Reporting* explains that relevance and faithful representation are the two fundamental qualitative characteristics of useful financial information. It also sets out and explains four further qualities which enhance the usefulness of information that is relevant and faithfully represented.

(a)   Briefly explain what is meant by:

   (i)   Relevance
   (ii)   Faithful representation

   according to the *Conceptual Framework for Financial Reporting*.

(b)   State the four enhancing qualitative characteristics of useful financial information.

Task 2.9

(a)   What is the objective of general purpose financial reporting according to the IASB *Conceptual Framework for Financial Reporting*?

(b)   Give THREE reasons why users might be interested in the information contained in financial statements.

Task 2.10

'As a professional, you should behave with courtesy and consideration towards anyone with whom you come into contact.'

State the fundamental ethical principle defined above.

....

Task 2.11

State TWO safeguards created by the profession that protect against threats to compliance with the fundamental ethical principles.

....

Task 2.12

Matt, an accountant in practice, has been working as a manager on work for an important client of his firm. The work is almost at an end and the information produced by Matt will be used by the client's bank to assess whether to increase its lending to the client. The Finance Director of the client has approached Matt and informally discussed the possibility of a high-profile finance position in his department, stating that the role would be his if the information presents the company in a favourable light.

State TWO threats to the fundamental principles of professional ethics identified by this situation.

....

Task 2.13

Ruchita, an accountant in practice, has been offered a referral fee by another accountant to introduce a client to its business.

State TWO of Ruchita's ethical principles that are threatened by this arrangement.

....

Task 2.14

A member of the public has asked you as an accountant to provide them with a second opinion on advice they have received from another firm. However, you will not have access to the books and records the other firm used to prepare their advice because they are still holding onto them.

State the fundamental principle you would be in breach of if you were to provide a second opinion without the books and records.

....

Task 2.15

Professional distance is most closely associated with which ethical principle?

··

Task 2.16

An accountant in business has an annual bonus that is related to the company's reported profits that they help to determine.

Which threat to fundamental ethical principles might be caused by this situation?

··

Task 2.17

Jane is an accountant working in practice. During a recent assignment she identified a number of significant threats to her objectivity.

State TWO examples of safeguards Jane could put in place to eliminate the threats or reduce them to an acceptable level.

··

Chapters 3 to 5 – Drafting financial statements

Note. This chapter provides tasks on the material in Chapter 3 *The statement of financial position*, Chapter 4 *The statements of financial performance* and Chapter 5 *The statement of cash flows*. These topics are highly integrated and tested together, so the tasks are combined in one chapter.

Task 3.1

You have a friend who is a shareholder in a small private company. She has been looking at the company's latest financial statements and is slightly confused by some of the terms used in the statement of financial position, in particular by the terms labelled 'current'. On checking the internet she has found out that these terms are defined in something called IAS 1, but she has been unable to find any further information.

Write short notes to explain how IAS 1 *Presentation of Financial Statements* defines the following terms:

(a)   Current assets
(b)   Current liabilities

....

Task 3.2

IAS 1 *Presentation of Financial Statements* requires some items to be disclosed as separate line items in the financial statements and others to be disclosed in the notes.

1   Depreciation
2   Revenue
3   Closing inventories
4   Finance cost
5   Dividends

Which two of the above have to be shown as line items in the statement of profit or loss and other comprehensive income, rather than in the notes to the financial statements?

1 and 4	
3 and 5	
2 and 3	
2 and 4	

....

Task 3.3

Salmon Ltd has incurred a substantial Irrecoverable debt amounting to 15% of its profit before tax. In accordance with IAS 1 *Presentation of Financial Statements*, how should this item be presented in Salmon Ltd's statement of profit or loss and other comprehensive income and/or notes to the financial statements?

Not disclosed separately and treated as a distribution cost	
Disclosed as an extraordinary item	
Not disclosed separately and treated as an administrative expense	
Its nature and amount disclosed separately	

Task 3.4

Given below is the trial balance for Paparazzi Ltd as at 30 June 20X2.

	£000	£000
Land and buildings – cost	2,100	
Plant and machinery – cost	1,050	
Motor vehicles – cost	1,000	
Retained earnings at 1 July 20X1		1,131
Share capital		2,500
Share premium		300
Trade receivables	2,500	
Trade payables		1,400
Inventories at 1 July 20X1	690	
Accruals		50
Prepayments	40	
Sales		14,700
Purchases	10,780	
Land and buildings – accumulated depreciation 30 June 20X2		280
Plant and machinery – accumulated depreciation 30 June 20X2		194
Motor vehicles – accumulated depreciation 30 June 20X2		404
Bank	567	
7% bank loan (repayable 20X9)		1,200
Allowance for doubtful debts 30 June 20X2		92
Dividend paid	120	
Interest paid	84	
Distribution costs	1,200	
Administrative expenses	2,120	
	22,251	22,251

Further information:

- The inventories at 30 June 20X2 cost £710,000
- The Tax charge for the year is estimated at £130,000

(a) **Draft the statement of profit or loss and other comprehensive income for Paparazzi Ltd for the year ended 30 June 20X2.**

Paparazzi Ltd – Statement of profit or loss and other comprehensive income for the year ended 30 June 20X2

	£000
Revenue	
Cost of sales	
Gross profit	
Distribution costs	
Administrative expenses	
Profit/(loss) from operations	
Finance costs	
Profit/(loss) before tax	
Tax	
Profit/(loss) for the period from continuing operations	

Working

Cost of sales	£000
Opening inventories	
Purchases	
Closing inventories	

(b) **Draft the statement of financial position for Paparazzi Ltd as at 30 June 20X2**

(Complete the left hand column by writing in the correct line item from the list provided.)

Paparazzi Ltd – Statement of financial position as at 30 June 20X2

	£000
ASSETS	
Non-current assets	
▼	
Current assets	
▼	
▼	
▼	
Total assets	
EQUITY AND LIABILITIES	
Equity	
▼	
▼	
▼	
Total equity	
Non-current liabilities	
▼	
Current liabilities	
▼	
▼	
Total liabilities	
Total equity and liabilities	

Bank loan
Cash and cash equivalents
Inventories
Property, plant and equipment
Retained earnings
Share capital
Share premium
Tax liabilities
Trade and other payables
Trade and other receivables

Workings

Property, plant and equipment	£000
Land and buildings – cost	
Plant and equipment – cost	
Motor vehicles – cost	
Accumulated depreciation – land and buildings	
Accumulated depreciation – plant and equipment	
Accumulated depreciation – motor vehicles	

Trade and other receivables	£000
Trade and other receivables	
Allowance for doubtful debts	
Prepayments	

Retained earnings	£000
Retained earnings at 1 July 20X1	
Total profit for the year	
Dividends paid	

Trade and other payables	£000
Trade payables	
Accruals	

Task 3.5

You have been asked to help prepare the financial statements of Benard Ltd for the year ended 31 October 20X7. The company's trial balance as at 31 October 20X7 is shown below.

Benard Ltd – Trial balance as at 31 October 20X7

	Debit £000	Credit £000
Share capital		12,000
Trade and other payables		3,348
Property, plant and equipment – cost	58,463	
Property, plant and equipment – accumulated depreciation as at 31 October 20X7		27,974
Trade and other receivables	6,690	
Accruals		387
7% bank loan repayable 20Y2		16,000
Cash at bank	1,184	
Retained earnings as at 1 November 20X6		12,345
Interest	560	
Sales		50,197
Purchases	34,792	
Distribution costs	6,654	
Administrative expenses	4,152	
Inventories as at 1 November 20X6	8,456	
Dividends paid	1,300	
	122,251	122,251

Further information

- The sales figure in the trial balance does not include the credit sales for October 20X7 of £3,564,000.

- The inventories at the close of business on 31 October 20X7 cost £9,786,000.

- The company paid £48,000 insurance costs in June 20X7, which covered the period from 1 July 20X7 to 30 June 20X8. This was included in administrative expenses in the trial balance.

- Interest on the bank loan for the last six months of the year has not been included in the accounts in the trial balance.

- The Tax charge for the year has been calculated as £1,254,000.

(a) **Draft the statement of profit or loss and other comprehensive income for Benard Ltd for the year ended 31 October 20X7.**

Benard Ltd – Statement of profit or loss and other comprehensive income for the year ended 31 October 20X7

	£000
Revenue	
Cost of sales	
Gross profit	
Distribution costs	
Administrative expenses	
Profit/(loss) from operations	
Finance costs	
Profit/(loss) before tax	
Tax	
Profit/(loss) for the period from continuing operations	

Workings

(Complete the left hand column by writing in the correct narrative from the list provided.)

Cost of sales	£000
 ▼	
▼	
▼	

Picklist:

Accruals
Closing inventories
Credit sales for October 20X7
Opening inventories
Prepayments
Purchases

Administrative expenses	£000
▼	
▼	

Picklist:

Accruals
Administrative expenses
Prepayments

(b) Draft the statement of financial position for Benard Ltd as at 31 October 20X7

(Complete the left hand column by writing in the correct line item from the list provided.)

Benard Ltd – Statement of financial position as at 31 October 20X7

		£000
ASSETS		
Non-current assets		
	▼	
Current assets		
	▼	
	▼	
	▼	
Total assets		
EQUITY AND LIABILITIES		
Equity		
	▼	
	▼	
Total equity		
Non-current liabilities		
	▼	
Current liabilities		
	▼	
	▼	
Total liabilities		
Total equity and liabilities		

Picklist:

Bank loan
Cash and cash equivalents
Inventories
Property, plant and equipment
Retained earnings
Share capital
Tax payable
Trade and other payables
Trade and other receivables

Workings

(Complete the left hand column by writing in the correct narrative from the list provided.)

Trade and other receivables		£000
	▼	
	▼	
	▼	

Picklist:

Accruals: trial balance
Administrative expenses accrual
Administrative expenses prepaid
Additional interest accrual
Credit sales for October 20X7
Prepayments
Trade and other payables
Trade and other receivables

Retained earnings	£000
▼	
▼	
▼	

Picklist:

Dividends paid
Other comprehensive income for the year
Retained earnings at 1 November 20X6
Total comprehensive income for the year
Total profit for the year

Trade and other payables	£000
▼	
▼	
▼	

Picklist for narratives:

Accruals: trial balance
Administrative expenses accrual
Administrative expenses prepayment
Additional interest accrual
Credit sales for October 20X7
Dividends
Prepayments
Tax payable
Trade and other payables
Trade and other receivables

Task 3.6

You have been asked to help prepare the financial statements of Laxdale Ltd for the year ended 31 October 20X8. The company's trial balance as at 31 October 20X8 is shown below.

Laxdale Ltd – Trial balance as at 31 October 20X8

	Debit £000	Credit £000
Share capital		25,000
Trade and other payables		2,798
Land and buildings – cost	35,152	
Land and buildings – accumulated depreciation at 1 November 20X7		7,000
Plant and equipment – cost	12,500	
Plant and equipment – accumulated depreciation at 1 November 20X7		7,400
Trade and other receivables	5,436	
Accruals		436
8% bank loan repayable 20Y2		15,000
Cash at bank	9,774	
Retained earnings		9,801
Interest	600	
Sales		58,411
Purchases	41,620	
Distribution costs	5,443	
Administrative expenses	4,789	
Inventories as at 1 November 20X7	9,032	
Dividends paid	1,500	
	125,846	125,846

Further information

- The inventories at the close of business on 31 October 20X8 were valued at £7,878,000.

- Depreciation is to be provided for the year to 31 March 20X1 as follows:

  Buildings   2% per annum   Straight line basis

  Plant and equipment   20% per annum   Reducing (diminishing) balance basis

  Depreciation is apportioned as follows:

	%
Cost of sales	40
Distribution costs	40
Administrative expenses	20

  Land, which is non-depreciable, is included in the trial balance at a cost of £15,152,000.

- The company began a series of television adverts for the company's range of products on 1 October 20X8 at a cost of £45,000. The adverts were to run for three months and were to be paid for in full at the end of December 20X8. Advertising expenses are included in distribution costs.

- Interest on the bank loan for the last six months of the year has not been included in the accounts in the trial balance.

- The tax charge for the year has been calculated as £970,000.

- All of the operations are continuing operations.

(a) **Draft the statement of profit or loss and other comprehensive income for Laxdale Ltd for the year ended 31 October 20X8.**

Laxdale Ltd – Statement of profit or loss and other comprehensive income for the year ended 31 October 20X8

	£000
Revenue	
Cost of sales	
Gross profit	
Distribution costs	
Administrative expenses	
Profit/(loss) from operations	
Finance costs	
Profit/(loss) before tax	
Tax	
Profit/(loss) for the period from continuing operations	

Workings

(Complete the left hand column by writing in the correct narrative from the list provided.)

Cost of sales		£000
	▼	
	▼	
	▼	
	▼	

Picklist:

Accruals
Closing inventories
Depreciation
Opening inventories
Prepayments
Purchases

BPP
LEARNING MEDIA

Distribution costs	£000
▼	
▼	
▼	

Picklist:

Accruals
Depreciation
Distribution costs
Prepayments

Administrative expenses	£000
▼	
▼	

Picklist:

Accruals
Administrative expenses
Depreciation
Prepayments

(b) **Draft the statement of financial position for Laxdale Ltd as at 31 October 20X8.**

(Complete the left hand column by writing in the correct line item from the list provided.)

Laxdale Ltd – Statement of financial position as at 31 October 20X8

	£000
ASSETS	
Non-current assets	
▼	
Current assets	
▼	
▼	
▼	
Total assets	
EQUITY AND LIABILITIES	
Equity	
▼	
▼	
Total equity	
Non-current liabilities	
Current liabilities	
Total liabilities	
Total equity and liabilities	

Picklist:

Bank loan
Cash and cash equivalents
Inventories
Property, plant and equipment
Retained earnings
Share capital
Tax liabilities
Trade and other payables
Trade and other receivables

Workings

(Complete the left hand column by writing in the correct narrative from the list provided.)

Property, plant and equipment	£000
▼	
▼	
▼	
▼	

Picklist:

Accumulated depreciation – land and buildings
Accumulated depreciation – plant and equipment
Land and buildings – cost
Plant and equipment – cost

Retained earnings	£000
▼	
▼	
▼	

Picklist:

Dividends paid
Other comprehensive income for the year
Retained earnings at 1 November 20X7
Total comprehensive income for the year
Total profit for the year

Trade and other payables	£000

Picklist:

Accruals: trial balance
Additional distribution costs accrual
Additional distribution costs prepaid
Additional interest accrual
Dividends
Prepayments
Tax payable
Trade and other payables
Trade and other receivables

Task 3.7

You have been asked to help prepare the financial statements of Cappielow Ltd for the year ended 31 March 20X1. The company's trial balance as at 31 March 20X1 is shown below.

Cappielow Ltd – Trial balance as at 31 March 20X1

	Debit £000	Credit £000
Share capital		10,000
Revaluation reserve at 1 April 20X0		2,000
Trade and other payables		1,347
Property, plant and equipment – cost/value	36,780	
Property, plant and equipment – accumulated depreciation at 31 March 20X1		19,876
Trade and other receivables	2,133	
Accruals		129
6% bank loan repayable 20X6		12,000
Cash at bank	7,578	
Retained earnings at 1 April 20X0		2,595
Interest	720	
Sales		35,547
Purchases	27,481	
Distribution costs	1,857	
Administrative expenses	2,235	
Inventories as at 1 April 20X0	3,790	
Dividends paid	920	
	83,494	83,494

Further information:

- The inventories at the close of business on 31 March 20X1 were valued at £4,067,000.

- Depreciation has already been provided on property, plant and equipment for the year ended 31 March 20X1.

- On 31 March 20X1 items of plant with a cost of £12,750,000 and accumulated depreciation of £3,100,000 were found to have a fair value less costs of disposal of £8,500,000 and a value in use of £8,200,000. Any adjustment should be included in cost of sales.

- Land, which is non-depreciable, is included in the trial balance at a value of £5,150,000. It is to be revalued at £7,500,000 and this revaluation is to be included in the financial statements for the year ended 31 March 20X1.

- The company hired some office copiers for the period 1 March to 30 June 20X1. The contract price for the four months was £164,000 and this was paid in full on 3 March.

- The company sourced extra warehousing space, for the storage of goods prior to their sale, for a period of three months from 1 February to 30 April 20X1. The invoice for the full three months of £114,000 was paid on 16 April. No entry has been made in the accounts for this transaction.

- The tax charge for the year has been calculated as £874,000.

- On 15 April 20X1 one of the company's customers went into liquidation. Trade receivables at 31 March 20X1 include a balance of £95,000 owed by this customer. The directors have been advised that they are unlikely to receive any of this amount.

- All of the operations are continuing operations.

(a) Draft the statement of profit or loss and other comprehensive income for Cappielow Ltd for the year ended 31 March 20X1.

(b) Draft the statement of changes in equity for Cappielow Ltd for the year ended 31 March 20X1.

(c) Draft the statement of financial position for Cappielow Ltd as at 31 March 20X1.

Note. Additional notes and disclosures are not required.

Cappielow Ltd – Statement of profit or loss and other comprehensive income for the year ended 31 March 20X1

	£000
Revenue	
Cost of sales	
Gross profit	
Distribution costs	
Administrative expenses	
Profit/(loss) from operations	
Finance costs	
Profit/(loss) before tax	
Tax	
Profit/(loss) for the period from continuing operations	
Other comprehensive income for the year	
Gain on revaluation of land	
Total comprehensive income for the year	

Workings

(Complete the left hand column by writing in the correct narrative from the list provided.)

Cost of sales	£000
▼	
▼	
▼	
▼	

Picklist:

Accruals
Closing inventories
Impairment loss
Opening inventories
Prepayment
Purchases

Distribution costs		£000
	▼	
	▼	

Picklist:

Accruals
Distribution costs
Irrecoverable debt
Prepayment

Administrative expenses		£000
	▼	
	▼	
	▼	

Picklist:

Accruals
Administrative expenses
Irrecoverable debt
Impairment loss
Prepayment

Cappielow Ltd – Statement of changes in equity for the year ended 31 March 20X1

	Share capital £000	Revaluation surplus £000	Retained earnings £000	Total equity £000
Balance at 1 April 20X0				
Changes in equity				
Total comprehensive income				
Dividends				
Balance at 31 March 20X1				

Cappielow Ltd – Statement of financial position as at 31 March 20X1

(Complete the left hand column by writing in the correct line item from the list provided.)

	£000
ASSETS	
Non-current assets	
▼	
Current assets	
▼	
▼	
▼	
Total assets	

	£000
EQUITY AND LIABILITIES	
Equity	
▼	
▼	
▼	
Total equity	
Non-current liabilities	
▼	
Current liabilities	
▼	
▼	
Total liabilities	
Total equity and liabilities	

Picklist:

Bank loan
Cash and cash equivalents
Inventories
Property, plant and equipment
Retained earnings
Revaluation reserve
Share capital
Tax payable
Trade and other payables
Trade and other receivables

Workings

(Complete the left hand column by writing in the correct narrative from the list provided.)

Property, plant and equipment	£000
▼	
▼	
▼	

Picklist:

Impairment loss
Property, plant and equipment: accumulated depreciation
Property, plant and equipment: cost/value

Trade and other receivables	£000
▼	
▼	
▼	

Picklist:

Accruals: trial balance
Administrative expenses accrued
Administrative expenses prepaid
Irrecoverable debt
Distribution costs accrued
Distribution costs prepaid
Trade and other payables
Trade and other receivables

Revaluation reserve	£000
▼	
▼	

Picklist:

Dividends paid
Other comprehensive income for the year
Retained reserves at 1 April 20X0
Revaluation reserve at 1 April 20X0
Total comprehensive income for the year
Total profit for the year

Retained earnings	£000
▼	
▼	
▼	

Picklist:

Dividends paid
Other comprehensive income for the year
Retained earnings at 1 April 20X0
Revaluation reserve at 1 April 20X0
Total comprehensive income for the year
Total profit for the year

Trade and other payables	£000
▼	
▼	
▼	

Picklist:

Accruals: trial balance
Administrative expenses accrued
Administrative expenses prepaid
Distribution costs accrued
Distribution costs prepaid
Dividends
Irrecoverable debt
Tax payable
Trade and other payables
Trade and other receivables

Task 3.8

You have been asked to help prepare the financial statements of Pine Ltd for the year ended 31 March 20X1. The company's trial balance as at 31 March 20X1 is shown below.

Pine Ltd – Trial balance as at 31 March 20X1

	Debit £000	Credit £000
Share capital		50,000
Revaluation reserve at 1 April 20X0		12,000
Trade and other payables		5,342
Land & buildings – value/cost	81,778	
accumulated depreciation at 1 April 20X0		14,000
Plant and equipment – cost	24,000	
accumulated depreciation at 1 April 20X0		8,000
Trade and other receivables	9,886	
Accruals		517
4% bank loan repayable 20X8		16,000
Cash and cash equivalents	1,568	
Retained earnings at 1 April 20X0		7,945
Interest paid	640	
Sales		80,908
Purchases	53,444	
Distribution costs	9,977	
Administrative expenses	6,755	
Inventories at 1 April 20X0	5,064	
Dividends paid	1,600	
	194,712	194,712

Further information:

- The inventories at the close of business on 31 March 20X1 cost £7,004,000.

- Land, which is not depreciated, is included in the trial balance at a value of £41,778,000. It is to be revalued at £51,000,000 and this revaluation is to be included in the financial statements for the year ended 31 March 20X1.

- Depreciation is to be provided for the year to 31 March 20X1 as follows:

  Buildings   5% per annum   Straight line basis

  Plant and equipment 25% per annum   Diminishing (reducing) balance basis

  Depreciation is apportioned as follows:

	%
Cost of sales	60
Distribution costs	30
Administrative expenses	10

- Trade receivables include a debt of £24,000 which is to be written off. Irrecoverable (bad) debts are to be classified as administrative expenses.

- Distribution costs of £160,000 owing at 31 March 20X1 are to be provided for.

- The Tax charge for the year has been calculated as £1,254,000.

- All of the operations are continuing operations.

(a) Draft the statement of profit or loss and other comprehensive income for Pine Ltd for the year ended 31 March 20X1.

(b) Draft the statement of changes in equity for Pine Ltd for the year ended 31 March 20X1.

(c) Draft the statement of financial position for Pine Ltd as at 31 March 20X1.

Pine Ltd – Statement of profit or loss and other comprehensive income for the year ended 31 March 20X1

	£000
Revenue	
Cost of sales	
Gross profit	
Distribution costs	
Administrative expenses	
Profit from operations	
Finance costs	
Profit before tax	
Tax	
Profit for the period from continuing operations	
Other comprehensive income for the year	
Total comprehensive income for the year	

Workings

(Complete the left hand column by writing in the correct narrative from the list provided.)

Cost of sales	£000
▼	
▼	
▼	
▼	

Picklist:

Accruals
Closing inventories
Depreciation
Opening inventories
Prepayments
Purchases

Distribution costs	£000
▼	
▼	
▼	

Picklist:

Accruals
Depreciation
Distribution costs
Irrecoverable debt
Prepayments

Administrative expenses	£000
▼	
▼	
▼	

Picklist:

Accruals
Administrative expenses
Depreciation
Irrecoverable debt
Prepayments

Pine Ltd – Statement of changes in equity for the year ended 31 March 20X1

	Share capital £000	Revaluation surplus £000	Retained earnings £000	Total equity £000
Balance at 1 April 20X0				
Changes in equity				
Total comprehensive income				
Dividends				
Issue of share capital				
Balance at 31 March 20X1				

Pine Ltd – Statement of financial position as at 31 March 20X1

(Complete the left hand column by writing in the correct line item from the list provided.)

	£000
ASSETS	
Non-current assets	
▼	
Current assets	
▼	
▼	
▼	
Total assets	

	£000
EQUITY AND LIABILITIES	
Equity	
 ▼	
▼	
▼	
Total equity	
Non-current liabilities	
▼	
Current liabilities	
▼	
▼	
Total liabilities	
Total equity and liabilities	

Picklist:

Bank loan
Cash and cash equivalents
Inventories
Property, plant and equipment
Retained earnings
Revaluation reserve
Share capital
Tax liability
Trade and other payables
Trade and other receivables

Workings

(Complete the left hand column by writing in the correct narrative from the list provided.)

Property, plant and equipment		£000
	▼	
	▼	
	▼	
	▼	

Picklist:

Accumulated depreciation – land and buildings
Accumulated depreciation – plant and equipment
Land and buildings – value
Plant and equipment – cost

Trade and other receivables		£000
	▼	
	▼	

Picklist:

Accruals: trial balance
Additional distribution costs accrual
Additional distribution costs prepaid
Irrecoverable debts
Prepayments
Trade and other payables
Trade and other receivables

Revaluation reserve		£000
	▼	
	▼	

Picklist:

Dividends paid
Other comprehensive income for the year
Retained reserves at 1 April 20X0
Revaluation reserve at 1 April 20X0
Total comprehensive income for the year
Total profit for the year

Retained earnings		£000
	▼	
	▼	
	▼	

Picklist:

Dividends paid
Other comprehensive income for the year
Retained earnings at 1 April 20X0
Revaluation reserve at 1 April 20X0
Total comprehensive income for the year
Total profit for the year

Trade and other payables		£000
	▼	
	▼	
	▼	

Picklist:

Accruals: trial balance
Additional distribution costs accrued
Additional distribution costs prepaid
Dividends
Irrecoverable debts
Prepayments
Taxation liability
Trade and other payables
Trade and other receivables

Task 3.9

You have been asked to help prepare the financial statements of Bookham Ltd for the year ended 30 June 20X1. The company's trial balance as at 30 June 20X1 is shown below.

Trial balance:

	Debit £000	Credit £000
Sales		78,241
Purchases	36,148	
Distribution costs	7,249	
Administrative expenses	27,338	
Inventories at 1 July 20X0	6,328	
Dividends paid	600	
Interest paid	1,520	
Share capital		32,000
Retained earnings at 1July 20X0		7,462
Bank loan repayable		17,000
Trade and other payables		6,813
Tax		60
Property, plant and equipment at cost	64,229	
Property, plant and equipment – accumulated depreciation at 30 June 20X1		17,867
Trade receivables	12,447	
Allowance for doubtful debts at 1July 20X0		236
Cash at bank	3,820	
	159,679	159,679

Further information:

- The share capital of the company consists of ordinary shares with a nominal value of £1.

- The inventories at the close of business on 30 June 20X1 cost £7,493,000.

- Insurance expenditure of £156,000, in respect of the period 1 May 20X1 to 30 April 20X2, was paid on 17 April 20X1. This payment is included in distribution costs in the trial balance.

- Costs of £5,000 relating to the routine servicing of photocopiers in the general administration office have been included in the cost of property, plant and equipment in the trial balance.

- The allowance for doubtful debts is to increase by £47,000. Bookham Ltd classifies doubtful debts as an administrative expense.

- The Tax balance of £60,000 included in the trial balance was the result of an over-estimate of the tax liability for the previous year. The Tax charge in respect of the profits for the current year to 30 June 20X1 is estimated to be £1,486,000.

- Land included in property, plant and equipment at a carrying amount of £14,000,000 is to be revalued at the end of the year at £19,000,000.

- All of the operations are continuing operations.

(a) **Draft the statement of profit or loss and other comprehensive income for Bookham Ltd for the year ended 30 June 20X1.**

(b) **Draft the statement of changes in equity for Bookham Ltd for the year ended 30 June 20X1.**

(c) **Draft the statement of financial position for Bookham Ltd as at 30 June 20X1.**

Note. Additional notes and disclosures are not required.

Bookham Ltd – Statement of profit or loss and other comprehensive income for the year ended 30 June 20X1

	£000
Revenue	
Cost of sales	
Gross profit	
Distribution costs	
Administrative expenses	
Profit from operations	

	£000
Finance costs	
Profit before tax	
Tax	
Profit for the period from continuing operations	
Other comprehensive income for the year	
Total comprehensive income for the year	

Workings

Costs of sales	£000
▼	
▼	
▼	

Picklist:

Accrual
Closing inventories
Doubtful debts adjustment
Opening inventories
Prepayment
Purchases
Service costs

Distribution costs	£000
▼	
▼	

Picklist:

Accrual
Depreciation
Distribution costs
Doubtful debts adjustment
Prepayment
Service costs

Administrative expenses	£000
▼	
▼	
▼	

Picklist:

Accrual
Administrative expenses
Doubtful debts adjustment
Prepayment
Service costs

Tax	£000
▼	
▼	

Picklist:

Current year
Previous year

Bookham Ltd – Statement of changes in equity for the year ended 30 June 20X1

	Share capital £000	Revaluation reserve £000	Retained earnings £000	Total equity £000
Balance at 1 July 20X0				
Changes in equity				
Total comprehensive income				
Dividends				
Balance at 30 June 20X1				

Bookham Ltd – Statement of financial position as at 30 June 20X1.

	£000
ASSETS	
Non-current assets	
▼	
Current assets	
▼	
▼	
▼	
Total assets	
EQUITY AND LIABILITIES	
Equity	
▼	
▼	
▼	
Total equity	
Non-current liabilities	
▼	
Current liabilities	
▼	
▼	
Total liabilities	
Total equity and liabilities	

Picklist:

Bank loans
Cash and cash equivalents
Inventories
Property, plant and equipment
Retained earnings
Revaluation reserve
Share capital
Tax liability
Trade and other payables
Trade and other receivables

Workings

Property, plant and equipment	£000
▼	
▼	
▼	
▼	

Picklist:

Accumulated depreciation
Property, plant and equipment – cost
Revaluation
Servicing costs

Trade and other receivables	£000
▼	
▼	
▼	

Picklist:

Accrual
Allowance for doubtful debts
Prepayment
Trade and other payables
Trade receivables

53

Retained earnings	£000
▼	
▼	
▼	

Picklist:

Dividends paid
Profit for the year
Retained earnings at 1 July 20X0

Task 3.10

A decrease in trade receivables is deducted from profit before tax in the reconciliation of profit before tax to net cash from operating activities.

Is this statement True or False?

True	
False	

Task 3.11

Which of these transactions would be reported in a statement of cash flows?

1 A bonus issue of shares
2 Dividends paid

1 only	
2 only	
Both 1 and 2	
Neither 1 nor 2	

Task 3.12

In preparing a company's statement of cash flows complying with IAS 7 *Statements of Cash Flows*, which, if any, of the following items could form part of the calculation of cash flow from financing activities?

1   Proceeds of sale of premises
2   Dividends received
3   Bonus issue of shares

1 only	
2 only	
3 only	
None of them	

Task 3.13

Which of the following assertions about statement of cash flows is/are correct?

1   A statement of cash flows prepared using the direct method produces a different figure for operating cash flow from that produced if the indirect method is used.

2   Rights issues of shares do not feature in statements of cash flows.

3   A surplus on revaluation of a non-current asset will not appear as an item in a statement of cash flows.

4   A profit on the sale of a non-current asset will appear as an item under Cash Flows from Investing Activities in a statement of cash flows.

1 and 4	
2 and 3	
3 only	
2 and 4	

Task 3.14

The following extract is from the financial statements of Pompeii, a limited liability company at 31 October:

	20X9 £000	20X8 £000
EQUITY AND LIABILITIES		
Share capital	120	80
Share premium	60	40
Retained earnings	85	68
	265	188
Non-current liabilities		
Bank loan	100	150
	365	338

What is the cash flow from financing activities to be disclosed in the statement of cash flows for the year ended 31 October 20X9?

£60,000 inflow	
£10,000 inflow	
£110,000 inflow	
£27,000 inflow	

Task 3.15

The following information is available about the plant, property and equipment of Lok Co, for the year to 31 December 20X3.

	£000
Carrying amount of assets at beginning of the year	462
Carrying amount of assets at end of the year	633
Increase in revaluation surplus during the year	50
Disposals during the year, at cost	110
Accumulated depreciation on the assets disposed of	65
Depreciation charge for the year	38

What will be included in cash flows from investing activities for the year, in a statement of cash flows that complies with IAS 7 *Statement of Cash Flows*?

£104,000	
£159,000	
£166,000	
£204,000	

Task 3.16

An extract from a company's statement of profit or loss for the year ended 31 December 20X1 is given:

	£
Revenue	560,000
Cost of sales	300,000
Gross profit	260,000
Other expenses	160,000
Profit from operations	100,000
Finance costs	(10,000)
Profit before tax	90,000

Other expenses include £20,000 of depreciation. Interest paid was £10,000. The tax paid for the year was £25,000.

Extracts from the statement of financial position are also given below:

	20X1 £	20X0 £
Inventories	30,000	25,000
Trade receivables	40,000	42,000
Trade payables	28,000	32,000

Prepare a reconciliation of profit before tax to net cash from operating activities using the indirect method.

Reconciliation of profit before tax to net cash from operating activities

	£
Profit before tax	
Depreciation	
Finance costs	
Increase/decrease in inventories	
Increase/decrease in trade receivables	
Increase/decrease in trade payables	
Cash generated from operations	
Interest paid	
Tax paid	
Net cash from operating activities	

....

Task 3.17

Given below is an extract from a company's statement of financial position:

| | Year ended 31 March | |
	20X2 £000	20X1 £000
Trade payables	340	380
Tax	100	94
Accrued interest	8	13

The statement of profit or loss shows that interest payable for the year was £32,400 and the Tax charge was £98,000.

Calculate the figures that would appear in the statement of cash flows for:

(a) Interest paid

£ _____

(b) Tax paid

£ _____

··

Task 3.18

An extract from a company's statement of financial position is given below:

| | Year ended 30 June | |
	20X2 £000	20X1 £000
Property, plant and equipment at cost	1,340	1,250
Less – accumulated depreciation	(560)	(480)
	780	770

During the year items with a cost of £140,000 and net carrying amount of £98,000 were sold at a loss of £23,000.

Calculate the figures for:

(a) **Proceeds of the sale of property, plant and equipment in the year**

£ [   ]

(b) **The depreciation charge for the year**

£ [   ]

(c) **Cash paid to acquire property, plant and equipment during the year**

£ [   ]

....

Task 3.19

During the year ended 30 April 20X2 a company made a profit of £110,000. On 1 May 20X1 there were already 500,000 £1 ordinary shares in issue. On that date the company issued a further 200,000 ordinary shares at a price of £1.40 per share.

During the year the company revalued some of its non-current assets upwards by £70,000. An ordinary dividend of £35,000 was paid.

Share capital and reserves at 1 May 20X1 (before accounting for the share issue) were as follows:

	£
£1 ordinary shares	500,000
Share premium	100,000
Revaluation reserve	30,000
Retained earnings	180,000
	810,000

Draft a statement of changes in equity for the year ended 30 April 20X2.

Statement of changes in equity for the year ended 30 April 20X2

	Share capital £	Share premium £	Revaluation reserve £	Retained earnings £	Total equity £
Balance at 1 May 20X1					
Changes in equity					
Total comprehensive income					
Dividends					
Issue of share capital					
Balance at 30 April 20X2					

Task 3.20

You are presented with the following information for Evans Ltd.

Evans Ltd – Statement of profit or loss for the year ended 31 October 20X1

	£000
Continuing operations	
Revenue	2,000
Cost of sales	(1,350)
Gross profit	650
Gain on disposal of non-current assets	10
Distribution costs	(99)
Administrative expenses	(120)
Profit from operations	441
Finance costs	(23)
Profit before tax	418
Tax	(125)
Profit for the period from continuing operations	293

Evans Ltd – Statements of financial position as at 31 October

	20X1		20X0	
	£000	£000	£000	£000
ASSETS				
Non-current assets				
Property, plant and equipment		1,180		1,010
Current assets				
Inventories	486		505	
Trade receivables	945		657	
Cash	2		10	
		1,433		1,172
Total assets		2,613		2,182
EQUITY AND LIABILITIES				
Equity				
Share capital	1,200		1,000	
Share premium	315		270	
Retained earnings	363		110	
Total equity		1,878		1,380
Non-current liabilities				
12% bank loan		50		150
Current liabilities				
Trade payables	560		546	
Tax payable	125		106	
		685		652
Total liabilities		735		802
Total equity and liabilities		2,613		2,182

Additional information for the year ended 31 October 20X1

- Vehicles which had cost £155,000 were sold during the year when their net carrying amount was £65,000.

- The total depreciation charge for the year was £190,000.

- There were no prepaid or accrued expenses at the beginning or end of the year.

- Dividends of £40,000 were paid during the year.

(a) **Prepare a reconciliation of profit before tax to net cash from operating activities for Evans Ltd for the year ended 31 October 20X1.**

Reconciliation of profit before tax to net cash from operating activities

	£000
Profit before tax	
Adjustments for:	
Depreciation	
Finance costs	
Gain on disposal of property, plant and equipment	
Adjustment in respect of inventories	
Adjustment in respect of trade receivables	
Adjustment in respect of trade payables	
Cash generated by operations	
Interest paid	
Tax paid	
Net cash from operating activities	

(b) **Prepare the statement of cash flows for Evans Ltd for the year ended 31 October 20X1.**

Evans Ltd – Statement of cash flows for the year ended 31 October 20X1

	£000
Net cash from operating activities	
Investing activities	
Purchase of property, plant and equipment	
Proceeds on disposal of property, plant and equipment	
Net cash used in investing activities	
Financing activities	
Proceeds of share issue	
Repayment of bank loan	
Dividends paid	
Net cash from financing activities	
Net increase/(decrease) in cash and cash equivalents	
Cash and cash equivalents at the beginning of the year	
Cash and cash equivalents at the end of the year	

Workings

Proceeds on disposal of property, plant and equipment (PPE)	£000
Carrying amount of PPE sold	
Gain on disposal	

Purchase of property, plant and equipment (PPE)	£000
PPE at start of year	
Depreciation charge	
Carrying amount of PPE sold	
PPE at end of year	
Total PPE additions	

(c) **Draft the statement of changes in equity for Evans Ltd for the year ended 31 October 20X1.**

Evans Ltd – Statement of changes in equity for the year ended 31 October 20X1

	Share capital £000	Other reserves £000	Retained earnings £000	Total equity £000
Balance at 1 November 20X0				
Changes in equity				
Profit for the year				
Dividends				
Issue of share capital				
Balance at 31 October 20X1				

Task 3.21

For the year ended 31 October 20X7 you have been asked to prepare:

- A reconciliation between profit before tax and net cash from operating activities.

- A statement of cash flows for Lochnagar Ltd.

The statements of financial position of Lochnagar Ltd for the past two years and the most recent statement of profit or loss are set out as follows:

Lochnagar Ltd

Statement of profit or loss for the year ended 31 October 20X7

	£000
Continuing operations	
Revenue	22,400
Cost of sales	(12,320)
Gross profit	10,080
Gain on disposal of property, plant and equipment	224
Distribution costs	(4,704)
Administrative expenses	(2,240)
Profit from operations	3,360
Finance costs – interest on loans	(91)
Profit before tax	3,269
Tax	(1,344)
Profit for the period from continuing operations	1,925

Lochnagar Ltd

Statements of financial position as at 31 October

	20X7 £000	20X6 £000
ASSETS		
Non-current assets		
Property, plant and equipment	25,171	24,100
Current assets		
Inventories	3,696	2,464
Trade and other receivables	3,360	2,464
Cash and cash equivalents	0	129
	7,056	5,057
Total assets	32,227	29,157
EQUITY AND LIABILITIES		
Equity		
Share capital	2,200	2,000
Share premium	800	500
Retained earnings	24,990	23,065
Total equity	27,990	25,565
Non-current liabilities		
Bank loans	1,300	800
Current liabilities		
Trade and other payables	1,232	1,848
Tax liability	1,344	944
Bank overdraft	361	0
	2,937	2,792
Total liabilities	4,237	3,592
Total equity and liabilities	32,227	29,157

Further information

- The total depreciation charge for the year was £3,545,000.

- Property, plant and equipment costing £976,000 with accumulated depreciation of £355,000 was sold in the year at a profit of £224,000.

- All sales and purchases were on credit. Other expenses were paid for in cash.

(a) **Prepare a reconciliation of profit before tax to net cash from operating activities for Lochnagar Ltd for the year ended 31 October 20X7.**

(Complete the left hand column by writing in the correct line item from the list provided.)

Lochnagar Ltd

Reconciliation of profit before tax to net cash from operating activities for the year ended 31 October 20X7

	£000
▼	
Adjustments for:	
▼	
▼	
▼	
▼	
▼	
▼	
Cash generated by operations	
▼	
▼	
Net cash from operating activities	

Picklist:

Adjustment in respect of inventories
Adjustment in respect of trade payables
Adjustment in respect of trade receivables
Depreciation
Finance costs
Gain on disposal of property, plant and equipment
Interest paid
New bank loans
Proceeds on disposal of property, plant and equipment
Profit after tax
Profit before tax
Profit from operations
Purchases of property, plant and equipment
Tax paid

(b) **Prepare the statement of cash flows for Lochnagar Ltd for the year ended 31 October 20X7.**

(Complete the left hand column by writing in the correct line item from the list provided.)

Lochnagar Ltd

Statement of cash flows for the year ended 31 October 20X7

	£000
Net cash from operating activities	
Investing activities	
▼	
▼	
Net cash used in investing activities	
Financing activities	
▼	
▼	
Net cash from financing activities	
Net increase/(decrease) in cash and cash equivalents	
Cash and cash equivalents at the beginning of the year	
Cash and cash equivalents at the end of the year	

Picklist:

Adjustment in respect of inventories
Adjustment in respect of trade payables
Adjustment in respect of trade receivables
New bank loans
Proceeds of share issue
Proceeds on disposal of property, plant and equipment
Purchases of property, plant and equipment

Workings

(Complete the left hand column by writing in the correct narrative from the list provided.)

Proceeds on disposal of property, plant and equipment (PPE)	£000
▼	
▼	

Picklist:

Carrying amount of PPE sold
Depreciation charge
Gain on disposal
PPE at end of year
PPE at start of year

Purchases of property, plant and equipment (PPE)	£000
PPE at start of year	
▼	
▼	
▼	
Total PPE additions	

Picklist:

Carrying amount of PPE sold
Depreciation charge
Gain on disposal of PPE
PPE at end of year

Task 3.22

You have been asked to prepare the statement of cash flows for Thehoose Ltd, for the year ended 31 March 20X9. The most recent statement of profit or loss and statements of financial position of Thehoose Ltd for the past two years are set out below.

Thehoose Ltd

Statement of profit or loss for the year ended 31 March 20X9

	£000
Continuing operations	
Revenue	37,680
Cost of sales	(22,608)
Gross profit	15,072
Gain on disposal of property, plant and equipment	376
Distribution costs	(6,782)
Administrative expenses	(3,014)
Profit from operations	5,652
Finance costs	(280)
Profit before tax	5,372
Tax	(1,484)
Profit for the period from continuing operations	3,888

Thehoose Ltd

Statements of financial position as at 31 March

	20X9 £000	20X8 £000
ASSETS		
Non-current assets		
Property, plant and equipment	27,570	21,340
Current assets		
Inventories	5,426	4,069
Trade and other receivables	3,768	4,145
Cash and cash equivalents	335	0
	9,529	8,214
Total assets	37,099	29,554
EQUITY AND LIABILITIES		
Equity		
Share capital	4,500	3,000
Share premium	3,000	2,000
Retained earnings	21,854	17,966
Total equity	29,354	22,966
Non-current liabilities		
Bank loans	4,000	1,500
Current liabilities		
Trade and other payables	2,261	4,069
Tax liability	1,484	887
Bank overdraft	–	132
	3,745	5,088
Total liabilities	7,745	6,588
Total equity and liabilities	37,099	29,554

Further information:

- The total depreciation charge for the year was £3,469,000.

- Property, plant and equipment costing £764,000, with accumulated depreciation of £347,000, were sold in the year.

- All sales and purchases were on credit. Other expenses were paid for in cash.

(a) **Prepare a reconciliation of profit before tax to net cash from operating activities for Thehoose Ltd for the year ended 31 March 20X9.**

(Complete the left hand column by writing in the correct line item from the list provided.)

Thehoose Ltd

Reconciliation of profit before tax to net cash from operating activities for the year ended 31 March 20X9

	£000
▼	
Adjustments for:	
▼	
▼	
▼	
▼	
▼	
▼	
Cash generated by operations	
▼	
▼	
Net cash from operating activities	

Picklist:

Adjustment in respect of inventories
Adjustment in respect of trade payables
Adjustment in respect of trade receivables
Depreciation
Finance costs
Gain on disposal of property, plant and equipment
Interest paid
New bank loans
Proceeds on disposal of property, plant and equipment
Profit after tax
Profit before tax
Profit from operations
Purchases of property, plant and equipment
Tax paid

(b) **Prepare the statement of cash flows for Thehoose Ltd for the year ended 31 March 20X9.**

(Complete the left hand column by writing in the correct line item from the list provided.)

Thehoose Ltd

Statement of cash flows for the year ended 31 March 20X9

	£000
Net cash from operating activities	
Investing activities	
▼	
▼	
Net cash used in investing activities	
Financing activities	
▼	
▼	
Net cash from financing activities	
Net increase/(decrease) in cash and cash equivalents	
Cash and cash equivalents at the beginning of the year	
Cash and cash equivalents at the end of the year	

Picklist:

Adjustment in respect of inventories
Adjustment in respect of trade payables
Adjustment in respect of trade receivables
Dividends paid
New bank loans
Proceeds of share issue
Proceeds on disposal of property, plant and equipment
Purchases of property, plant and equipment

Workings

(Complete the left hand column by writing in the correct narrative from the list provided.)

Proceeds on disposal of property, plant and equipment (PPE)	£000
▼	
▼	

Picklist:

Carrying amount of PPE sold
Depreciation charge
Gain on disposal
PPE at end of year
PPE at start of year

Purchases of property, plant and equipment (PPE)	£000
PPE at start of year	
▼	
▼	
▼	
Total PPE additions	

Picklist:

Carrying amount of PPE sold
Depreciation charge
Gain on disposal of PPE
PPE at end of year

Task 3.23

You have been asked to prepare a statement of cash flows and a statement of changes in equity for Adlington Ltd for the year ended 31 October 20X9. The most recent statement of profit or loss and statements of financial position of the company for the past two years are set out below.

Adlington Ltd

Statement of profit or loss for the year ended 31 October 20X9

	£000
Continuing operations	
Revenue	45,500
Cost of sales	(27,300)
Gross profit	18,200
Gain on disposal of property, plant and equipment	455
Distribution costs	(6,825)
Administrative expenses	(5,005)
Profit from operations	6,825
Finance costs – interest on loan	(595)
Profit before tax	6,230
Tax	(1,757)
Profit for the period from continuing operations	4,473

Adlington Ltd

Statements of financial position as at 31 October

	20X9 £000	20X8 £000
ASSETS		
Non-current assets		
Property, plant and equipment	31,989	22,246
Current assets		
Inventories	6,552	4,914
Trade and other receivables	4,550	4,641
Cash and cash equivalents	450	0
	11,552	9,555
Total assets	43,541	31,801
EQUITY AND LIABILITIES		
Equity		
Share capital	10,000	8,000
Share premium	4,000	3,000
Retained earnings	15,462	11,489
Total equity	29,462	22,489
Non-current liabilities		
Bank loan	8,500	3,000
Current liabilities		
Trade and other payables	3,822	4,368
Tax liabilities	1,757	658
Bank overdraft	–	1,286
	5,579	6,312
Total liabilities	14,079	9,312
Total equity plus liabilities	43,541	31,801

Additional data

- The total depreciation charged for the year was £4,398,000.

- Property, plant and equipment costing £568,000 with accumulated depreciation of £226,000 was sold in the year.

- All sales and purchases were on credit. Other expenses were paid for in cash.

- A dividend of £500,000 was paid during the year.

(a) **Prepare a reconciliation of profit before tax to net cash from operating activities for Adlington Ltd for the year ended 31 October 20X9.**

(Complete the left hand column by writing in the correct line item from the list provided.)

Reconciliation of profit before tax to net cash from operating activities for the year ended 31 October 20X9

	£000
▼	
Adjustments for:	
▼	
▼	
▼	
▼	
▼	
▼	
Cash generated from operations	
▼	
▼	
Net cash from operating activities	

Picklist:

Adjustment in respect of inventories
Adjustment in respect of trade payables
Adjustment in respect of trade receivables
Depreciation
Finance costs
Gain on disposal of property, plant and equipment
Interest paid
New bank loans
Proceeds on disposal of property, plant and equipment
Profit after tax
Profit before tax
Profit from operations
Purchases of property, plant and equipment
Tax paid

(b) **Prepare the statement of cash flows for Adlington Ltd for the year ended 31 October 20X9.**

(Complete the left hand column by writing in the correct line item from the list provided.)

Adlington Ltd

Statement of cash flows for the year ended 31 October 20X9

	£000
Net cash from operating activities	
Investing activities	
▼	
▼	
Net cash used in investing activities	
Financing activities	
▼	
▼	
▼	
Net cash from financing activities	
Net increase/(decrease) in cash and cash equivalents	
Cash and cash equivalents at the beginning of the year	
Cash and cash equivalents at the end of the year	

Picklist:

Adjustment in respect of inventories
Adjustment in respect of trade payables
Adjustment in respect of trade receivables
Dividends paid
New bank loans
Proceeds of share issue
Proceeds on disposal of property, plant and equipment
Purchases of property, plant and equipment

Workings

(Complete the left hand column by writing in the correct narrative from the list provided.)

Proceeds on disposal of property, plant and equipment (PPE)		£000
	▼	
	▼	

Picklist:

Carrying amount of PPE sold
Depreciation charge
Gain on disposal
PPE at end of year
PPE at start of year

Purchases of property, plant and equipment (PPE)		£000
PPE at start of year		
	▼	
	▼	
	▼	
Total PPE additions		

Picklist:

Carrying amount of PPE sold
Depreciation charge
Gain on disposal of PPE
PPE at end of year

(c) **Draft the statement of changes in equity for Adlington Ltd for the year ended 31 October 20X9.**

(Complete the left hand column by writing in the correct line item from the list provided.)

Adlington Ltd

Statement of changes in equity for the year ended 31 October 20X9

	Share capital £000	Other reserves £000	Retained earnings £000	Total equity £000
Balance at 1 November 20X8				
Changes in equity				
Profit for the year				
Dividends				
Issue of share capital				
Balance at 31 October 20X9				

Task 3.24

Set out below is the statement of cash flows for Primrose Ltd for the year ended 31 May 20X5.

Primrose Ltd

Statement of cash flows for the year ended 31 May 20X5

	£000	£000
Cash flows from operating activities		
Profit before tax	1,032	
Adjustments for:		
Depreciation	700	
Loss on sale of tangible non-current assets	20	
Finance costs	10	
Increase in inventories	(80)	
Increase in trade receivables	(130)	
Increase in trade payables	85	
Net cash generated from operating activities	1,637	
Interest paid	(10)	
Tax paid	(145)	
Dividends paid	(270)	
Net cash from operating activities		1,212
Cash flow from investing activities		
Purchase of tangible non-current assets	(2,800)	
Receipts from sales of tangible non-current assets	180	
Net cash used in investing activities		(2,620)
Cash flows from financing activities		
Proceeds from issue of share capital	1,280	
Repayment of long-term borrowing	(100)	
Net cash generated from financing activities		1,180
Net increase/(decrease) in cash and cash equivalents		(228)
Cash and cash equivalents at the beginning of period		170
Cash and cash equivalents at end of period		(58)

Comment on the financial position of Primrose Ltd as shown by the above statement of cash flows.

∙∙∙

BPP
LEARNING MEDIA

Task 3.25

Briefly state some of the ways in which companies could manipulate their year-end cash position.

....

Task 3.26

You have been asked to prepare the statement of cash flows and statement of changes in equity for Forthbank Ltd for the year ended 31 March 20X1.

The most recent statement of profit or loss and statement of financial position (with comparatives for the previous year) of Forthbank Ltd are set out below.

Forthbank Ltd – Statement of profit or loss for the year ended 31 March 20X1

Continuing operations	£000
Revenue	54,000
Cost of sales	(32,400)
Gross profit	21,600
Dividends received	650
Loss on disposal of property, plant and equipment	(110)
Distribution costs	(11,420)
Administrative expenses	(4,860)
Profit from operations	5,860
Finance costs	(301)
Profit before tax	5,559
Tax	(1,113)
Profit for the period from continuing operations	4,446

Forthbank Ltd – Statement of financial position as at 31 March 20X1

	20X1 £000	20X0 £000
ASSETS		
Non-current assets		
Property, plant and equipment	26,660	19,140
Current assets		
Inventories	5,832	4,860
Trade and other receivables	5,400	4,320
Cash and cash equivalents	587	0
	11,819	9,180
Total assets	38,479	28,320
EQUITY AND LIABILITIES		
Equity		
Share capital	8,000	6,000
Share premium	3,000	2,000
Retained earnings	18,826	14,840
Total equity	29,826	22,840
Non-current liabilities		
Bank loans	4,300	800
	4,300	800
Current liabilities		
Trade payables	3,240	3,564
Tax liabilities	1,113	908
Bank overdraft	0	208
	4,353	4,680
Total liabilities	8,653	5,480
Total equity and liabilities	38,479	28,320

Further information:

- The total depreciation charge for the year was £3,366,000.
- Property, plant and equipment costing £812,000 with accumulated depreciation of £475,000 was sold in the year.
- All sales and purchases were on credit. Other expenses were paid for in cash.
- A dividend of £460,000 was paid during the year.

(a) **Prepare a reconciliation of profit before tax to net cash from operating activities for Forthbank Ltd for the year ended 31 March 20X1.**

(Complete the left hand column by writing in the correct line item from the list provided.)

Reconciliation of profit before tax to net cash from operating activities

	£000
▼	
Adjustments for:	
▼	
▼	
▼	
▼	
▼	
▼	
▼	
Cash generated by operations	
▼	
▼	
Net cash from operating activities	

Picklist:

Adjustment in respect of inventories
Adjustment in respect of trade payables
Adjustment in respect of trade receivables
Depreciation
Dividends received
Finance costs
Interest paid
Loss on disposal of property, plant and equipment
New bank loans
Proceeds on disposal of property, plant and equipment
Profit after tax
Profit before tax
Profit from operations
Purchases of property, plant and equipment
Tax paid

(b) **Prepare the statement of cash flows for Forthbank Ltd for the year ended 31 March 20X1.**

(Complete the left hand column by writing in the correct line item from the list provided.)

Forthbank Ltd

Statement of cash flows for the year ended 31 March 20X1

	£000
Net cash from operating activities	
Investing activities	
▼	
▼	
▼	
Net cash used in investing activities	
Financing activities	
▼	
▼	
▼	
Net cash from financing activities	
Net increase/(decrease) in cash and cash equivalents	
Cash and cash equivalents at the beginning of the year	
Cash and cash equivalents at the end of the year	

BPP
LEARNING MEDIA

Picklist:

Adjustment in respect of inventories
Adjustment in respect of trade payables
Adjustment in respect of trade receivables
Dividends paid
Dividends received
New bank loans
Proceeds of share issue
Proceeds on disposal of property, plant and equipment
Purchases of property, plant and equipment

Workings

(Complete the left hand column by writing in the correct narrative from the list provided.)

Proceeds on disposal of property, plant and equipment (PPE)	£000
▼	
▼	

Picklist:

Carrying amount of PPE sold
Depreciation charge
Loss on disposal
PPE at end of year
PPE at start of year

Purchases of property, plant and equipment (PPE)	£000
PPE at start of year	
▼	
▼	
▼	
Total PPE additions	

Picklist for narratives:

Carrying amount of PPE sold
Depreciation charge
Loss on disposal of PPE
PPE at end of year

(c)   **Draft the statement of changes in equity for Forthbank Ltd for the year ended 31 March 20X1.**

Forthbank Ltd

Statement of changes in equity for the year ended 31 March 20X1

	Share capital £000	Other reserves £000	Retained earnings £000	Total equity £000
Balance at 1 April 20X0				
Changes in equity				
Profit for the year				
Dividends				
Issue of share capital				
Balance at 31 March 20X1				

Chapter 6 – Property, plant and equipment

Task 6.1

The components of the cost of a major item of equipment are given below.

	£
Purchase price	780,000
Import duties	117,000
Site preparation	30,000
Installation	28,000
General overheads	50,000
	1,005,000

What amount should be recognised as the cost of the asset, according to IAS 16 *Property, Plant and Equipment*?

£888,000	
£897,000	
£955,000	
£1,005,000	

Task 6.2

A property was purchased on 1 April 20X0 for £160,000. Depreciation policy is to depreciate properties over a period of 40 years. On 1 April 20X2 the property was revalued to £200,000.

What is the depreciation charge for the year ended 31 March 20X3?

£4,000	
£4,211	
£5,000	
£5,263	

Task 6.3

A machine was purchased on 1 January 20X0 for £80,000 and was depreciated over a period of ten years using the straight-line method. On 1 January 20X2 it was decided that the machine had a total useful life of just seven years.

What is the depreciation charge for the year ending 31 December 20X2?

£9,143	
£11,429	
£12,800	
£18,286	

Task 6.4

On 1 January 20X0 a building was purchased for £240,000. At that date its useful life was 50 years. On 1 January 20X4 it was revalued to £460,000 with no change in estimated useful life. On 31 December 20X5 the building was sold for £500,000.

What is the profit on disposal?

£40,000	
£58,400	
£60,000	
£288,800	

Task 6.5

Lingfield Ltd purchases a machine for £20,000 on 1 July 20X0. The machine is estimated to have a useful economic life of four years, after which it can be sold for £4,000. The company depreciates the machine using the straight line method, charging a full year's depreciation in both the year of purchase and sale. Lingfield Ltd prepares its financial statements to 30 June each year.

What will be the carrying amount of the machine at 30 June 20X3?

£4,000	
£5,000	
£8,000	
£12,000	

Task 6.6

Which of the following statements are correct with regard to property, plant and equipment (PPE)?

1   A revaluation reserve arises when an item of PPE is sold at a profit.
2   All non-current assets must be depreciated.

1 only	
2 only	
Both	
Neither of them	

Task 6.7

The directors of Sydenham Ltd have recently purchased a new item of manufacturing equipment. The invoiced price of the equipment was £37,000, delivery costs were £1,600, and installation and testing costs were £4,500. As part of the process of testing the equipment, the company produced some samples, which were slightly imperfect and were sold for £1,800. After the equipment had been successfully installed and tested the company incurred costs of £3,000 in training staff to use it.

Prepare brief notes for the directors of Sydenham Ltd to cover the following:

(a) **When should items of property, plant and equipment be recognised as assets?**

(b) **Which costs should be included on initial recognition of property, plant and equipment?**

(c) **Calculate the amount that should be recognised in property, plant and equipment as the cost of the new item of manufacturing equipment.**

Chapter 7 – Intangible assets and inventories

Task 7.1

The directors of Dorchester Ltd are concerned that one of its machines might have become impaired. The following information applies:

	£
Carrying amount	19,600
Fair value	18,500
Costs of disposal	300
Value in use	18,400

What is the amount of impairment loss that will be recognised in the statement of profit or loss, in accordance with IAS 36 *Impairment of Assets*?

£NIL	
£1,100	
£1,200	
£1,400	

Task 7.2

You have been asked to help prepare the financial statements of Sandringham Ltd for the year ended 30 September 20X4 and to advise the directors on the accounting treatment of certain items.

Prepare brief notes to answer the following questions that have been asked by the directors of Sandringham Ltd. Where appropriate, make reference to relevant accounting standards.

(a) **(i)** **Why is an adjustment made for closing inventories in the financial statements?**

(ii) **How should inventories be valued in the financial statements?**

(b) **(i)** **When would an impairment review of non-current assets be necessary?**

(ii) **What would you do in an impairment review?**

Task 7.3

State the criteria which must be met under IAS 38 *Intangible Assets* if development expenditure is to be capitalised.

....

Task 7.4

What are the main characteristics of goodwill which distinguish it from other intangible assets?

....

Task 7.5

Internally generated goodwill should be measured at fair value.

Is this statement True or False?

True	
False	

....

Task 7.6

An asset has a carrying amount of £125,000. Its fair value less costs of disposal is £120,000 and its value in use is £130,000, so the asset should be measured at £120,000.

Is this statement True or False?

True	
False	

....

Task 7.7

Fowey Ltd has four assets which the directors consider may have become impaired.

	Carrying amount £	Fair value less costs of disposal £	Value in use £
(i)	10,000	12,000	14,000
(ii)	8,000	9,000	5,800
(iii)	7,000	3,800	7,200
(iv)	9,000	4,300	5,200

Which of the above assets will be impaired according to IAS 36 _Impairment of Assets_?

(i) only	
(i) and (iii)	
(ii) and (iv)	
(iv) only	

Task 7.8

During June 20X6, a company made the following purchases of inventory.

1 June	25 units @	£140 per unit
15 June	15 units @	£160 per unit

On 30 June it sold 30 units at a price of £150 per unit. The company uses the first-in, first-out (FIFO) method of valuation.

What is the value of closing inventories at 30 June 20X6?

£1,400	
£1,475	
£1,500	
£1,600	

Task 7.9

Bovey Ltd holds three distinct types of inventory in its warehouse at the end of its accounting year, which are valued as follows:

Product	FIFO (cost) £	NRV £
I	11,300	12,800
II	7,600	5,900
III	15,200	18,400
	34,100	37,100

At what value should inventories be stated in Bovey Ltd's financial statements according to IAS 2 _Inventories_?

£32,400	
£34,000	
£34,100	
£37,100	

Chapter 8 – Further accounting standards

Task 8.1

A company estimated that its tax liability for the year ended 30 June 20X1 was £113,000. During the year to 30 June 20X2 the amount actually paid to Her Majesty's Revenue and Customs (HMRC) was £108,000. The estimate for the tax liability for the year ended 30 June 20X2 is £129,000.

What amounts should be recognised in the financial statements for the year ended 30 June 20X2?

Tax expense (profit or loss)	Tax payable (statement of financial position)
£124,000	£124,000
£124,000	£129,000
£129,000	£129,000
£134,000	£129,000

Task 8.2

A company leases some plant on 1 January 20X4. The cash price of the plant is £9,000, and the company leases it for four years, paying four annual instalments of £3,000 beginning on 31 December 20X4.

The company uses the sum-of-the-digits method to allocate interest.

What is the interest charge for the year ended 31 December 20X5?

£750	
£500	
£900	
£1,000	

Task 8.3

A company leases some plant on 1 January 20X4. The cash price is £9,000, and the company is to pay four annual instalments of £3,000, beginning on 1 January 20X4.

The company uses the sum-of-the-digits method to allocate interest.

What is the interest charge for the year ended 31 December 20X5?

£750	
£500	
£900	
£1,000	

Task 8.4

An asset is hired under a finance lease with a deposit of £30,000 on 1 January 20X1 plus 8 six monthly payments in arrears of £20,000 each. The fair value of the asset is £154,000. The finance charge is to be allocated using the sum-of-the-digits method.

What is the finance charge for the year ending 31 December 20X3?

£7,000	
£8,000	
£10,000	
£11,000	

Task 8.5

CS acquired a machine, using a finance lease, on 1 January 20X4. The machine had an expected useful life of 12,000 operating hours, after which it would have no residual value.

The finance lease was for a five-year term with rentals of £20,000 per year payable in arrears. The cost price of the machine was £80,000 and the implied interest rate is 7.93% per year. CS used the machine for 2,600 hours in 20X4 and 2,350 hours in 20X5

The actuarial method is used to allocate interest to accounting periods over the lease term.

What are the current liability and the non-current liability figures required by IAS 17 *Leases* to be shown in CS's statement of financial position at 31 December 20X5?

Current liability	Non-current liability	
£25,908	£35,967	
£51,605	£35,812	
£15,908	£35,967	
£35,908	£15,397	

Task 8.6

A company leases an asset on 1 January 20X1. The terms of the lease are to pay a deposit immediately of £575 followed by seven annual instalments of £2,000 payable in arrears. The present value of minimum lease payments is £10,000.

The interest rate implicit in the lease is 11% and the actuarial method is used to allocate interest to accounting periods over the lease term.

What is the current finance lease liability in the statement of financial position for the year ended 31 December 20X1?

£931	
£2,000	
£963	
£1,069	

Task 8.7

An asset with a fair value of £15,400 is acquired under a finance lease on 1 January 20X1 with a deposit on that date of £4,000 and four further annual payments on 31 December each year. The interest rate implicit in the lease is 15% and the actuarial method is used to allocate interest to accounting periods over the lease term.

What is the total lease obligation (liability) at 31 December 20X1?

£7,400	
£9,110	
£10,250	
£13,110	

Task 8.8

Trent Ltd entered into a finance lease agreement on 1 April 20X5. The fair value of the asset was £76,000 and Trent Ltd agreed to make four annual payments of £25,000 starting on 31 March 20X6. The rate of interest implicit in the lease is 12%. Trent Ltd uses the actuarial method to account for finance lease interest.

What is the finance charge to profit or loss relating to the lease for the year ended 31 March 20X6?

£6,120	
£9,120	
£9,600	
£25,000	

Task 8.9

Define a 'contingent asset' and a 'contingent liability', and explain how each should be treated in the financial statements.

BPP
LEARNING MEDIA

Task 8.10

The directors of a company are reviewing the company's most recent draft financial statements and the following points have been raised for discussion:

(a) Shortly after the end of the reporting period a major customer of the company went into liquidation because of heavy trading losses and it is expected that little or nothing will be recoverable for the debt.

In the financial statements the debt has been written off, but one of the directors has pointed out that, as an event after the reporting period, the debt should not in fact be written off but disclosure should be made by note to this year's financial statements, and the debt written off next year.

(b) An ex-director of the company has commenced an action against the company claiming substantial damages for wrongful dismissal. The company's solicitors have advised that the ex-director is unlikely to succeed with his claim. The solicitors' estimates of the company's potential liabilities are:

	£
Legal costs (to be incurred whether the claim is successful or not)	50,000
Settlement of claim if successful	500,000
	550,000

At present there is no provision or note for this contingency.

State with reasons whether you consider the accounting treatments in the draft financial statements, as described above, are acceptable. Include in your answer, where appropriate, an explanation of the relevant provisions of IFRSs/IASs.

Task 8.11

At 30 April 20X7 Ellison Ltd has the following two legal claims outstanding:

1   A legal action against the company filed in February 20X8. Ellison Ltd has been advised that it is probable that the liability will materialise.

2   A legal action taken by the company against another entity, started in March 20X4. Ellison Ltd has been advised that it is probable that it will win the case.

According to IAS 37 *Provisions, Contingent Liabilities and Contingent Assets*, how should the company report these legal actions in its financial statements for the year ended 30 April 20X7?

Legal action 1	Legal action 2	
Disclose in a note to the financial statements	No disclosure	
Recognise a provision	No disclosure	
Recognise a provision	Disclose in a note to the financial statements	
Recognise a provision	Recognise the income	

Task 8.12

Which of the following events after the end of the reporting period would normally be classified as adjusting, according to IAS 10 *Events After the Reporting Period*?

Destruction of a major non-current asset	
Discovery of error or fraud	
Issue of shares	
Purchases of a major non-current asset	

Task 8.13

Teign Ltd prepares its financial statements to 30 September each year. The following events took place between 30 September and the date on which the financial statements were authorised for issue.

(i) The company made a major purchase of plant and machinery.

(ii) A customer who owed the company money at 30 September was declared bankrupt.

Which of the above is likely to be classified as an adjusting event according to IAS 10 *Events After the Reporting Period*?

(i) only	
(ii) only	
Both	
Neither of them	

Task 8.14

On 1 September 20X9 Usk Ltd sold goods to Chertsey Ltd. The two companies have agreed that Chertsey Ltd can return any items that are still unsold at 30 November 20X9. All the goods remained in the inventories of Chertsey Ltd at 30 September 20X9. Based on past sales, Usk estimates that 20% of the goods will be returned.

In accordance with IFRS 15 *Revenue from Contracts with Customers*, Usk Ltd should not recognise any revenue from this transaction in its financial statements for the year ended 30 September 20X9.

Is this statement True or False?

True	
False	

Task 8.15

Brondby Ltd is about to enter into two leases for items of equipment. The terms of the first lease require the company to make lease payments of £5,000 per annum with a lease term of five years. The fair value of the equipment is £20,000 and its economic life is six years. The second lease is for a term of two years and Brondby Ltd is required to make lease payments of £200 per month. The fair value of this item of equipment is £9,000 and its economic life is seven years.

The directors of Brondby Ltd understand that the accounting treatment of each lease will depend upon whether it is to be classified as a finance lease or as an operating lease, but are unsure as to the requirements of IAS 17 *Leases*, both in terms of when a lease should be classified as a finance lease or as an operating lease, and how the two types of lease should be accounted for.

Prepare brief notes for the directors of Brondby Ltd to cover the following:

(a) **When should a lease be classified as a finance lease and when should it be classified as an operating lease according to IAS 17 *Leases*?**

(b) **(i)** **Explain how a finance lease is accounted for in the financial statement of the lessee at the beginning of the lease term only.**

(ii) **Explain how an operating lease is accounted for in the financial statements of the lessee.**

(c) **Which of the two leases Brondby Ltd is about to enter into would be classified as a finance lease, if any?**

Task 8.16

You have been asked to help prepare the financial statements of Merched Ltd for the year ended 31 March 20X3. Legal proceedings have been started against the company because of faulty products supplied to a customer. The company's lawyers advise that it is probable that the entity will be found liable for damages of £250,000.

Explain how you would treat the probable damages arising from the legal proceedings in the financial statements. Refer, where relevant, to accounting standards.

Task 8.17

Houghton Ltd owns and operates a department store. During the year, the directors decided to offer refunds to dissatisfied customers, provided that these were claimed within three months of the date the goods were purchased. There are large notices explaining this policy on every floor of the store. Since the policy was introduced, refunds have been claimed on roughly 2% of all sales.

Prepare brief notes for the directors of Houghton Ltd to answer the following questions:

(a) **When should a provision be recognised, according to IAS 37 *Provisions, Contingent Liabilities and Contingent Assets*?**

(b) **How should the policy of refunding customers be treated in the financial statements for the year?**

(c) **How should the policy of refunding customers be disclosed in the notes to the financial statements?**

....

Task 8.18

Talland Ltd purchases goods for resale. The directors of the company would like you to clarify the accounting treatment of inventories and when to recognise revenue arising from the sale of goods. Answer the following queries of the directors.

(a) **What are inventories, according to IAS 2 *Inventories*? How are inventories measured? What is included in the cost of inventories?**

(b) **What is revenue, according to IFRS 15 *Revenue from Contracts with Customers*? How should it be measured? When should revenue be recognised?**

....

Chapter 9 – Group accounts: the consolidated statement of financial position

Task 9.1

Erewash Ltd has rights to variable returns from its involvement in Amber Ltd and has the ability to affect those returns through its power over Amber Ltd. In relation to Erewash Ltd, Amber Ltd is:

A parent	
A simple investment	
A subsidiary	

Task 9.2

IFRS 3 Business Combinations identifies key requirements of the acquisition method.

(i)   Identifying the acquirer

(ii)   Determining the acquisition date

(iii)   Recognising and measuring the identifiable assets acquired, liabilities assumed and any non-controlling interest in the acquiree

(iv)   Recognising and measuring goodwill or a gain from a bargain purchase

Which of the above statements are key requirements of the acquisition method?

Elements (i) and (iii) only	
Elements (ii), (iii) and (iv) only	
Elements (i), (ii) and (iv) only	
All of the above	

Task 9.3

The directors of Lavendar plc are considering acquiring a subsidiary. They are unclear about the criteria for an entity to be a parent of a subsidiary, and would like you to clarify this for them. They would like to write off any goodwill that arises on the acquisition of the subsidiary immediately, and have asked for your opinion on the correct accounting treatment.

Prepare brief notes to answer the following questions that have been asked by the directors of Lavendar plc:

(a) **What are the criteria for an entity being the parent of a subsidiary?**

(b) **Explain the accounting treatment that has to be adopted for the goodwill in the consolidated statement of financial position of Lavendar plc**

Note. Your answer should make reference to relevant accounting standards.

Task 9.4

On 1 January 20X1 X plc purchased 75% of the ordinary share capital of Y Ltd when the retained earnings of Y Ltd stood at £240,000. At 31 December 20X1 the summarised statements of financial position of the two companies were as follows.

	X plc £000	Y Ltd £000
Assets		
Property, plant and equipment	800	400
Investment in Y Ltd	350	–
Current assets	170	130
	1,320	530
Equity and liabilities		
Share capital	800	200
Retained earnings	420	280
	1,220	480
Current liabilities	100	50
	1,320	530

Draft a consolidated statement of financial position for X plc and its subsidiary as at 31 December 20X1.

X plc
Consolidated statement of financial position as at 31 December 20X1

	£000
Assets	
Goodwill	
Property, plant and equipment	
Current assets	
Equity and liabilities	
Share capital	
Retained earnings	
Non-controlling interest	
Current liabilities	

Workings

Goodwill	£000
Consideration	
Non-controlling interest at acquisition	
Net assets acquired	

Retained earnings	£000
X plc	
Y Ltd – attributable to X plc	

Non-controlling interest (NCI) at acquisition	£000
Share capital – attributable to NCI	
Retained earnings – attributable to NCI	

Non-controlling interest (NCI) at year end	£000
Share capital – attributable to NCI	
Retained earnings – attributable to NCI	

Task 9.5

Fertwrangler Ltd has one subsidiary, Voncarryon Ltd, which it acquired on 1 April 20X2. The statement of financial position of Voncarryon Ltd as at 31 March 20X3 is set out below.

Voncarryon Ltd
Summarised statement of financial position as at 31 March 20X3

	£000
Non-current assets	3,855
Current assets	4,961
Total assets	8,816
Equity	
Share capital	2,000
Share premium	1,000
Retained earnings	1,770
	4,770
Non-current liabilities	1,500
Current liabilities	2,546
Total equity and liabilities	8,816

Further information

- The share capital of Voncarryon Ltd consists of ordinary shares of £1 each. There have been no changes to the balances of share capital and share premium during the year. No dividends were paid by Voncarryon Ltd during the year.

- Fertwrangler acquired 1,200,000 shares in Voncarryon Ltd on 1 April 20X2 at a cost of £3,510,000.

- At 1 April 20X2 the balance on the retained earnings reserve of Voncarryon Ltd was £1,350,000.

- The fair value of the non-current assets of Voncarryon Ltd at 1 April 20X2 was £4,455,000. The book value of the assets at 1 April 20X2 was £4,055,000. The revaluation has not been reflected in the books of Voncarryon Ltd.

- Goodwill arising on consolidation had suffered an impairment loss of £66,000 by 31 March 20X3.

- At 31 March 20X3 the balance on the retained earnings reserve of Fertwrangler Ltd was £5,610,000.

- Non-controlling interest is measured at the proportionate share of the fair value of Voncarryon's net assets.

(a) **Calculate the goodwill figure relating to the acquisition of Voncarryon Ltd that will appear in the consolidated statement of financial position of Fertwrangler Ltd as at 31 March 20X3.**

£

(b) **Calculate the non-controlling interest figure that will appear in the consolidated statement of financial position of Fertwrangler Ltd at 31 March 20X3.**

£

(c) **Calculate the balance on the consolidated retained earnings reserve that will appear in the consolidated statement of financial position of Fertwrangler Ltd at 31 March 20X3.**

£

Task 9.6

The Managing Director of Dumyat plc has asked you to prepare the statement of financial position for the group. Dumyat plc has one subsidiary, Devon Ltd. The statements of financial position of the two companies as at 31 October 20X7 are set out below.

Statements of financial position as at 31 October 20X7

	Dumyat plc £000	Devon Ltd £000
ASSETS		
Non-current assets		
Property, plant and equipment	65,388	31,887
Investment in Devon Ltd	26,000	
	91,388	31,887
	£000	**£000**
Current assets		
Inventories	28,273	5,566
Trade and other receivables	11,508	5,154
Receivable from Devon Ltd	4,000	0
Cash and cash equivalents	2,146	68
	45,927	10,788
Total assets	137,315	42,675
EQUITY AND LIABILITIES		
Equity		
Share capital	25,000	12,000
Share premium	12,000	4,000
Retained earnings	55,621	17,092
Total equity	92,621	33,092

	Dumyat plc £000	Devon Ltd £000
Non-current liabilities		
Long-term loans	25,000	4,000
Current liabilities		
Trade and other payables	13,554	1,475
Payable to Dumyat plc	0	4,000
Tax liabilities	6,140	108
	19,694	5,583
Total liabilities	44,694	9,583
Total equity and liabilities	137,315	42,675

You have been given the following further information.

- The share capital of Devon Ltd consists of ordinary shares of £1 each. Ownership of these shares carries voting rights in Devon Ltd. There have been no changes to the balances of share capital and share premium during the year. No dividends were paid or proposed by Devon Ltd during the year.

- Dumyat plc acquired 9,000,000 shares in Devon Ltd on 1 November 20X6.

- At 1 November 20X6 the balance of retained earnings of Devon Ltd was £12,052,000.

- The fair value of the non-current assets of Devon Ltd at 1 November 20X6 was £28,800,000. The book value of the non-current assets at 1 November 20X6 was £25,800,000. The revaluation has not been recorded in the books of Devon Ltd (ignore any effect on the depreciation for the year).

- The directors of Dumyat plc have concluded that goodwill has not been impaired during the year.

- The non-controlling interest is measured at the proportionate share of the fair value of Devon Ltd's net assets.

Draft a consolidated statement of financial position for Dumyat plc and its subsidiary as at 31 October 20X7. (Complete the left hand column by writing in the correct line item from the list provided.)

113

Dumyat plc
Consolidated statement of financial position as at 31 October 20X7

	£000
ASSETS	
Non-current assets	
▼	
▼	
Current assets	
▼	
▼	
▼	
Total assets	
EQUITY AND LIABILITIES	
Equity	
▼	
▼	
▼	
Non-controlling interest	
Total equity	
Non-current liabilities	
▼	
Current liabilities	
▼	
▼	
Total liabilities	
Total equity and liabilities	

Picklist:

Cash and cash equivalents
Goodwill
Inventories
Long term loans
Property, plant and equipment
Retained earnings
Share capital
Share premium
Tax payable
Trade and other payables
Trade and other receivables

Workings

(Complete the left hand column by writing in the correct narrative from the list provided.)

Goodwill		£000
	▼	
	▼	
	▼	

Picklist:

Consideration
Non-controlling interest at acquisition
Net assets acquired

Retained earnings		£000
	▼	
	▼	

Picklist:

Devon Ltd – attributable to Dumyat plc
Dumyat plc
Revaluation

Non-controlling interest (NCI) at acquisition	£000
▼	
▼	
▼	
▼	

Picklist:

Current assets – attributable to NCI
Non-current assets – attributable to NCI
Price paid
Retained earnings – attributable to NCI
Revaluation reserve – attributable to NCI
Share capital – attributable to NCI
Share premium – attributable to NCI

Non-controlling interest (NCI) at year end	£000
▼	
▼	
▼	
▼	

Picklist:

Current assets – attributable to NCI
Non-current assets – attributable to NCI
Price paid
Retained earnings – attributable to NCI
Revaluation reserve – attributable to NCI
Share capital – attributable to NCI
Share premium – attributable to NCI

Task 9.7

The Managing Director of Tolsta plc has asked you to prepare the statement of financial position for the group. Tolsta plc has one subsidiary, Balallan Ltd. The statements of financial position of the two companies as at 31 October 20X8 are set out below.

Statements of financial position as at 31 October 20X8

	Tolsta plc £000	Balallan Ltd £000
ASSETS		
Non-current assets		
Property, plant and equipment	47,875	31,913
Investment in Balallan Ltd	32,000	
	79,875	31,913
Current assets		
Inventories	25,954	4,555
Trade and other receivables	14,343	3,656
Cash and cash equivalents	1,956	47
	42,253	8,258
Total assets	122,128	40,171

	Tolsta plc £000	Balallan Ltd £000
EQUITY AND LIABILITIES		
Equity		
Share capital	45,000	12,000
Share premium	12,000	6,000
Retained earnings	26,160	11,340
Total equity	83,160	29,340
Non-current liabilities		
Long-term loans	20,000	7,000
Current liabilities		
Trade and other payables	14,454	3,685
Tax liabilities	4,514	146
	18,968	3,831
Total liabilities	38,968	10,831
Total equity and liabilities	122,128	40,171

Further information

- The share capital of Balallan Ltd consists of ordinary shares of £1 each. Ownership of these shares carries voting rights in Balallan Ltd. There have been no changes to the balances of share capital and share premium during the year. No dividends were paid or proposed by Balallan Ltd during the year.

- Tolsta plc acquired 8,000,000 shares in Balallan Ltd on 1 November 20X7.

- At 1 November 20X7 the balance of retained earnings of Balallan Ltd was £9,750,000.

- The fair value of the non-current assets of Balallan Ltd at 1 November 20X7 was £31,100,000. The book value of the non-current assets at 1 November 20X7 was £26,600,000. The revaluation has not been recorded in the books of Balallan Ltd (ignore any effect on the depreciation for the year).

- Included in Trade and other receivables for Tolsta plc and in Trade and other payables for Balallan Ltd is an inter-company transaction for £2,000,000 that took place in early October 20X8.

- The directors of Tolsta plc have concluded that goodwill has been impaired by £2,100,000 during the year.

- The non-controlling interest is measured as the proportionate share of the fair value of Balallan Ltd's net assets.

Draft a consolidated statement of financial position for Tolsta plc and its subsidiary as at 31 October 20X8.

Tolsta plc

Consolidated statement of financial position as at 31 October 20X8

	£000
ASSETS	
Non-current assets	
Intangible assets: goodwill	
Property, plant and equipment	
Current assets	
Inventories	
Trade and other receivables	
Cash and cash equivalents	
Total assets	

	£000
EQUITY AND LIABILITIES	
Equity	
Share capital	
Share premium	
Retained earnings	
Non-controlling interest	
Total equity	
Non-current liabilities	
Long-term loan	
Current liabilities	
Trade and other payables	
Tax liabilities	
Total liabilities	
Total equity and liabilities	

Workings

(Complete the left hand column by writing in the correct narrative from the list provided.)

Goodwill		£000
	▼	
	▼	
	▼	
	▼	

Picklist:

Impairment
Consideration
Non-controlling interest at acquisition
Net assets acquired

Retained earnings		£000
	▼	
	▼	
	▼	

Picklist:

Balallan Ltd – attributable to Tolsta plc
Impairment
Revaluation
Tolsta plc

Non-controlling interest (NCI) at acquisition	£000
▼	
▼	
▼	
▼	

Picklist:

Current assets – attributable to NCI
Impairment
Non-current assets – attributable to NCI
Price paid
Retained earnings – attributable to NCI
Revaluation reserve – attributable to NCI
Share capital – attributable to NCI
Share premium – attributable to NCI

Non-controlling interest (NCI) at year end	£000
▼	
▼	
▼	
▼	

Picklist:

Current assets – attributable to NCI
Impairment
Non-current assets – attributable to NCI
Price paid
Retained earnings – attributable to NCI
Revaluation reserve – attributable to NCI
Share capital – attributable to NCI
Share premium – attributable to NCI

Task 9.8

Ard plc has one subsidiary, Ledi Ltd. The summarised statements of financial position of the two companies as at 31 March 20X9 are set out below.

Summarised statements of financial position as at 31 March 20X9

	Ard plc £000	Ledi Ltd £000
ASSETS		
Non-current assets		
Property, plant and equipment	45,210	27,480
Investment in Ledi Ltd	23,000	
	68,210	27,480
Current assets	32,782	10,835
Total assets	100,992	38,315
EQUITY AND LIABILITIES		
Equity		
Share capital	50,000	20,000
Retained earnings	21,526	9,740
Total equity	71,526	29,740
Non-current liabilities	14,000	4,000
Current liabilities	15,466	4,575
Total equity and liabilities	100,992	38,315

Further information

- The share capital of Ledi Ltd consists of ordinary shares of £1 each. Ownership of these shares carries voting rights in Ledi Ltd. There have been no changes to the balances of share capital and share premium during the year. No dividends were paid or proposed by Ledi Ltd during the year.

- Ard plc acquired 12,000,000 shares in Ledi Ltd on 1 April 20X8.

- On 1 April 20X8 the balance of retained earnings of Ledi Ltd was £7,640,000.

- Included in Trade and other receivables for Ard plc and in Trade and other payables for Ledi Ltd is an inter-company transaction for £3,000,000 that took place in early March 20X9.

- The directors of Ard plc have concluded that goodwill has been impaired by £1,600,000 during the year.

Draft a consolidated statement of financial position for Ard plc and its subsidiary as at 31 March 20X9.

Ard plc

Consolidated statement of financial position as at 31 March 20X9

	£000
ASSETS	
Non-current assets	
Intangible assets: goodwill	
Property, plant and equipment	
Current assets	
Total assets	
EQUITY AND LIABILITIES	
Equity	
Share capital	
Retained earnings	
Non-controlling interest	
Total equity	
Non-current liabilities	
Current liabilities	
Total liabilities	
Total equity and liabilities	

Workings

(Complete the left hand column by writing in the correct narrative from the list provided.)

Goodwill		£000
	▼	
	▼	
	▼	
	▼	

Picklist:

Impairment
Consideration
Non-controlling interest at acquisition
Net assets acquired

Retained earnings		£000
	▼	
	▼	
	▼	

Picklist:

Ard plc
Impairment
Ledi Ltd – attributable to Ard plc

Non-controlling interest (NCI) at acquisition	£000
▼	
▼	

Picklist:

Current assets – attributable to NCI
Impairment
Non-current assets – attributable to NCI
Price paid
Retained earnings – attributable to NCI
Share capital – attributable to NCI

Non-controlling interest (NCI) at year end	£000
▼	
▼	

Picklist:

Current assets – attributable to NCI
Impairment
Non-current assets – attributable to NCI
Price paid
Retained earnings – attributable to NCI
Share capital – attributable to NCI

....

Task 9.9

The Managing Director of Glebe plc has asked you to prepare the statement of financial position for the group. Glebe plc acquired 70% of the issued share capital of Starks Ltd on 1 April 20X0. At that date Starks Ltd had issued share capital of £10,000,000 and retained earnings of £11,540,000.

The summarised statements of financial position of the two companies as at 31 March 20X1 are set out below.

	Glebe plc £000	Starks Ltd £000
ASSETS		
Investment in Starks Ltd	18,000	
Non-current assets	36,890	25,600
Current assets	22,364	7,835
Total assets	77,254	33,435
EQUITY AND LIABILITIES		
Equity		
Share capital	40,000	10,000
Retained earnings	12,249	16,650
Total equity	52,249	26,650
Non-current liabilities	13,000	5,000
Current liabilities	12,005	1,785
Total liabilities	25,005	6,785
Total equity and liabilities	77,254	33,435

Additional data

- The fair value of the non-current assets of Starks Ltd at 1 April 20X0 was £26,300,000. The book value of the non-current assets at 1 April 20X0 was £23,900,000. The revaluation has not been recorded in the books of Starks Ltd (ignore any effect on the depreciation for the year).

- The directors of Glebe plc have concluded that goodwill has been impaired by £400,000 during the year.

- Glebe plc has decided non-controlling interests will be valued at their proportionate share of net assets.

Draft a consolidated statement of financial position for Glebe plc and its subsidiary as at 31 March 20X1.

Glebe plc

Consolidated statement of financial position as at 31 March 20X1

	£000
ASSETS	
Non-current assets	
Intangible assets: goodwill	
Property, plant and equipment	
Current assets	
Total assets	
EQUITY AND LIABILITIES	
Equity	
Share capital	
Retained earnings	
Non-controlling interest	
Total equity	
Non-current liabilities	
Current liabilities	
Total liabilities	
Total equity and liabilities	

Workings

(Complete the left hand column by writing in the correct narrative from the list provided.)

Goodwill	£000
▼	
▼	
▼	
▼	

Picklist:

Impairment
Consideration
Non-controlling interest at acquisition
Net assets acquired

Retained earnings	£000
▼	
▼	
▼	

Picklist:

Glebe plc
Impairment
Revaluation
Starks Ltd – attributable to Glebe plc

Non-controlling interest (NCI) at acquisition	£000
▼	
▼	
▼	

Picklist:

Current assets – attributable to NCI
Impairment
Non-current assets – attributable to NCI
Price paid
Retained earnings – attributable to NCI
Revaluation reserve – attributable to NCI
Share capital – attributable to NCI

Non-controlling interest (NCI) at year end	£000
▼	
▼	
▼	

Picklist:

Current assets – attributable to NCI
Impairment
Non-current assets – attributable to NCI
Price paid
Retained earnings – attributable to NCI
Revaluation reserve – attributable to NCI
Share capital – attributable to NCI

....

Chapter 10 – Group accounts: further aspects

Task 10.1

	P plc £000	S Ltd £000
Continuing operations		
Revenue	4,600	2,210
Cost of sales	(2,700)	(1,320)
Gross profit	1,900	890
Other income – dividend from S Ltd	70	–
Operating expenses	(870)	(430)
Profit before tax	1,100	460
Tax	(300)	(120)
Profit for the period from continuing operations	800	340

Draft a consolidated statement of profit or loss income for P plc and its subsidiary for the year ended 31 March 20X2.

Consolidated statement of profit or loss for the year ended 31 March 20X2

	£000
Continuing operations	
Revenue	
Cost of sales	
Gross profit	
Other income	
Operating expenses	
Profit before tax	
Tax	
Profit for the period from continuing operations	

	£000
Attributable to:	
Equity holders of the parent	
Non-controlling interests	

Task 10.2

C plc purchased 60% of the shares in D Ltd a number of years ago. The statements of profit or loss for each company for the year ended 31 December 20X1 are given below.

	C plc £000	D Ltd £000
Continuing operations		
Revenue	38,600	14,700
Cost of sales	(25,000)	(9,500)
Gross profit	13,600	5,200
Other income – dividend from D Ltd	300	–
Operating expenses	(7,700)	(2,900)
Profit before tax	6,200	2,300
Tax	(1,600)	(600)
Profit for the period from continuing operations	4,600	1,700

You are also given the following information.

* During the year C plc sold goods which had cost £4,000,000 to D Ltd for £5,000,000. All of the goods were still in the inventory of D Ltd at the year-end.

Draft a consolidated statement of profit or loss for C plc and its subsidiary for the year ended 31 December 20X1.

C plc
Consolidated statement of profit or loss for the year ended 31 December 20X1

	£000
Continuing operations	
Revenue	
Cost of sales	
Gross profit	
Other income	
Operating expenses	
Profit before tax	
Tax	
Profit for the period from continuing operations	
Attributable to:	
Equity holders of the parent	
Non-controlling interests	

Workings

Revenue	£000
C plc	
D Ltd	
Total inter-company adjustment	

Cost of sales	£000
C plc	
D Ltd	
Total inter-company adjustment	

Task 10.3

The managing director of Aswall plc has asked you to prepare the draft consolidated statement of profit or loss for the group. The company has one subsidiary, Unsafey Ltd. The statements of profit or loss for the two companies for the year ended 31 March 20X4 are set out below.

Statements of profit or loss for the year ended 31 March 20X4

	Aswall plc £000	Unsafey Ltd £000
Continuing operations		
Revenue	32,412	12,963
Cost of sales	(14,592)	(5,576)
Gross profit	17,820	7,387
Other income – dividend from Unsafey Ltd	1,500	–
Distribution costs	(5,449)	(1,307)
Administrative expenses	(3,167)	(841)
Profit from operations	10,704	5,239
Finance costs	(1,960)	(980)
Profit before tax	8,744	4,259
Tax	(2,623)	(1,063)
Profit for the period from continuing operations	6,121	3,196

Further information:

- Aswall plc owns 75% of the ordinary share capital of Unsafey Ltd.

- During the year Unsafey Ltd sold goods which had cost £1,200,000 to Aswall plc for £1,860,000. None of the goods had been sold by Aswall plc by the end of the year.

Draft a consolidated statement of profit or loss for Aswall plc and its subsidiary for the year ended 31 March 20X4.

Aswall plc

Consolidated statement of profit or loss for the year ended 31 March 20X4

	£000
Continuing operations	
Revenue	
Cost of sales	
Gross profit	
Other income	
Distribution costs	
Administrative expenses	
Profit from operations	
Finance costs	
Profit before tax	
Tax	
Profit for the period from continuing operations	
Attributable to:	
Equity holders of the parent	
Non-controlling interest	

135

Workings

Revenue	£000
Aswall plc	
Unsafey Ltd	
Total inter-company adjustment	

Cost of sales	£000
Aswall plc	
Unsafey Ltd	
Total inter-company adjustment	

Non-controlling interest (NCI)	£000
Profit for the period attributable to NCI	
Unrealised profit attributable to NCI	

....

Task 10.4

Danube plc has one subsidiary, Inn Ltd.

Extracts from their statements of profit or loss for the year ended 31 March 20X2 are shown below:

	Danube plc £000	Inn Ltd £000
Continuing operations		
Revenue	15,800	5,400
Cost of sales	(8,500)	(2,800)
Gross profit	7,300	2,600
Other income	300	–
Operating expenses	(3,300)	(1,230)
Profit from operations	4,300	1,370

Additional data

- Danube plc acquired 75% of the ordinary share capital of Inn Ltd on 1 April 20X1.

- During the year Inn Ltd sold goods which had cost £600,000 to Danube plc for £1,000,000. Half of these goods still remain in the inventories of Danube plc at the end of the year.

- Other income of Danube plc included a dividend received from Inn Ltd.

- Inn ltd had paid a dividend of 400,000 on 1 March 20X2.

Draft the consolidated statement of profit or loss for Danube plc and its subsidiary up to and including the profit from operations line for the year ended 31 March 20X2.

Danube plc

Consolidated statement of profit or loss for the year ended 31 March 20X2

	£000
Continuing operations	
Revenue	
Cost of sales	
Gross profit	
Other income	
Operating expenses	
Profit from operations	

Workings

Revenue	£000
Danube plc	
Inn Ltd	
Total inter-company adjustment	

Cost of sales	£000
Danube plc	
Inn Ltd	
Total inter-company adjustment	

Task 10.5

The managing director of Wewill plc has asked you to prepare the draft consolidated statement of profit or loss for the group. The company has one subsidiary, Rokyu Ltd. The statements of profit or loss for the two companies for the year ended 31 March 20X4 are set out below.

Statements of profit or loss for the year ended 31 March 20X4

	Wewill plc £000	Rokyu Ltd £000
Continuing operations		
Revenue	36,400	14,600
Cost of sales	(20,020)	(6,935)
Gross profit	16,830	7,665
Other income – dividend from Rokyu Ltd	860	–
Distribution costs	(6,552)	(3,358)
Administrative expenses	(4,004)	(1,898)
Profit from operations	6,684	2,409
Finance costs	(675)	(154)
Profit before tax	6,009	2,255
Tax	(1,468)	(445)
Profit for the period from continuing operations	4,541	1,810

Additional data:

- Wewill plc acquired 80% of the ordinary share capital of Rokyu Ltd on 1 April 20X3.

- During the year Wewill plc sold goods which had cost £1,000,000 to Rokyu Ltd for £1,400,000. None of the goods had been sold by Rokyu Ltd by the end of the year.

Draft a consolidated statement of profit or loss for Wewill plc and its subsidiary for the year ended 31 March 20X4.

Wewill plc

Consolidated statement of profit or loss for the year ended 31 March 20X4

	£000
Continuing operations	
Revenue	
Cost of sales	
Gross profit	
Other income	
Distribution costs	
Administrative expenses	
Profit from operations	
Finance costs	
Profit before tax	
Tax	
Profit for the period from continuing operations	
Attributable to:	
Equity holders of the parent	
Non-controlling interest	

Workings

Revenue	£000
Wewill plc	
Rokyu Ltd	
Total inter-company adjustment	

Cost of sales	£000
Wewill plc	
Rokyu Ltd	
Total inter-company adjustment	

Task 10.6

Beadnell plc acquired 100% of the issued share capital and voting rights of Catton Ltd on 1 January 20X0.

The consolidated cost of sales of Beadnell plc and its subsidiary undertaking for the year ended 31 December 20X0, before taking into account any adjustments required in respect of the information below, is £200,000.

Additional data

During the year Beadnell plc sold goods which had cost £40,000 to Catton Ltd for £50,000. 60% of these goods still remain in inventories at the end of the year.

The consolidated cost of sales for the year ending 31 December 20X0 will be:

£144,000	
£150,000	
£156,000	
£160,000	

Chapter 11 – Interpreting financial statements

Calculating ratios

Task 11.1

Given below is a summarised statement of profit or loss and a summarised statement of financial position for a company.

Statement of profit or loss for the year ended 30 April 20X2

	£000
Continuing operations	
Revenue	989
Cost of sales	(467)
Gross profit	522
Operating expenses	(308)
Profit from operations	214
Interest payable	(34)
Profit before tax	180
Tax	(48)
Profit for the period from continuing operations	132

Statement of financial position as at 30 April 20X2

	£000
Non-current assets	1,200
Current assets	700
	1,900
Share capital and reserves	1,000
Non-current liabilities: long-term loan	400
Current liabilities	500
	1,900

Calculate the following ratios to the nearest ONE DECIMAL PLACE.

(a)	Gross profit percentage		%
(b)	Operating profit percentage		%
(c)	Return on capital employed		%
(d)	Asset turnover (net assets)		times
(e)	Interest cover		times

Task 11.2

Given below are extracts from a company's statement of profit or loss and statement of financial position.

Statement of profit or loss for the year ended 30 June 20X2 – extract

	£
Revenue	772,400
Cost of sales	507,400
Gross profit	265,000

Statement of financial position as at 30 June 20X2 – extract

	£
Inventories	58,600
Trade receivables	98,400
Trade payables	86,200
Bank overdraft	6,300

Calculate the following ratios to the nearest ONE DECIMAL PLACE.

(a)	Current ratio		:1
(b)	Quick (acid test) ratio		:1
(c)	Trade receivables collection period		days
(d)	Inventory turnover		times
(e)	Inventory holding period		days

Task 11.3

You have been asked to calculate ratios for Midsummer Ltd in respect of its financial statements for the year ending 31 March 20X4 to assist a shareholder in his analysis of the company. The shareholder has given you Midsummer's statement of profit or loss and the summarised statement of financial position prepared for internal purposes. These are set out below.

Midsummer Ltd

Statement of profit or loss for the year ended 31 March 20X4

	£000
Continuing operations	
Revenue	8,420
Cost of sales	(3,536)
Gross profit	4,884
Distribution costs	(1,471)
Administrative expenses	(1,224)
Profit from operations	2,189
Finance costs	(400)
Profit before tax	1,789
Tax	(465)
Profit for the period from continuing operations	1,324

Midsummer Ltd

Summarised statement of financial position as at 31 March 20X4

	£000
ASSETS	
Non-current assets	15,132
Current assets	4,624
Total assets	19,756
EQUITY AND LIABILITIES	
Equity	
Share capital	6,000
Share premium	2,000
Retained earnings	4,541
Total equity	12,541
Non-current liabilities: long term loan	5,000
Current liabilities	2,215
Total liabilities	7,215
Total equity plus liabilities	19,756

(a) **State the formulae that are used to calculate each of the following ratios:**

(Write in the correct formula from the list provided)

(i) Return on capital employed [▼]

Formulae:

Profit after tax/Total equity × 100
Profit from operations/Total equity × 100
Profit after tax/Total equity + Non-current liabilities × 100
Profit from operations/Total equity + Non-current liabilities × 100

(ii) Operating profit percentage ⬛▼

Formulae:

Profit from operations/Revenue × 100
Profit from operations/Total assets × 100
Profit from operations/Total equity + Non-current liabilities × 100
Profit from operations/Finance costs × 100

(iii) Gross profit percentage ⬛▼

Formulae:

Gross profit/Total equity × 100
Gross profit/Revenue × 100
Gross profit/Total assets × 100
Gross profit/Total assets – Current liabilities

(iv) Asset turnover (net assets) ⬛▼

Formulae:

Revenue/Total assets – Current liabilities
Revenue/Total assets – Total liabilities
Total assets – Current liabilities/Revenue
Total assets – Total liabilities/Revenue

(v) Gearing ⬛▼

Formulae:

Current assets/Current liabilities
Revenue/Total assets – Current liabilities
Non-current liabilities/Total equity + Non-current liabilities
Profit after tax/Number of issued ordinary shares

(b) Calculate the ratios to the nearest ONE DECIMAL PLACE.

(i)	Return on capital employed		%
(ii)	Operating profit percentage		%
(iii)	Gross profit percentage		%
(iv)	Asset turnover (net assets)		times
(v)	Gearing		%

Task 11.4

A shareholder in Drain Ltd has asked you to help her by analysing the financial statements of the company for the year ended 31 March 20X6. These are set out below.

Drain Ltd
Statement of profit or loss for the year ended 31 March 20X6

	£000
Continuing operations	
Revenue	21,473
Cost of sales	(9,878)
Gross profit	11,595
Distribution costs	(4,181)
Administrative expenses	(3,334)
Profit from operations	4,080
Finance costs	(350)
Profit before tax	3,730
Tax	(858)
Profit for the period from continuing operations	2,872

Drain Ltd
Statement of financial position as at 31 March 20X6

	£000
ASSETS	
Non-current assets	
Property, plant and equipment	27,781
Current assets	
Inventories	1,813
Trade receivables	3,000
Cash and cash equivalents	62
	4,875
Total assets	32,656
EQUITY AND LIABILITIES	
Equity	
Share capital	5,000
Retained earnings	20,563
	25,563
Non-current liabilities	
Bank loans	5,000
Current liabilities	
Trade and other payables	1,235
Tax liabilities	858
	2,093
Total liabilities	7,093
Total equity and liabilities	32,656

(a) **State the formulae that are used to calculate each of the following ratios:**

(Write in the correct formula from the list provided)

(i) Gross profit percentage ▼

Formulae:

Gross profit/Total equity × 100
Gross profit/Revenue × 100
Gross profit/Total assets × 100
Gross profit/Total assets – Current liabilities

(ii) Operating profit percentage ▼

Formulae:

Profit from operations/Revenue × 100
Profit from operations/Total assets × 100
Profit from operations/Total equity + Non-current liabilities × 100
Profit from operations/Finance costs × 100

(iii) Current ratio ▼

Formulae:

Total assets/Total liabilities
Current assets – Inventories/Current liabilities
Current assets/Current liabilities
Total assets – Inventories/Total liabilities

(iv) Quick (acid test) ratio ▼

Formulae:

Current assets/Current liabilities
Total assets – Inventories/Total liabilities
Total assets/Total liabilities
Current assets – Inventories/Current liabilities

(v) Inventory holding period ▼

Formulae:

Inventories/Cost of sales × 365
Inventories/Revenue × 365
Cost of sales/Inventories × 365
Revenue/Inventories × 365

(b) **Calculate the ratios to the nearest ONE DECIMAL PLACE.**

(i) Gross profit percentage	%
(ii) Operating profit percentage	%
(iii) Current ratio	:1
(iv) Quick (acid test) ratio	:1
(v) Inventory holding period	days

Task 11.5

You have been asked to calculate ratios for Route Ltd in respect of its financial statements for the year ending 31 March 20X7.

Route Ltd's statement of profit or loss and statement of financial position are set out below.

Route Ltd

Statement of profit or loss for the year ended 31 March 20X7

	£000
Continuing operations	
Revenue	20,562
Cost of sales	(11,309)
Gross profit	9,253
Distribution costs	(4,841)
Administrative expenses	(3,007)
Profit from operations	1,405
Finance costs – interest on bank loan	(800)
Profit before tax	605
Tax	(133)
Profit for the period from continuing operations	472

BPP
LEARNING MEDIA

Route Ltd

Statement of financial position as at 31 March 20X7

	£000
ASSETS	
Non-current assets	
Property, plant and equipment	23,982
Current assets	
Inventories	4,012
Trade and other receivables	2,241
Cash and cash equivalents	84
	6,337
Total assets	30,319
EQUITY AND LIABILITIES	
Equity	
Share capital	4,000
Retained earnings	9,413
Total equity	13,413
Non-current liabilities	
Bank loans	14,000
Current liabilities	
Trade and other payables	2,773
Tax liabilities	133
	2,906
Total liabilities	16,906
Total equity and liabilities	30,319

(a) **State the formulae that are used to calculate each of the following ratios:**

(Write in the correct formula from the list provided)

(i) Operating expenses/revenue percentage

Formulae:

Administrative expenses/Revenue × 100
Distribution costs + administrative expenses/Revenue × 100
Distribution costs/Revenue × 100
Revenue/Distribution costs + administrative expenses × 100

(ii) Current ratio

Formulae:

Total assets/Total liabilities
Current assets – Inventories/Current liabilities
Current assets/Current liabilities
Total assets – Inventories/Total liabilities

(iii) Quick (acid test) ratio

Formulae:

Current assets/Current liabilities
Total assets – Inventories/Total liabilities
Total assets/Total liabilities
Current assets – Inventories/Current liabilities

(iv) Gearing ratio

Formulae:

Current assets/Current liabilities
Revenue/Total assets – Current liabilities
Non-current liabilities/Total equity + Non-current liabilities
Profit after tax/Number of issued ordinary shares

(v) Interest cover

▼

Formulae:

Finance costs/Profit from operations
Finance costs/Revenue
Profit from operations/Finance costs
Revenue/Finance costs

(b) **Calculate the ratios to the nearest ONE DECIMAL PLACE.**

(i)	Operating expenses/revenue percentage	%
(ii)	Current ratio	:1
(iii)	Quick (acid test) ratio	:1
(iv)	Gearing ratio	%
(v)	Interest cover	times

Task 11.6

You have been asked to calculate ratios for Orford Ltd in respect of its financial statements for the year ending 31 October 20X8.

Orford Ltd's statement of profit or loss and statement of financial position are set out below.

Orford Ltd

Statement of profit or loss for the year ended 31 October 20X8

	£000
Continuing operations	
Revenue	4,900
Cost of sales	(2,597)
Gross profit	2,303
Distribution costs	(1,225)
Administrative expenses	(490)
Profit from operations	588
Finance costs	(161)
Profit before tax	427
Tax	(64)
Profit for the period from continuing operations	363

Orford Ltd

Statement of financial position as at 31 October 20X8

	£000
ASSETS	
Non-current assets	
Property, plant and equipment	8,041
Current assets	
Inventories	649
Trade receivables	392
Cash and cash equivalents	0
	1,041
Total assets	9,082
EQUITY AND LIABILITIES	
Equity	
Share capital	2,500
Retained earnings	3,741
Total equity	6,241
Non-current liabilities	
Bank loans	2,300
Current liabilities	
Trade payables	286
Tax liabilities	64
Bank overdraft	191
	541
Total liabilities	2,841
Total equity and liabilities	9,082

(a) **State the formulae that are used to calculate each of the following ratios:**

(Write in the correct formula from the list provided)

(i) Return on shareholders' funds

Formulae:

Profit after tax/Total equity × 100
Profit before tax/Total equity × 100
Profit from operations/Total equity × 100
Profit from operations/Total equity + Non-current liabilities × 100

(ii) Inventory holding period

Formulae:

Inventories/Cost of sales × 365
Inventories/Revenue × 365
Cost of sales/Inventories × 365
Revenue/Inventories × 365

(iii) Trade receivables collection period

Formulae:

Trade payables/Cost of sales × 365
Trade receivables/Cost of sales × 365
Revenue/Trade receivables × 365
Trade receivables/Revenue × 365

(iv) Trade payables payment period

Formulae:

Trade payables/Revenue × 365
Trade payables/Cost of sales × 365
Revenue/Trade payables × 365
Cost of sales/Trade payables × 365

(v) Working capital cycle

▼

Formulae:

Current assets/Current liabilities
Current assets – Inventories/Current liabilities
Inventory days + Receivable days – Payable days
Inventory days + Receivable days + Payable days

(b) **Calculate the ratios to the nearest ONE DECIMAL PLACE.**

(i) Return on shareholders' funds		%
(ii) Inventory holding period		days
(iii) Trade receivables collection period		days
(iv) Trade payables payment period		days
(v) Working capital cycle		days

Task 11.7

You have been asked to calculate ratios for Tower Ltd in respect of its financial statements for the year ending 31 October 20X9.

Tower Ltd's statement of profit or loss and statement of financial position as follows:

Tower Ltd

Statement of profit or loss for the year ended 31 October 20X9

	£000
Continuing operations	
Revenue	27,800
Cost of sales	(14,178)
Gross profit	13,622
Distribution costs	(6,950)
Administrative expenses	(3,892)
Profit from operations	2,780
Finance costs	(840)
Profit before tax	1,940
Tax	(894)
Profit for the period from continuing operations	1,046

Tower Ltd

Statement of financial position as at 31 October 20X9

	£000
ASSETS	
Non-current assets	
Property, plant and equipment	23,016
Current assets	
Inventories	3,261
Trade receivables	1,946
Cash and cash equivalents	–
	5,207
Total assets	28,223
EQUITY AND LIABILITIES	
Equity	
Share capital	8,500
Retained earnings	5,037
Total equity	13,537
Non-current liabilities	
Bank loans	12,000
Current liabilities	
Trade payables	1,276
Tax liabilities	894
Bank overdraft	516
	2,686
Total liabilities	14,686
Total equity and liabilities	28,223

(a) **State the formulae that are used to calculate each of the following ratios:**

(Write in the correct formula from the list provided)

(i) Gearing

▼

Formulae:

Current assets/Current liabilities > 100
Revenue/Total assets – Current liabilities × 100
Non-current liabilities/Total equity + Non-current liabilities × 100
Profit after tax/Number of issued ordinary shares × 100

(ii) Interest cover

▼

Formulae:

Finance costs/Profit from operations
Finance costs/Revenue
Profit from operations/Finance costs
Revenue/Finance costs

(iii) Current ratio

▼

Formulae:

Total assets/Total liabilities
Current assets – Inventories/Current liabilities
Current assets/Current liabilities
Total assets – Inventories/Total liabilities

(iv) Trade receivables collection period

▼

Formulae:

Trade payables/Cost of sales × 365
Trade receivables/Cost of sales × 365
Revenue/Trade receivables × 365
Trade receivables/Revenue × 365

(v) Trade payables payment period

▼

Formulae:

Trade payables/Revenue × 365
Trade payables/Cost of sales × 365
Revenue/Trade payables × 365
Cost of sales/Trade payables × 365

(b) **Calculate the ratios to the nearest ONE DECIMAL PLACE.**

(i)	Gearing		%
(ii)	Interest cover		times
(iii)	Current ratio		:1
(iv)	Trade receivables collection period		days
(v)	Trade payables payment period		days

Task 11.8

You have been asked to calculate ratios for Jewel Ltd in respect of its financial statements for the year ending 31 March 20X1 to assist your manager in his analysis of the company.

Jewel Ltd's statement of profit or loss and statement of financial position are set out below.

Jewel Ltd – Statement of profit or loss for the year ended 30 September 20X1

	£000
Continuing operations	
Revenue	36,000
Cost of sales	(19,800)
Gross profit	16,200
Distribution costs	(6,840)
Administrative expenses	(6,120)
Profit from operations	3,240
Finance costs	(280)
Profit before tax	2,960
Tax	(2,094)
Profit for the period from continuing operations	866

Jewel Ltd – Statement of financial position as at 30 September 20X1

	£000
ASSETS	
Non-current assets	
Property, plant and equipment	26,908
Current assets	
Inventories	2,376
Trade receivables	3,960
Cash and cash equivalents	787
	7,123
Total assets	34,031
EQUITY AND LIABILITIES	
Equity	
Share capital	12,000
Retained earnings	14,155
Total equity	26,155
Non-current liabilities	
Bank loans	4,000
	4,000
Current liabilities	
Trade payables	1,782
Tax liabilities	2,094
	3,876
Total liabilities	7,876
Total equity and liabilities	34,031

(a) **State the formulae that are used to calculate each of the following ratios:**

(Write in the correct formula from the list provided)

(i) Gross profit percentage

Formulae:

Gross profit/Revenue × 100
Gross profit/Total assets × 100
Gross profit/Total equity × 100
Gross profit/Total equity + Non-current liabilities × 100

(ii) Operating profit percentage

Formulae:

Profit from operations/Finance costs × 100
Profit from operations/Revenue × 100
Profit from operations/Total assets × 100
Profit from operations/Total equity + Non-current liabilities × 100

(iii) Return on shareholders' funds

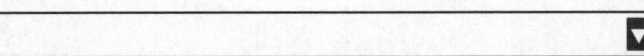

Formulae:

Profit after tax/Total equity × 100
Profit before tax/Total equity × 100
Profit from operations/Total equity × 100
Profit from operations/Total equity + Non-current liabilities × 100

(iv) Quick (acid test) ratio

Formulae:

Current assets/Current liabilities
Total assets/Total liabilities
Current assets – Inventories/Current liabilities
Total assets – Inventories/Total liabilities

(v) Operating expenses/revenue percentage

▼

Formulae:

Administrative expenses/Revenue × 100
Distribution costs + Administrative expenses/Revenue × 100
Distribution costs/Revenue × 100
Revenue/Distribution costs + Administrative expenses × 100

(b) **Calculate the ratios to the nearest ONE DECIMAL PLACE.**

(i)	Gross profit percentage	%
(ii)	Operating profit percentage	%
(iii)	Return on shareholders' funds	%
(iv)	Quick (acid test) ratio	:1
(v)	Operating expenses/revenue percentage	%

Interpreting financial statements

Task 11.9

Given below is a range of financial ratios for two companies that both operate in the retail trade.

	Rigby Ltd	Rialto Ltd
Gross profit percentage	60%	32%
Operating profit percentage	28%	10%
Asset turnover	0.80 times	2.2 times
ROCE	22%	22%
Current ratio	2.0	1.8
Quick ratio	1.2	0.4
Inventory turnover	4.8 times	10.3 times
Trade receivables collection period	41 days	3 days
Trade payables payment period	62 days	70 days
Gearing	33%	50%
Interest cover	16 times	5 times

(a)   **Comment upon what the ratios indicate about each business.**

(b)   **One of the businesses is a supermarket and the other is a jeweller who supplies some goods on credit to long standing customers. Identify, with reasons, which business is which.**

••

Task 11.10

Duncan Tweedy wishes to invest some money in one of two private companies. He has obtained the latest financial statements for Byrne Ltd and May Ltd prepared for internal purposes. As part of his decision making process he has asked you to assess the relative profitability of the two companies, based on the following ratios.

	Byrne Ltd	May Ltd
Return on capital employed	21.5%	32.1%
Gross profit percentage	59.0%	67.0%
Operating profit percentage	25.0%	36.0%

Prepare a report for Duncan Tweedy that:

(a) Uses each ratio to comment on the relative profitability of the companies

(b) Concludes, with reasons, which company is the more profitable.

Task 11.11

A colleague has asked you to take over an assignment. He has been helping a shareholder of Youngernst Ltd to understand the financial statements of the company for the past two years. The shareholder is interested in finding out how well the company has managed working capital. Your colleague has obtained the financial statements of Youngernst Ltd for the past two years and has calculated the following ratios:

	20X3	20X2
Ratio		
Current ratio	2.8:1	2.3:1
Quick (acid test) ratio	0.6:1	1.1:1
Trade receivables collection period	48 days	32 days
Trade payables payment period	27 days	30 days
Inventory holding period	84 days	67 days

Prepare notes for a meeting with the shareholder that include:

(a) **Your comments on the change in the ratios of Youngernst Ltd over the two years, including an analysis of whether the change in each of the ratios shows that the management of the components of working capital has improved or deteriorated.**

(b) **A brief overall conclusion, based on the ratios above.**

Task 11.12

Madge Keygone is the managing director of Asbee Ltd. She has just returned from a meeting with one of the company's major shareholders. The shareholder was concerned about the current ratio, quick ratio, inventory holding period and trade receivables collection period and how they compared with the industry averages. Madge did not understand the shareholder's concern and has asked you to help her. She has calculated these ratios from the summarised financial statements of Asbee Ltd and has obtained the industry averages from computerised databases. These are set out below.

	Asbee Ltd	Industry average
Current ratio	2.3:1	1.9:1
Quick (acid test) ratio	0.8:1	0.9:1
Inventory holding period	176 days	98 days
Trade receivables collection period	51 days	47 days

Prepare a letter for Madge Keygone that includes the following.

(a) **Comments about how the ratios for Asbee Ltd compare with the industry averages and what this tells you about the company.**

(b) **A conclusion, based on the ratios above, as to whether the shareholder is right to be concerned.**

BPP
LEARNING MEDIA

Task 11.13

Leopold Scratchy plans to invest in shares in a private company. He has identified two companies that might be suitable, Partridge Ltd and Carington Ltd. He has obtained the latest financial statements of the companies in order to learn more about the risk inherent in, and return provided by, a potential investment in these companies. You have used these financial statements to compute the following ratios:

	Partridge Ltd	Carington Ltd
Gross profit percentage	59%	59%
Operating profit percentage	23%	15%
Return on shareholders' funds	38%	29%
Gearing	45%	5%

Both companies have the same number of £1 ordinary shares and approximately the same amount of shareholders' funds (share capital and reserves).

Prepare a report for Leopold Scratchy that includes:

(a) **Comments on the relative risk and return of the two companies based on the ratios above.**

(b) **A conclusion, with reasons based on the ratios above, as to which of the two companies would provide Leopold with the best return on his investment and which of the two companies would be the safer investment.**

Task 11.14

Peter Stewart is a shareholder in Hillhead Ltd. He wishes to assess the efficiency and effectiveness of the management of the company. He has asked you to assist him by analysing the financial statements of the company for the last two years. You have computed the following ratios to assist you in your analysis.

	20X2	20X1
Gross profit percentage	40.0%	45.0%
Operating profit percentage	9.5%	7.5%
Inventory holding period	86.7 days	65.7 days
Trade receivables collection period	55.9 days	40.2 days

The financial statements show that sales have risen by 14% in the period.

Prepare a report for Peter Stewart that includes:

(a) **A comment on the relative performance of the company for the two years based on the ratios calculated and what this tells you about the company.**

(b) **ONE suggestion as to how EACH of the ratios might be improved.**

Task 11.15

Nancy Charlton is considering buying shares in Limden Ltd and has asked you to assist her in determining the level of profitability and risk of the company. You have computed the following ratios in respect of Limden Ltd's financial statements for the last two years to assist you in your analysis.

	20X1	20X0
Gross profit percentage	46.0%	42.0%
Operating profit percentage	6.5%	8.0%
Return on shareholders' funds	7.4%	10.8%
Gearing	35.2%	22.4%
Interest cover	2.9 times	7.5 times

Prepare a report to Nancy that includes:

(a) **A comment on the relative performance of the company for the two years based on the ratios calculated and what this tells you about the company.**

(b) **Advice, with reasons based on the ratios you have calculated, on whether or not Nancy should invest.**

Task 11.16

Two companies, River and Mountain, trade in the same market. Susan Smith, a client, has asked for your advice on which of the companies to invest in, based on the ratios calculated for the year ended 31 October 20X6.

	River	Mountain
Gross profit percentage	45.4%	50.5%
Operating profit percentage	21.5%	15.4%
Asset turnover ratio	1.1 times	0.6 times
Current ratio	1.1:1	1.2:1
Quick ratio	0.6:1	0.3:1
Trade receivables collection period	59.1 days	89.8 days

Additional information: River has sales revenue of £284,000 and Mountain has sales revenue of £305,000.

Prepare a report to Susan that includes:

(a) **A discussion of the relative performance of the two companies based on the ratios calculated and what this tells you about the company.**

(b) **Advice, with reasons based on the ratios you have calculated, on which company Susan should invest in.**

Task 11.17

Ratio analysis is a useful tool, but should not be relied on exclusively when interpreting financial statements.

State five limitations of ratio analysis.

Task 11.18

The directors of Knole Ltd are concerned about the company's liquidity and cash flow. At the beginning of the current year the company had a positive cash balance of nearly £500,000 but by the year end this had become an overdraft of just over £1,500,000. The directors cannot understand how this has happened.

The company purchased new plant and equipment during the year, but there should have been enough cash available to cover this expenditure. Knole Ltd is highly profitable and has been able to raise finance by increasing its bank loans and by issuing new share capital during the year.

The directors have given you the financial statements for the past two years. You have used these to prepare a reconciliation of the profit from operations to net cash from operating activities. You have also calculated some ratios. The reconciliations and the ratios are set out below.

Knole Ltd

Reconciliation of profit from operations to net cash inflow from operating activities for the year ended 31 October

	20X8 £000	20X7 £000
Profit from operations	13,200	11,060
Adjustments for:		
Depreciation	4,777	3,745
Gain on disposal of property, plant and equipment	(880)	(570)
Decrease/(Increase) in inventories	(4,840)	(3,606)
Decrease/(Increase) in trade receivables	(2,640)	(1,208)
(Decrease)/Increase in trade payables	(2,420)	(1,320)
Cash generated by operations	7,197	8,101
Tax paid	(944)	(885)
Interest paid	(280)	(105)
Net cash from operating activities	5,973	7,111

Ratios	20X8	20X7
Current ratio	3.6:1	2.5:1
Quick (acid test) ratio	1.7:1	1.3:1
Gearing	7.2%	4.1%

Prepare a report for the Directors of Knole Ltd that includes:

(a) **Comments upon the change in net cash from operating activities between 20X7 and 20X8.**

(b) **A comment on the relative liquidity and financial position of the company for the two years based on the ratios calculated and what this tells you about the company.**

Note. If you were preparing the reconciliation in a statement of cash flows question, you would start off with profit before tax rather than profit from operations.

....

Answer Bank

Answer Bank

Chapter 1

Task 1.1

(a) **Limited liability** means that the maximum amount that an owner stands to lose, in the event that the company becomes insolvent and cannot pay off its debts, is their share of the capital in the business.

(b) (i) **Limited liability** (see Part (a)) means that the investment is less risky for the owner.

(ii) **Ease of raising finance.** Providers of finance may be more prepared to lend to a company with limited liability as it is less risky than a sole trader or partnership.

(iii) **Perpetual succession.** With a partnership, a new partnership must be formed when one partner dies or retires. A share in a company is transferable.

(iv) **Tax** advantages. Limited companies are taxed as separate entities and are subject to company tax on their profits. Partners and sole traders are personally liable for tax on their share of the business profits. Company tax tends to be less than personal tax.

(c) Any two of:

(i) Compliance with national legislation

(ii) Compliance with national accounting standards and/or International Financial Reporting Standards

(iii) Formation and annual registration costs

Task 1.2

Differences between share capital and loan capital.

(a) **Share capital** is held by shareholders, who are the **owners** of a company. **Loan capital** is a **liability,** and holders of loan capital are **creditors**.

(b) **Shareholders** receive **dividends** (appropriations of profit) whereas **loan stockholders** are entitled to **interest** (an expense in the statement of profit or loss).

(c) Loan stockholders can take legal action against a company if their interest is not paid when due, whereas **shareholders cannot enforce the payment of dividends**.

(d) Loan stock interest must be paid even if there are no profits. **Dividends are only paid when profits allow**.

Task 1.3

£125,000	✓
£500,000	
£750,000	
£150,000	

Task 1.4

£50,000	
£12,500	✓
£62,500	
£60,000	

50,000 × 25p

Task 1.5

Total interest payable for the year.

£	24,000	(12% × 200,000)

Journal

Account name	Debit £	Credit £
Interest payable	10,000	
Accruals		10,000

This is five months' interest (12% × 200,000 × 5/12)

Task 1.6

(a) Definitions:

- Assets are resources controlled by the entity as a result of past events and from which future economic benefits are expected to flow to the entity.

- Liabilities are present obligations of the entity arising from past events, the settlement of which is expected to result in an outflow of resources embodying economic benefits from the entity.

- Equity is the owners' residual interest in the assets of the entity after deducting all its liabilities.

(b) Transaction 1 would increase inventories, an asset, by £120 and also increase trade payables, a liability, by £120.

Transaction 2 would decrease the asset inventories by £120, but increase the asset cash by £180. Thus there would be a net increase in assets of £60. In the other half of the statement of financial position, equity would increase by £60, being the profit made on the sale.

(c) The accounting equation after the two transactions would be:

ASSETS LESS LIABILITIES = EQUITY

(i)   £1,320 – £920   = £400

(ii) £1,380 – £920   = £460

Task 1.7

(a) Accruals basis

Accrual accounting shows the effects of transactions and other events and circumstances on a reporting entity's economic resources and claims in the periods in which those effects occur, even if the resulting cash receipts and payments occur in a different period.

This is important to users because information about an entity's economic resources and claims and changes in these during a period is more useful in assessing an entity's past and future performance than information based solely on cash receipts and payments during that period.

(b) Cash flow basis

Information about a reporting entity's cash flows shows users how the reporting entity obtains and spends cash, including information about its borrowing and repayment of debt, cash dividends paid to investors and other factors that may affect its liquidity or solvency. Cash flow information

helps users to understand a reporting entity's operations and its financing and investing activities.

Information about a reporting entity's cash flows during a period also helps users to assess the entity's ability to generate cash in the future.

Task 1.8

Silver Ltd – Statement of profit or loss for the year ended 31 December 20X3

	£000
Revenue	31,500
Cost of sales (3,390 + 18,900 – 4,640)	(17,650)
Gross profit	13,850
Operating expenses	(7,400)
Profit from operations	6,450
Finance costs	(250)
Profit before tax	6,200
Tax	(1,450)
Profit for the year	4,750

Silver Ltd – Statement of financial position as at 31 December 20X3

	£000
ASSETS	
Non-current assets	
Property, plant and equipment (17,700 – 4,250)	13,450
Current assets	
Inventories	4,640
Trade and other receivables	4,300
Cash and cash equivalents	2,250
	11,190
Total assets	24,640
EQUITY AND LIABILITIES	
Equity	
Share capital	5,000
Retained earnings (6,540 + 4,750)	11,290
Total equity	16,290
Non-current liabilities	
Bank loan	4,000
Current liabilities	
Trade and other payables	2,900
Tax payable	1,450
	4,350
Total liabilities	8,350
Total equity and liabilities	24,640

Chapter 2

Task 2.1

The IFRS Advisory Committee	
The stock exchange	
The International Accounting Standards Board	✓
The government	

The role of the IASB is to develop and publish International Financial Reporting Standards.

Task 2.2

1 only	✓
1 and 2 only	
1, 2 and 3	
1 and 3 only	

The responsibility of the financial statements rests with the directors, whether or not those financial statements are audited. Some of the duties of directors are statutory duties, laid down in law, including the duty to act within their powers, promote the success of the company and exercise reasonable skill and care.

Task 2.3

1 and 2	
2 only	
1, 2 and 3	✓
1 and 3 only	

All three statements are true.

Note. Based on the information available at the time this book was written, we anticipate that the tasks in this section would be human marked in the real assessment.

Task 2.4

GAAP stands for **Generally Accepted Accounting Principles**. In most countries GAAP does not have any statutory or regulatory authority or definition, but the major components are normally:

- Accounting standards (eg International Financial Reporting Standards)

- National company law (eg Companies Act 2006 in the UK)

- Stock exchange requirements (for companies quoted on a recognised stock exchange)

Task 2.5

(a) The IASB's *Conceptual Framework* states that **existing and potential investors, lenders and other creditors** are the primary users of general purpose financial reports (financial statements).

These are the people who **provide capital** (finance) to an entity, either in the form of share capital (equity) as owners, or in the form of loans.

(b) The statement of financial position shows the current assets and current liabilities of the company for the current year and the preceding year and the notes to the financial statements provide further information (for example, total receivables are analysed into trade receivables, other receivables and prepayments). The user can observe the movements in working capital and can also calculate ratios that measure working capital management. He or she can also interpret this information in the context of the financial statements as a whole. For example, the statement of profit or loss and other comprehensive income (with comparative figures) shows whether revenue and expenses are increasing or decreasing, which may help to explain any unusual movements in working capital. The statement of cash flows will provide additional information on liquidity and should help him or her to assess the extent to which the directors' management of working capital is affecting the company's cash flows.

(c) The IASB's *Conceptual Framework* defines equity as the residual amount found by deducting all of the entity's liabilities from all of the entity's assets. It consists of the capital that the owners have invested, plus accumulated profits, less dividends (or other amounts) paid to the owners. This can be expressed as:

Assets less liabilities = equity

Equity = contributions from owners plus income less expenses less distributions to owners

Income (profits or gains) is increases in equity (net assets) other than contributions from owners. Expenses are decreases in equity (net assets) other than distributions to owners.

Task 2.6

Information is **material** if omitting or misstating it could **influence decisions** that users make on the basis of financial information.

The judgement as to whether an item is material or immaterial is subjective. **Materiality** may be considered in the context of individual items within the financial statements or the statements as a whole. The nature of the item has to be considered, to decide whether to judge it in relative or absolute terms.

Materiality may depend upon context in the following ways.

(a)   If the treatment of the item reverses a trend or turns a profit into a loss or affects the solvency ratios in the statement of financial position, then materiality must be judged in a narrower context.

(b)   If the profits are unusually low, or there is a loss, then materiality should be judged against the more normal trading pattern.

(c)   A relatively small item should not be assumed to be immaterial, as in the context the user may have expected the figure to be substantially larger.

(d)   If an item must be disclosed by statute, then materiality takes on a different meaning. An example is directors' emoluments.

Note. Only three of the above points were needed.

Task 2.7

(a)   The IASB's *Conceptual Framework* defines the elements of financial statements as follows.

(i)   Assets are resources controlled by an entity as a result of past events and from which future economic benefits are expected to flow to the entity.

(ii)   Liabilities are present obligations of an entity arising from past events, the settlement of which is expected to result in an outflow of resources embodying economic benefits from the entity.

(iii)   Equity is the owners' residual interest in the assets of an entity after deducting all its liabilities.

(b) Inventories are an asset because:

- They are the result of a past event (the purchase of goods); and

- The purchase of inventories gives rise to future economic benefits because it results in a future inflow of cash when the inventories are sold.

Task 2.8

(a) (i) Information is relevant if it is capable of making a difference in the decisions made by users.

(ii) If financial information faithfully represents the economic phenomena that it purports to represent, it is:

- Complete;
- Neutral; and
- Free from error.

(b) The four enhancing qualitative characteristics of useful financial information are:

- Comparability
- Verifiability
- Timeliness
- Understandability

Task 2.9

(a) The objective of general purpose financial reporting is to provide financial information about the reporting entity that is useful to existing and potential investors, lenders and other creditors in making decisions about providing resources to the entity.

(b) The introduction to the *Conceptual Framework* lists the following decisions that users may need to make, based on the information in general purpose financial statements prepared for external users:

- To decide when to buy, hold or sell an equity investment.

- To assess the stewardship or accountability of management.

- To assess the ability of the entity to pay and provide other benefits to its employees.

- To assess the security for amounts lent to the entity.

- To determine taxation policies.

- To determine distributable profits and dividends.

BPP
LEARNING MEDIA

- To prepare and use national income statistics.
- To regulate the activities of entities.

Note. Candidates only needed to give THREE of the above.

Task 2.10

Professional behaviour.

'The principle of professional behaviour imposes an obligation on members to comply with relevant laws and regulations and avoid any action that may bring disrepute to the profession.'

Task 2.11

Correct answers include:

Education, training and experience requirements on entry

Continuing professional development (CPD)

Corporate governance regulations

Professional standards

Professional or regulatory monitoring and disciplinary procedures

External review of financial reports, returns, communications or information produced by members

Note. Candidates only needed to give TWO of the above.

Task 2.12

Self-interest and intimidation.

The self-interest threat comes from the high-profile role on offer if the information is presented favourably. The intimidation threat is implied from the situation – if it is not favourable he will not get the role.

Task 2.13

The correct answers are:
- Objectivity
- Professional competence and due care

Task 2.14

Professional competence and due care.

Professional competence is at risk if you do not base your opinion on the same set of facts as the other accountant or if you have insufficient evidence to make a decision.

••

Task 2.15

Professional distance is closely associated with the ethical principle of objectivity.

••

Task 2.16

An accountant that has a financial interest in their employer might face a self-interest threat.

••

Task 2.17

There is more than one possible correct answer to this question. Credit will be given for any relevant answer.

Examples of safeguards might include:

Withdrawing from the assignment team

Put supervisory procedures in place to ensure her work is reviewed

Discuss the matter with senior management in the firm

••

Chapter 3 to 5 (combined)

Note. This chapter provides tasks on the material in Chapter 3 *The statement of financial position*, Chapter 4 *The statements of financial performance* and Chapter 5 *The statement of cash flows*. These topics are highly integrated and tested together, so the tasks are combined in one chapter.

Task 3.1

(a)   An asset is a current asset if:

- It is cash or a cash equivalent (a short term investment or deposit that can be easily converted into cash); or

- The entity expects to collect, sell or consume it within its normal operating cycle; or

- It is held primarily for trading and is expected to be realised (received) within twelve months after the reporting period.

(b)   A liability is a current liability if:

- The entity expects to settle it in its normal operating cycle; or

- It is held primarily for trading and is due to be settled (paid) within twelve months after the reporting period.

Task 3.2

1 and 4	
3 and 5	
2 and 3	
2 and 4	✓

Task 3.3

Not disclosed separately and treated as a distribution cost	
Disclosed as an extraordinary item	
Not disclosed separately and treated as an administrative expense	
Its nature and amount disclosed separately	✓

Task 3.4

(a) Paparazzi Ltd

Statement of profit or loss and other comprehensive income for the year ended 30 June 20X2

	£000
Revenue	14,700
Cost of sales (W)	(10,760)
Gross profit	3,940
Distribution costs	(1,200)
Administrative expenses	(2,120)
Profit/(loss) from operations	620
Finance costs	(84)
Profit/(loss) before tax	536
Tax	(130)
Profit/(loss) for the period from continuing operations	406

Workings

Cost of sales	£000
Opening inventories	690
Purchases	10,780
Closing inventories	(710)
	10,760

(b) **Paparazzi Ltd**

Statement of financial position as at 30 June 20X2

	£000
ASSETS	
Non-current assets	
Property, plant and equipment (W)	3,272
Current assets	
Inventories	710
Trade and other receivables (W)	2,448
Cash and cash equivalents	567
	3,725
Total assets	6,997
EQUITY AND LIABILITIES	
Equity	
Share capital	2,500
Share premium	300
Retained earnings (W)	1,417
Total equity	4,217
Non-current liabilities	
Bank loan	1,200
Current liabilities	
Trade and other payables (W)	1,450
Tax liabilities	130
	1,580
Total liabilities	2,780
Total equity and liabilities	6,997

Workings

Property, plant and equipment	£000
Land and buildings – cost	2,100
Plant and equipment – cost	1,050
Motor vehicles – cost	1,000
Accumulated depreciation – land and buildings	(280)
Accumulated depreciation – plant and equipment	(194)
Accumulated depreciation – motor vehicles	(404)
	3,272

Trade and other receivables	£000
Trade and other receivables	2,500
Allowance for doubtful debts	(92)
Prepayments	40
	2,448

Retained earnings	£000
Retained earnings at 1 July 20X1	1,131
Total profit for the year	406
Dividends paid	(120)
	1,417

Trade and other payables	£000
Trade payables	1,400
Accruals	50
	1,450

Task 3.5

(a) Benard Ltd

Statement of profit or loss and other comprehensive income for the year ended 31 October 20X7

	£000
Revenue (50,197 + 3,564)	53,761
Cost of sales (W)	(33,462)
Gross profit	20,299
Distribution costs	(6,654)
Administrative expenses (W)	(4,120)
Profit/(loss) from operations	9,525
Finance costs (560 + 560)	(1,120)
Profit/(loss) before tax	8,405
Tax	(1,254)
Profit/(loss) for the period from continuing operations	7,151

Workings

Cost of sales	£000
Opening inventories	8,456
Purchases	34,792
Closing inventories	(9,786)
	33,462

Administrative expenses	£000
Administrative expenses	4,152
Prepayments (48 × 8/12)	(32)
	4,120

(b) **Benard Ltd**

Statement of financial position as at 31 October 20X7

	£000
ASSETS	
Non-current assets	
Property, plant and equipment (58,463 – 27,974)	30,489
Current assets	
Inventories	9,786
Trade and other receivables (W)	10,286
Cash and cash equivalents	1,184
	21,256
Total assets	51,745
EQUITY AND LIABILITIES	
Equity	
Share capital	12,000
Retained earnings (W)	18,196
Total equity	30,196
Non-current liabilities	
Bank loan	16,000
Current liabilities	
Trade and other payables (W)	4,295
Tax payable	1,254
	5,549
Total liabilities	21,549
Total equity and liabilities	51,745

Workings

Trade and other receivables	£000
Trade and other receivables	6,690
Credit sales for October 20X7	3,564
Administrative expenses prepaid	32
	10,286

Retained earnings	£000
Retained earnings at 1 November 20X6	12,345
Total profit for the year	7,151
Dividends paid	(1,300)
	18,196

Trade and other payables	£000
Trade and other payables	3,348
Accruals: trial balance	387
Additional interest accrual	560
	4,295

Task 3.6

(a) Laxdale Ltd

Statement of profit or loss and other comprehensive income for the year ended 31 October 20X8

	£000
Revenue	58,411
Cost of sales (W)	(43,342)
Gross profit	15,069
Distribution costs (W)	(6,026)
Administrative expenses (W)	(5,073)
Profit/(loss) from operations	3,970
Finance costs (8% × 15,000)	(1,200)
Profit/(loss) before tax	2,770
Tax	(970)
Profit/(loss) for the period from continuing operations	1,800

Workings

Cost of sales	£000
Opening inventories	9,032
Purchases	41,620
Depreciation (40% × 1,420)	568
Closing inventories	(7,878)
	43,342

Distribution costs	£000
Distribution costs	5,443
Depreciation (40% × 1,420)	568
Accruals (45 × 1/3)	15
	6,026

Administrative expenses	£000
Administrative expenses	4,789
Depreciation (20% × 1,420)	284
	5,073

Depreciation	£000
Buildings (2% × 35,152 – 15,152)	400
Plant and equipment (20% × 12,500 – 7,400)	1,020
	1,420

(b)   Laxdale Ltd

Statement of financial position as at 31 October 20X8

	£000
ASSETS	
Non-current assets	
Property, plant and equipment (W)	31,832
Current assets	
Inventories	7,878
Trade and other receivables	5,436
Cash and cash equivalents	9,774
	23,088
Total assets	54,920
EQUITY AND LIABILITIES	
Equity	
Share capital	25,000
Retained earnings (W)	10,101
Total equity	35,101

	£000
Non-current liabilities	
Bank loan	15,000
Current liabilities	
Trade and other payables (W)	3,849
Tax liabilities	970
	4,819
Total liabilities	19,819
Total equity and liabilities	54,920

Workings

Property, plant and equipment	£000
Land and buildings – Cost	35,152
Plant and equipment – Cost	12,500
Accumulated depreciation – land and buildings (7,000 + 400)	(7,400)
Accumulated depreciation – plant and equipment (7,400 + 1,020)	(8,420)
	31,832

Retained earnings	£000
Retained earnings at 1 November 20X7	9,801
Total profit for the year	1,800
Dividends paid	(1,500)
	10,101

Trade and other payables	£000
Trade and other payables	2,798
Accruals: trial balance	436
Additional distribution costs accrual	15
Additional interest accrual	600
	3,849

Task 3.7

(a) Cappielow Ltd

Statement of profit or loss and other comprehensive income for the year ended 31 March 20X1

	£000
Revenue	35,547
Cost of sales (W)	(28,354)
Gross profit	7,193
Distribution costs (W)	(1,933)
Administrative expenses (W)	(2,207)
Profit/(loss) from operations	3,053
Finance costs	(720)
Profit/(loss) before tax	2,333
Tax	(874)
Profit/(loss) for the period from continuing operations	1,459
Other comprehensive income for the year	
Gain on revaluation of land (7,500 – 5,150)	2,350
Total comprehensive income for the year	3,809

Workings

Cost of sales	£000
Opening inventories	3,790
Purchases	27,481
Closing inventories	(4,067)
Impairment loss (12,750 – 3,100 – 8,500)	1,150
	28,354

Distribution costs	£000
Distribution costs	1,857
Accruals (114 × 2/3)	76
	1,933

Administrative expenses	£000
Administrative expenses	2,235
Prepayment (164 × ¾)	(123)
Irrecoverable debt	95
	2,207

(b) **Cappielow Ltd**

Statement of changes in equity for the year ended 31 March 20X1

	Share capital £000	Revaluation surplus £000	Retained earnings £000	Total equity £000
Balance at 1 April 20X0	10,000	2,000	2,595	14,595
Changes in equity				
Total comprehensive income		2,350	1,459	3,809
Dividends	0	0	(920)	(920)
Balance at 31 March 20X1	10,000	4,350	3,134	17,484

(c) **Cappielow Ltd**

Statement of financial position as at 31 March 20X1

	£000
ASSETS	
Non-current assets	
Property, plant and equipment (W)	18,104
Current assets	
Inventories	4,067
Trade and other receivables (W)	2,161
Cash and cash equivalents	7,578
	13,806
Total assets	31,910

	£000
EQUITY AND LIABILITIES	
Equity	
Share capital	10,000
Revaluation reserve (W)	4,350
Retained earnings (W)	3,134
Total equity	17,484
Non-current liabilities	
Bank loan	12,000
Current liabilities	
Trade and other payables (W)	1,552
Tax payable	874
	2,426
Total liabilities	14,426
Total equity and liabilities	31,910

Workings

Property, plant and equipment	£000
Property, plant and equipment – Cost/value (36,780 + 2,350)	39,130
Property, plant and equipment – Accumulated depreciation	(19,876)
Impairment loss	(1,150)
	18,104

Trade and other receivables	£000
Trade and other receivables	2,133
Administrative expenses prepaid	123
Irrecoverable debt	(95)
	2,161

Revaluation reserve	£000
Revaluation reserve at 1 April 20X0	2,000
Other comprehensive income for the year	2,350
	4,350

Retained earnings	£000
Retained earnings at 1 April 20X0	2,595
Total profit for the year	1,459
Dividends paid	(920)
	3,134

Trade and other payables	£000
Trade and other payables	1,347
Accruals: trial balance	129
Distribution costs accrued	76
	1,552

Task 3.8

(a) Pine Ltd

Statement of profit or loss and other comprehensive income for the year ended 31 March 20X1

	£000
Revenue	80,908
Cost of sales (W)	(55,104)
Gross profit	25,804
Distribution costs (W)	(11,937)
Administrative expenses (W)	(7,379)
Profit from operations	6,488
Finance costs	(640)
Profit before tax	5,848
Tax	(1,254)
Profit for the period from continuing operations	4,594
Other comprehensive income for the year (Gain on revaluation of land (51,000 – 41,778))	9,222
Total comprehensive income for the year	13,816

Workings

Cost of sales	£000
Opening inventories	5,064
Purchases	53,444
Depreciation (60% × 6,000)	3,600
Closing inventories	(7,004)
	55,104

Distribution costs	£000
Distribution costs	9,977
Depreciation (30% × 6,000)	1,800
Accruals	160
	11,937

Administrative expenses	£000
Administrative expenses	6,755
Depreciation (10% × 6,000)	600
Irrecoverable debt	24
	7,379

Depreciation	£000
Buildings (5% × 81,778 – 41,778)	2,000
Plant and equipment (25% × (24,000 – 8,000))	4,000
	6,000

(b) Pine Ltd

Statement of changes in equity for the year ended 31 March 20X1

	Share capital £000	Other reserves £000	Retained earnings £000	Total equity £000
Balance at 1 April 20X0	50,000	12,000	7,945	69,945
Changes in equity				
Total comprehensive income	0	9,222	4,594	13,816
Dividends	0	0	(1,600)	(1,600)
Issue of share capital	0	0	0	0
Balance at 31 March 20X1	50,000	21,222	10,939	82,161

(c) **Pine Ltd**

Statement of financial position as at 31 March 20X1

	£000
ASSETS	
Non-current assets	
Property, plant and equipment (W)	87,000
Current assets	
Inventories	7,004
Trade and other receivables (W)	9,862
Cash and cash equivalents	1,568
	18,434
Total assets	105,434
EQUITY AND LIABILITIES	
Equity	
Share capital	50,000
Revaluation reserve (W)	21,222
Retained earnings (W)	10,939
Total equity	82,161
Non-current liabilities	
Bank loan	16,000
Current liabilities	
Trade and other payables (W)	6,019
Tax liability	1,254
	7,273
Total liabilities	23,273
Total equity and liabilities	105,434

Workings

Property, plant and equipment	£000
Land and buildings – value (81,778 + 9,222)	91,000
Plant and equipment – cost	24,000
Accumulated depreciation – land and buildings (14,000 + 2,000)	(16,000)
Accumulated depreciation – plant and equipment (8,000 + 4,000)	(12,000)
	87,000

Trade and other receivables	£000
Trade and other receivables	9,886
Irrecoverable debts	(24)
	9,862

Revaluation reserve	£000
Revaluation reserve at 1 April 20X0	12,000
Other comprehensive income for the year	9,222
	21,222

Retained earnings	£000
Retained earnings at 1 April 20X0	7,945
Total profit for the year	4,594
Dividends paid	(1,600)
	10,939

Trade and other payables	£000
Trade and other payables	5,342
Accruals: trial balance	517
Additional distribution costs accrual	160
	6,019

Task 3.9

Bookham Ltd

Statement of profit or loss and other comprehensive income for the year ended 30 June 20X1

	£000
Revenue	78,241
Cost of sales (W)	(34,983)
Gross profit	43,258
Distribution costs (W)	(7,119)
Administrative expenses (W)	(27,390)
Profit from operations	8,749
Finance costs	(1,520)
Profit before tax	7,229
Tax (W)	(1,426)
Profit for the period from continuing operations	5,803
Other comprehensive income for the year	5,000
Total comprehensive income for the year	10,803

Workings

Costs of sales	£000
Opening inventories	6,328
Purchases	36,148
Closing inventories	(7,493)
	34,983

Distribution costs	£000
Distribution costs	7,249
Prepayment (156 × 10/12)	(130)
	7,119

Administrative expenses	£000
Administrative expenses	27,338
Doubtful debts adjustment	47
Service costs	5
	27,390

Tax	£000
Current year	1,486
Previous year	(60)
	1,426

Bookham Ltd

Statement of changes in equity for the year ended 30 June 20X1

	Share capital £000	Revaluation reserve £000	Retained earnings £000	Total equity £000
Balance at 1 July 20X0	32,000		7,462	39,462
Changes in equity				
Total comprehensive income		5,000	5,803	10,803
Dividends			(600)	(600)
Balance at 30 June 20X1	32,000	5,000	12,665	49,665

Bookham Ltd – Statement of financial position as at 30 June 20X1

	£000
ASSETS	
Non-current assets	
Property, plant and equipment (W)	51,357
Current assets	
Inventories	7,493
Trade and other receivables (W)	12,294
Cash and cash equivalents	3,820
	23,607
Total assets	74,964
EQUITY AND LIABILITIES	
Equity	
Share capital	32,000
Retained earnings (W)	12,665
Revaluation reserve	5,000
Total equity	49,665
Non-current liabilities	
Bank loans	17,000
	17,000
Current liabilities	
Trade and other payables	6,813
Tax liability	1,486
	8,299
Total liabilities	25,299
Total equity and liabilities	74,964

Workings

Property, plant and equipment	£000
Property, plant and equipment – cost	64,229
Revaluation (19,000 – 14,000)	5,000
Accumulated depreciation	(17,867)
Servicing costs	(5)
	51,357

Trade and other receivables	£000
Trade receivables	12,447
Prepayment	130
Allowance for doubtful debts (236 + 47)	(283)
	12,294

Retained earnings	£000
Retained earnings at 1 July 20X0	7,462
Profit for the year	5,803
Dividends paid	(600)
	12,665

Task 3.10

True	
False	✓

A decrease in trade receivables means that less cash has been 'tied up' in working capital.

Task 3.11

1 only	
2 only	✓
Both 1 and 2	
Neither 1 nor 2	

Task 3.12

1 only	
2 only	
3 only	
None of them	✓

1   Proceeds from sale of premises appears under investing activities.
2   Dividends received appears under operating or investing activities.
3   A bonus issue of shares is not a cash flow.

Task 3.13

1 and 4	
2 and 3	
3 only	✓
2 and 4	

1   The direct and indirect methods will give the same figure.

2   A rights issue of shares is a cash flow.

3   Revaluations of non-current assets do not affect cash flows

4   The profit on sale of a non-current asset appears as an adjustment to profit in order to reach net cash flow from operations

Task 3.14

£60,000 inflow	
£10,000 inflow	✓
£110,000 inflow	
£27,000 inflow	

		£000
Cash flows from financing:		
Issue of share capital	(120 + 60) – (80 + 40)	60
Repayment of bank loan	(100 – 150)	(50)
		10

Task 3.15

£104,000	
£159,000	
£166,000	
£204,000	✓

	£000
Carrying amount of assets at beginning of the year	462
Increase in revaluation surplus during the year	50
Book value of assets disposed of (110 – 65)	(45)
Depreciation charge for the year	(38)
	429
Carrying amount of assets at end of the year	633
Purchases of property, plant and equipment during the year	204

Task 3.16

Reconciliation of profit before tax to net cash from operating activities

	£
Profit before tax	90,000
Depreciation	20,000
Finance costs	10,000
Increase in inventories (30,000 – 25,000)	(5,000)
Decrease in trade receivables (40,000 – 42,000)	2,000
Decrease in trade payables (28,000 – 32,000)	(4,000)
Cash generated from operations	113,000
Interest paid	(10,000)
Tax paid	(25,000)
Net cash from operating activities	78,000

....

Task 3.17

(a)

£	37,400

	£
Opening balance	13,000
Profit or loss	32,400
Closing balance	(8,000)
	37,400

(b)

£	92,000

	£
Opening balance	94,000
Profit or loss	98,000
Closing balance	(100,000)
	92,000

Task 3.18

(a)

£	19,000

(b)

£	80,000

(c)

£	132,000

Workings

Proceeds on disposal of property, plant and equipment	£000
Carrying amount of property, plant and equipment sold (140 – 98)	42
Loss on disposal	(23)
	19

Purchases of property, plant and equipment	£000
Property, plant and equipment at start of year	770
Depreciation charge (560 – 480)	(80)
Carrying amount of property, plant and equipment sold	(42)
Property, plant and equipment at end of year	(780)
Total purchases of property, plant and equipment additions (= 780 – (770 – 80 – 42))	(132)

Task 3.19

Statement of changes in equity for the year ended 30 April 20X2

	Share capital £	Share premium £	Revaluation reserve £	Retained earnings £	Total equity £
Balance at 1 May 20X1	500,000	100,000	30,000	180,000	810,000
Changes in equity					
Total comprehensive income			70,000	110,000	180,000
Dividends				(35,000)	(35,000)
Issue of share capital (200,000 × 1.4)	200,000	80,000			280,000
Balance at 30 April 20X2	700,000	180,000	100,000	255,000	1,235,000

Task 3.20

(a) Evans Ltd

Reconciliation of profit before tax to net cash from operating activities for the year ended 31 October 20X1

	£000
Profit before tax	418
Adjustments for	
Depreciation	190
Finance costs	23
Gain on disposal of property, plant and equipment	(10)
Adjustment in respect of inventories (505 – 486)	19
Adjustment in respect of trade receivables (945 – 657)	(288)
Adjustment in respect of trade payables (560 – 546)	14
Cash generated by operations	366
Interest paid	(23)
Tax paid	(106)
Net cash from operating activities	237

(b) Evans Ltd

Statement of cash flows for the year ended 31 October 20X1

	£000
Net cash from operating activities	237
Investing activities	
Purchase of property, plant and equipment (W)	(425)
Proceeds on disposal of property, plant and equipment (W)	75
Net cash used in investing activities	(350)
Financing activities	
Proceeds of share issue (1,200 – 1,000) + (315 – 270)	245
Repayment of bank loan (150 – 50)	(100)
Dividends paid	(40)
Net cash from financing activities	105
Net increase/(decrease) in cash and cash equivalents	(8)
Cash and cash equivalents at the beginning of the year	10
Cash and cash equivalents at the end of the year	2

Workings

Proceeds on disposal of property, plant and equipment (PPE)	£000
Carrying amount of PPE sold	65
Gain on disposal	10
	75

Purchases of property, plant and equipment (PPE)	£000
PPE at start of year	1,010
Depreciation charge	(190)
Carrying amount of PPE sold	(65)
PPE at end of year	(1,180)
Total PPE additions	(425)

(c) **Evans Ltd**

Statement of changes in equity for the year ended 31 October 20X1

	Share capital £000	Share premium £000	Retained earnings £000	Total equity £000
Balance at 1 November 20X0	1,000	270	110	1,380
Changes in equity				
Profit for the year			293	293
Dividends			(40)	(40)
Issue of share capital	200	45	–	245
Balance at 31 October 20X1	1,200	315	363	1,878

Task 3.21

(a)   Lochnagar Ltd

Reconciliation of profit before tax to net cash from operating activities for the year ended 31 October 20X7

	£000
Profit before tax	3,269
Adjustments for:	
Depreciation	3,545
Gain on disposal of property, plant and equipment	(224)
Finance costs	91
Adjustment in respect of inventories (3,696 – 2,464)	(1,232)
Adjustment in respect of trade receivables (3,360 – 2,464)	(896)
Adjustment in respect of trade payables (1,232 – 1,848)	(616)
Cash generated by operations	3,937
Interest paid	(91)
Tax paid	(944)
Net cash from operating activities	2,902

(b)   Lochnagar Ltd

Statement of cash flows for the year ended 31 October 20X7

	£000
Net cash from operating activities	2,902
Investing activities	
Purchases of property, plant and equipment (W)	(5,237)
Proceeds on disposal of property, plant and equipment (W)	845
Net cash used in investing activities	(4,392)
Financing activities	
Proceeds of share issue	500
New bank loans (1,300 – 800)	500
Net cash from financing activities	1,000
Net increase/(decrease) in cash and cash equivalents	(490)
Cash and cash equivalents at the beginning of the year	129
Cash and cash equivalents at the end of the year	(361)

Workings

Proceeds on disposal of property, plant and equipment (PPE)	£000
Carrying amount of PPE sold	621
Gain on disposal	224
	845

Purchases of property, plant and equipment (PPE)	£000
PPE at start of year	24,100
Depreciation charge	(3,545)
Carrying amount of PPE sold	(621)
PPE at end of year	(25,171)
Total PPE additions	(5,237)

Task 3.22

(a) **Thehoose Ltd**

Reconciliation of profit before tax to net cash from operating activities for the year ended 31 March 20X9

	£000
Profit before tax	5,372
Adjustments for:	
Depreciation	3,469
Gain on disposal of property, plant and equipment	(376)
Finance costs	280
Adjustment in respect of inventories (5,426 – 4,069)	(1,357)
Adjustment in respect of trade receivables (4,145 – 3,768)	377
Adjustment in respect of trade payables (4,069 – 2,261)	(1,808)
Cash generated by operations	5,957
Interest paid	(280)
Tax paid	(887)
Net cash from operating activities	4,790

(b) Thehoose Ltd

Statement of cash flows for the year ended 31 March 20X9

	£000
Net cash from operating activities	4,790
Investing activities	
Purchases of property, plant and equipment (W)	(10,116)
Proceeds on disposal of property, plant and equipment (W)	793
Net cash used in investing activities	(9,323)
Financing activities	
Proceeds of share issue: (4,500 + 3,000) – (3,000 + 2,000)	2,500
New bank loans: 4,000 – 1,500	2,500
Net cash from financing activities	5,000
Net increase/(decrease) in cash and cash equivalents	467
Cash and cash equivalents at the beginning of the year	(132)
Cash and cash equivalents at the end of the year	335

Workings

Proceeds on disposal of property, plant and equipment (PPE)	£000
Carrying amount of PPE sold	417
Gain on disposal	376
	793

Purchases of property, plant and equipment (PPE)	£000
PPE at start of year	21,340
Depreciation charge	(3,469)
Carrying amount of PPE sold	(417)
PPE at end of year	(27,570)
Total PPE additions	10,116

Task 3.23

(a) **Reconciliation of profit before tax to net cash from operating activities for the year ended 31 October 20X9**

	£000
Profit before tax	6,230
Adjustments for:	
Depreciation	4,398
Gain on disposal of property, plant and equipment	(455)
Finance costs	595
Adjustment in respect of inventories (4,914 – 6,552)	(1,638)
Adjustment in respect of trade receivables (4,641 – 4,550)	91
Adjustment in respect of trade payables (4,368 – 3,822)	(546)
Cash generated by operations	8,675
Tax paid	(658)
Interest paid	(595)
Net cash from operating activities	7,422

(b) Adlington Ltd

Statement of cash flows for the year ended 31 October 20X9

	£000
Net cash from operating activities	7,422
Investing activities	
Purchases of property, plant and equipment (W)	(14,483)
Proceeds on disposal of property, plant and equipment (W)	797
Net cash used in investing activities	(13,686)
Financing activities	
Proceeds of share issue: (10,000 + 4,000) – (8,000 + 3,000)	3,000
New bank loans: 8,500 – 3,000	5,500
Dividends paid	(500)
Net cash from financing activities	8,000
Net increase/(decrease) in cash and cash equivalents	1,736
Cash and cash equivalents at the beginning of the year	(1,286)
Cash and cash equivalents at the end of the year	450

Workings

Proceeds on disposal of property, plant and equipment (PPE)	£000
Carrying amount of PPE sold	342
Gain on disposal	455
	797

Purchases of property, plant and equipment (PPE)	£000
PPE at start of year	22,246
Depreciation charge	(4,398)
Carrying amount of PPE sold	(342)
PPE at end of year	(31,989)
Total PPE additions	14,483

(c) **Adlington Ltd**

Statement of changes in equity for the year ended 31 October 20X9

	Share capital £000	Other reserves £000	Retained earnings £000	Total equity £000
Balance at 1 November 20X8	8,000	3,000	11,489	22,489
Changes in equity				
Profit for the year	0	0	4,473	4,473
Dividends	0	0	(500)	(500)
Issue of share capital	2,000	1,000	0	3,000
Balance at 31 October 20X9	10,000	4,000	15,462	29,462

Task 3.24

Primrose is showing a **net decrease in cash** for the year ended 31 May 20X5, converting a positive balance into an overdraft. This is not good news. The **net cash flow from operating activities** is **impressive** at £1,637,000, but this is offset by the factors that are putting the company's **working capital under strain.**

The main cash outflow is the **purchase of non-current assets** for £2,800,000. This suggests that the company is **expanding**, perhaps too rapidly, although it is to be hoped that the non-current assets would **generate profits in future years.**

To finance this expansion, Primrose has **issued additional shares,** resulting in a cash inflow of £1,280,000. This will result in **future cash outflows** in the form of dividends, but it prevents gearing from becoming too high. **Long-term loans of £100,000 were repaid**, which will reduce interest payments in the future.

Inventories, trade receivables and trade payables have all increased, showing that the **company's working capital is under strain.** Credit customers are taking longer to pay, and therefore credit control may be an issue.

More information is needed about whether any expansion as resulted from additional revenue, and whether this is likely to continue.

....

Task 3.25

Generally, cash is less easy to manipulate than profit. However, there are ways in which the cash position at the year end can be manipulated.

(a)   **Selling non-current assets** just before the year end. This will have a long-term impact on profit, but will boost cash in the short term.

(b)   Offering **discounts** so that credit customers pay early. Of course this means that in the long term, less cash comes in.

(c)   **Delaying payments to suppliers**. Working capital will be unchanged, but cash will be higher.

(d)   **Cutting gross profit margins** to give a short term boost to sales.

(e)   **Cutting expenses**, for example advertising, which may be damaging in the long term.

....

Task 3.26

(a) **Forthbank Ltd**

Reconciliation of profit before tax to net cash from operating activities

	£000
Profit before tax	5,559
Adjustments for:	
Depreciation	3,366
Dividends received	(650)
Loss on disposal of property, plant and equipment	110
Finance costs	301
Adjustment in respect of inventories (5,832 – 4,860)	(972)
Adjustment in respect of trade receivables (5,400 – 4,320)	(1,080)
Adjustment in respect of trade payables (3,240 – 3,564)	(324)
Cash generated by operations	6,310
Tax paid	(908)
Interest paid	(301)
Net cash from operating activities	5,101

(b) **Forthbank Ltd**

Statement of cash flows for the year ended 31 March 20X1

	£000
Net cash from operating activities	5,101
Investing activities	
Purchases of property, plant and equipment (W)	(11,223)
Proceeds on disposal of property, plant and equipment (W)	227
Dividends received	650
Net cash used in investing activities	(10,346)

	£000
Financing activities	
Proceeds of share issue (11,000 – 8,000)	3,000
New bank loans (4,300 – 800)	3,500
Dividends paid	(460)
Net cash from financing activities	6,040
Net increase/(decrease) in cash and cash equivalents	795
Cash and cash equivalents at the beginning of the year	(208)
Cash and cash equivalents at the end of the year	587

Workings

Proceeds on disposal of property, plant and equipment (PPE)	£000
Carrying amount of PPE sold	337
Loss on disposal	(110)
	227

Purchases of property, plant and equipment (PPE)	£000
PPE at start of year	19,140
Depreciation charge	(3,366)
Carrying amount of PPE sold	(337)
PPE at end of year	(26,660)
Total PPE additions	(11,223)

(c) **Forthbank Ltd**

Statement of changes in equity for the year ended 31 March 20X1

	Share Capital £000	Other Reserves £000	Retained Earnings £000	Total Equity £000
Balance at 1 April 20X0	6,000	2,000	14,840	22,840
Changes in equity				
Profit for the year	0	0	4,446	4,446
Dividends	0	0	(460)	(460)
Issue of share capital	2,000	1,000	0	3,000
Balance at 31 March 20X1	8,000	3,000	18,826	29,826

Chapter 6

Task 6.1

£888,000	
£897,000	
£955,000	✓
£1,005,000	

General overheads should not be included in the cost of an item of property, plant and equipment.

Task 6.2

£4,000	
£4,211	
£5,000	
£5,263	✓

£200,000 ÷ 38 = £5,263

Task 6.3

£9,143	
£11,429	
£12,800	✓
£18,286	

Carrying amount at 1 January 20X2	=	£80,000 – (2 × 8,000)
	=	£64,000
Remaining useful life at 1 January 20X2	=	7 – 2 years
	=	5 years
Depreciation charge y/e 31 December 20X2	=	$\dfrac{£64,000}{5}$
	=	£12,800

Task 6.4

£40,000	
£58,400	
£60,000	✓
£288,800	

	£
Carrying amount at 31 December 20X5	
£460,000 – (2 × £460,000/46 years)	440,000
Disposal proceeds	500,000
Profit on disposal	60,000

Task 6.5

What will be the carrying amount of the machine at 30 June 20X3?

£4,000	
£5,000	
£8,000	✓
£12,000	

Working

	£
Cost at 1 July 20X0	20,000
Depreciation (3 years × [(20 – 4)/4]	(12,000)
Carrying amount at 30 June 20X3	8,000

Task 6.6

Which of the following statements are correct with regard to property, plant and equipment (PPE)?

1   A revaluation reserve arises when an item of PPE is sold at a profit.
2   All non-current assets must be depreciated.

1 only	
2 only	
Both	
Neither of them	✓

Task 6.7

Note. Based on the information available at the time this book was written, we anticipate that this task would be human marked in the real assessment.

(a)   IAS 16 states that items of property, plant, and equipment should be recognised as assets when two conditions are met:

- It is probable that future economic benefits associated with the item will flow to the entity; and

- The cost of the asset can be measured reliably.

(b)   The cost of an item of property, plant and equipment is:

- Its purchase price, including import duties and after deducting trade discounts and rebates; and

- Any costs directly attributable to bringing the item to the location and condition necessary for it to be capable of operating in the manner intended by management.

(c)   Cost of new item of manufacturing equipment:

	£
Invoiced price of the equipment	37,000
Delivery costs	1,600
Installation and testing costs	4,500
Proceeds from the sale of samples produced when testing equipment	(1,800)
Net costs	41,300

Chapter 7

Task 7.1

What is the amount of impairment loss that will be recognised in the statement of profit or loss, in accordance with IAS 36 *Impairment of Assets*?

Note. Fair value less costs of disposal is £18,200, which is less than value in use, so value in use of £18,400 is the recoverable amount. The impairment loss is the difference between the carrying amount of £19,600 and the recoverable amount, ie, £1,200.

£NIL	
£1,100	
£1,200	✓
£1,400	

Note. Based on the information available at the time this book was written, we anticipate that the tasks in this section would be human marked in the real assessment.

Task 7.2

(a) Inventories

(i) Financial statements are prepared on an accruals basis. This means that costs are matched with the revenues to which they relate. In addition, IAS 2 *Inventories* states that the carrying amount of inventories is recognised as an expense in the period in which the related revenue is recognised. Closing inventories are therefore recognised as an asset in the statement of financial position and carried forward to the next period, when they will be sold and the revenue will be recognised.

(ii) Closing inventories are valued at the lower of cost and net realisable value.

(b) **Impairment**

(i) IAS 36 *Impairment of Assets* requires an impairment review to be carried out if there is any indication that an asset has become impaired. An asset is impaired if its carrying amount is greater than its recoverable amount. IAS 36 also states that certain assets should be reviewed for impairment annually, even if there is no indication of impairment. These assets are goodwill acquired in a business combination and intangible assets with indefinite lives.

(ii) When an asset is reviewed for impairment, its carrying amount is compared with its recoverable amount. Recoverable amount is the higher of fair value less costs of disposal and value in use.

Task 7.3

(i) Probable future economic benefits will be generated by the asset

(ii) Intention to complete and use or sell the asset

(iii) Resources (technical/financial) adequate to complete and use or sell the asset

(iv) Ability to use or sell the asset

(v) Technical feasibility of completing the asset

(vi) Expenditure can be reliably measured

Task 7.4

Goodwill may be **distinguished from other intangible non-current** assets by reference to the following characteristics.

(a) It cannot exist independently of the business.

(b) Its value has **no reliable or predictable relationship to any costs** which may have been incurred.

(c) Its value arises from various intangible factors such as skilled employees, effective advertising or a strategic location. These indirect factors cannot be valued.

(d) The value of goodwill may **fluctuate widely** according to internal and external circumstances over relatively short periods of time.

(e) The assessment of the value of goodwill is **highly subjective**.

Task 7.5

True	
False	✓

IAS 38 *Intangible Assets* prohibits the recognition of internally generated goodwill.

···

Task 7.6

True	
False	✓

According to IAS 36 *Impairment of Assets*, an asset is impaired if its recoverable amount is lower than its carrying amount. An asset's recoverable amount is the higher of fair value less costs of disposal or value in use. This asset has a recoverable amount of £130,000, so it is not impaired and should continue to be measured at its carrying amount of £125,000.

···

Task 7.7

(i) only	
(ii) only	
(iii) only	
(iv) only	✓

IAS 36 states that an asset is impaired if its carrying amount exceeds its recoverable amount. Recoverable amount is the higher of fair value less costs of disposal and value in use.

···

Task 7.8

£1,400	
£1,475	
£1,500	✓
£1,600	

- The items sold are assumed to be the 25 units purchased on 1 June and 5 units purchased on 15 June.

- Therefore the items in inventory are 10 units purchased on 15 June.

- Net realisable value is lower than cost, so the value of inventories is: $10 \times 150 = £1,500$

···

Task 7.9

£32,400	✓
£34,000	
£34,100	
£37,100	

	£000
Inventories	
Product I (Cost: FIFO)	11,300
Product II (NRV)	5,900
Product III (Cost: FIFO)	15,200
	32,400

Chapter 8

Task 8.1

Tax expense (profit or loss)	Tax payable (statement of financial position)	
£124,000	£124,000	
£124,000	£129,000	✓
£129,000	£129,000	
£134,000	£129,000	

	£
Expense for current year	129,000
Less adjustment in respect of prior period	(5,000)
Tax expense in profit or loss	124,000
Tax payable (liability)	129,000

Task 8.2

£750	
£500	
£900	✓
£1,000	

$\frac{3}{10} \times £3,000 = £900$

Task 8.3

£750	
£500	
£900	
£1,000	✓

$\frac{2}{6} \times £3,000 = £1,000$

Task 8.4

£7,000	✓
£8,000	
£10,000	
£11,000	

	£
Deposit	30,000
Instalments (8 × £20,000)	160,000
	190,000
Fair value	154,000
Interest	36,000

Sum-of-the-digits = $\frac{8 \times 9}{2}$ = 36

6 months to June X1 $\frac{8}{36}$ × £36,000

Dec X1 $\frac{7}{36}$ × £36,000

June X2 $\frac{6}{36}$ × £36,000

Dec X2 $\frac{5}{36}$ × £36,000

June X3 $\frac{4}{36}$ × £36,000   =   £4,000

Dec X3 $\frac{3}{36}$ × £36,000   =   <u>£3,000</u>

<u>£7,000</u>

Task 8.5

Current liability	Non-current liability	
£25,908	£35,967	
£51,605	£35,812	
£15,908	£35,967	✓
£35,908	£15,397	

	£
Cost 1.1.X4	80,000
Interest 7.93%	6,344
Instalment	(20,000)
Balance 31.12.X4	66,344
Interest 7.93%	5,261
Instalment	(20,000)
Balance 31.12.X5	51,605
Interest 7.93%	4,092
Instalment	(20,000)
Balance 31.12.X6	35,697
Current liability (51,605 – 35,697) =	15,908
Non-current liability	35,697
Total balance at 31.12.X5	51,605

Task 8.6

£931		
£2,000		
£963		
£1,069		✓

Working

		Capital £		Interest £	Cash (memo) £
1.1.X	Asset	10,000			
1.1.X1	Deposit	(575)			
		9,425			
1.1.X1 – 31.12.X1	Interest		× 11% =	1,037	
31.12.X1	Instalment 1	(963)		(1,037)	2,000
Balance at 31.12.X1		8,462			
1.1.X2 – 31.12.X2	Interest		× 11% =	931	
31.12.X2	Instalment 2	(1,069)		(931)	2,000
Balance at 31.12.X2		7,393			

Task 8.7

£7,400	
£9,110	✓
£10,250	
£13,110	

Using the actuarial method, the liability at 31 December 20X1 is:

	£
Fair value	15,400
Less deposit	(4,000)
	11,400
Interest (11,400 × 15%)	1,710
Payment 31 December 20X1	(4,000)
	9,110

Task 8.8

£6,120	
£9,120	✓
£9,600	
£25,000	

Finance charge of £9,120 (76,000 × 12%)

Task 8.9

IAS 37 *Provisions, Contingent Assets and Contingent Liabilities* defines a **contingent asset as**:

'A possible asset that arises from past events and whose existence will be confirmed only by the occurrence of one or more uncertain future events not wholly within the control of the entity.'

A **contingent liability** is defined as:

(a)   A possible obligation that arises from past events and whose existence will be confirmed only by the occurrence of one or more uncertain future events not wholly within the entity's control, or

(b)   A present obligation that arises from past events but is not recognised because it is not probable that a transfer of economic benefits will be required to settle the obligation, or the amount of the obligation cannot be measured with sufficient reliability.

An entity **must not recognise a contingent asset**, because it could result in the recognition of profit that may never be realised. However, when the realisation of profit is virtually certain, then the related asset is not a contingent asset and its recognition is appropriate.

Contingent assets must be **disclosed in the notes** to the financial statements where an inflow of economic benefits is probable.

A **contingent liability must not be recognised**. It must be **disclosed** in the financial statements unless the possibility of a transfer of economic benefits is remote.

....

Task 8.10

(a)   **Events after the reporting period** are defined in IAS 10 as 'those events, favourable and unfavourable, that occur between the end of the reporting period and the date when the financial statements are authorised for issue.' Events after the reporting period may be either adjusting or non-adjusting in nature.

Adjusting events are those which provide evidence of conditions that existed at the reporting date.

This is an adjusting event because the news that the company went into liquidation after the end of the reporting period shows that it must have been in financial difficulty at the reporting date.

Because this is a major customer of the company the debt is likely to be material, and so per IAS 10 the financial statements should be adjusted.

A doubtful debt allowance for the full amount of this receivable should be made in the financial statements.

(b)   IAS 37 *Provisions, Contingent Liabilities and Contingent Assets* states that an entity should **never recognise a contingent liability.** The IAS requires a contingent liability to be disclosed by note unless the possibility of any outflow of economic benefits to settle it is remote.

The IAS also requires that a provision should be recognised only when an entity has an obligation that requires the transfer of economic benefits in settlement which can be measured sufficiently reliably.

As the claim is unlikely to succeed, the company does not have a present obligation and the potential settlement of £500,000 should be disclosed as a contingent liability. However, given that the legal costs of £50,000 must be paid whether the claim is successful or not, this amount should be provided for in the company's financial statements.

Task 8.11

Legal action 1	Legal action 2	
Disclose in a note to the financial statements	No disclosure	
Recognise a provision	No disclosure	
Recognise a provision	Disclose in a note to the financial statements	✓
Recognise a provision	Recognise the income	

Task 8.12

A	Destruction of a major non-current asset	
B	Discovery of error or fraud	✓
C	Issue of shares	
D	Purchases of a major non-current asset	

Task 8.13

(i) only	
(ii) only	✓
Both	
Neither of them	

Task 8.14

True	
False	✓

Under IFRS 15 *Revenue from Contracts with Customers,* Usk would have recognised revenue on the goods sold to Chertsey Ltd but reduced it by the expected value of returns. Instead of recognising revenue for these expected returns, Usk would recognise a refund liability. The inventory cost of items expected to be returned is also excluded from cost of sales and instead remains within inventory.

....

Task 8.15

(a)   A lease is classified as a finance lease if it is a lease that transfers substantially all the risks and rewards incidental to ownership of an asset to the lessee.

A lease is classified as an operating lease if it does not transfer substantially all the risks and rewards of ownership of an asset to the lessee.

(b)   **(i)**   If an entity leases an asset under a finance lease, it recognises the lease as an asset in the statement of financial position. It also recognises a liability for the outstanding lease payments. The asset and the liability are measured at the fair value of the leased asset, or the present value of the minimum lease payments (if this is lower).

(ii)   If an entity leases an asset under an operating lease, the lease payments are charged to profit or loss on a straight line basis unless another systematic basis is more appropriate. The leased asset is not recognised in the statement of financial position.

(c)   The first lease has a term (five years) which is for the major part of the useful life of the equipment (six years). The present value of the minimum lease payments is unknown, but from the information provided it is likely to amount to substantially all of the fair value of the leased asset (total lease payments of £25,000 compared with a fair value of £20,000). This indicates that the first lease should be classified as a finance lease.

The second lease is for only a small part of the total useful life of the equipment (two years out of seven). Again, the present value of the minimum lease payments is unknown, but total lease payments are £4,800 (£200 × 24) which is only just over 50% of the fair value of the item (the present value of the minimum lease payments would be less than £4,800). This indicates that the second lease is an operating lease.

....

Task 8.16

The treatment of the damages claim is governed by IAS 37 *Provisions, Contingent Liabilities and Contingent Assets*. According to IAS 37 a provision should be recognised when:

(a) An entity has a present obligation (legal or constructive) as a result of a past event.

(b) It is probable that a transfer of economic benefits will be required to settle the obligation.

(c) A reliable estimate can be made of the obligation.

For a provision to be recognised, the circumstances must meet each of these three criteria. In the case of the damages claim there is a present obligation (a) to pay damages. The lawyer has stated that this transfer of economic benefits is probable (b). In addition the amount of the claim has been estimated reliably (c) at £250,000, so a provision for this amount should be recognised in the financial statements.

Task 8.17

(a) IAS 37 *Provisions, Contingent Liabilities and Contingent Assets* states that a provision should be recognised when:

- An entity has a present obligation as a result of a past event. The obligation can be either legal or constructive; and

- It is probable that an outflow of resources embodying economic benefits will be required to settle the obligation; and

- A reliable estimate can be made of the amount of the obligation.

(b) Houghton Ltd has a constructive obligation to make the refunds because it has publicised its policy, leading its customers to expect that it will refund purchases. (The past obligating event is the sale of the product).

It is also probable that the company will actually have to make some refunds (an outflow of resources embodying economic benefits) in the next reporting period (refunds have already been claimed).

Although the precise amount of future claims is unknown it should be possible to make a reasonable estimate based on past experience. (IAS 37 explains that it is almost always possible to make a reliable estimate.)

Therefore Houghton Ltd should recognise a provision, based on its best estimate of the cost of refunds relating to goods sold in the last three months of the year.

(c) IAS 37 requires disclosure of the following information for each class of provision:

- The carrying amount at the beginning and end of the period
- Additional provisions made in the period
- Amounts used during the period
- Unused amounts reversed during the period

There should also be a narrative note giving:

- A brief description of the nature of the obligation and expected timing of any resulting transfers of economic benefit.

- An indication of the uncertainties about the amount or timing of those transfers of economic benefit.

Task 8.18

(a) Inventories are assets held by an entity that are for sale in the ordinary course of business.

IAS 2 *Inventories* requires inventories to be recognised in the financial statements at the lower of cost and net realisable value.

The cost of inventories should include the purchase price, import duties and other taxes, and transport, handling and other costs directly attributable to the acquisition of the finished goods. Essentially, all costs incurred in bringing the inventories to their present location and condition can be included.

(b) IFRS 15 *Revenue from Contracts with Customers* defines revenue as the 'income arising in the course of an entity's ordinary activities'.

IFRS 15 requires revenue to be measured at the transaction price, which is 'the amount of consideration to which an entity expects to be entitled in exchange for transferring promised goods or services to a customer, excluding amounts collected on behalf of third parties'.

Revenue from the sale of goods should be recognised when the performance obligation(s) in the contract is/are satisfied. There is a five step process for establishing the amount of revenue to recognise, and when it should be recognised:

(i) Identify the contract(s) with a customer.

(ii) Identify the performance obligations in the contract.

(iii) Determine the transaction price.

(iv) Allocate the transaction price to the performance obligations in the contract

(v) Recognise revenue when (or as) the entity satisfies a performance obligation.

Chapter 9

Task 9.1

A parent	
A simple investment	
A subsidiary	✓

Erewash Ltd **controls** Amber Ltd. An investor controls an investee when it is exposed, or has rights, to variable returns from its involvement with the investee and has the ability to affect those returns through its power over the investee (IFRS 10).

••

Task 9.2

Elements (i) and (iii) only	
Elements (ii), (iii) and (iv) only	
Elements (i), (ii) and (iv) only	
All of the above	✓

••

Task 9.3

(a) IFRS 10 *Consolidated Financial Statements* explains that an entity that has an investment in another entity should determine whether it is a parent by assessing whether it controls that other entity.

IFRS 10 states that an investor controls an investee if and only if the investor has all the following:

- Power over the investee

- Exposure, or rights, to variable returns from its involvement with the investee; and

- The ability to use its power over the investee to affect the amount of the investor's returns.

An investor has power over an investee when it has existing rights that give it the current ability to direct its relevant activities (the activities that significantly affect its returns). The most common form of rights that give power are voting rights, where an investor holds more than half the voting rights in its investee. However, an investor may have other rights that give it

power over its investee, even if it does not hold a majority of the voting rights. For example, it may have the right to appoint or remove the entity's board of directors, or other management personnel, or it may have legal or contractual rights to direct the entity's activities.

(b) IFRS 3 *Business Combinations states* that goodwill acquired in a business combination should be carried in the statement of financial position at cost less any impairment losses. The cost of goodwill is the difference between the cost of the investment and the fair value of the identifiable assets and liabilities acquired. Goodwill is not amortised, but must be reviewed for impairment annually. Therefore the directors of Lavendar cannot write off the goodwill on acquisition immediately.

Task 9.4

X plc

Consolidated statement of financial position as at 31 December 20X1

	£000
ASSETS	
Goodwill (W)	20
Property, plant and equipment (800 + 400)	1,200
Current assets (170 + 130)	300
	1,520
EQUITY AND LIABILITIES	
Share capital	800
Retained earnings (W)	450
Non-controlling interest (W)	120
Current liabilities (100 + 50)	150
	1,520

Workings

Goodwill	£000
Consideration	350
Non-controlling interests at acquisition	110
Net assets acquired (200 + 240)	(440)
	20

Retained earnings	£000
X plc	420
Y Ltd – attributable to X plc (75% × (280 – 240))	30
	450

Non-controlling interest (NCI) at acquisition	£000
Share capital – attributable to NCI (25% × 200)	50
Retained earnings – attributable to NCI (25% × 240)	60
	110

Non-controlling interest (NCI) at year end	£000
Share capital – attributable to NCI (25% × 200)	50
Retained earnings – attributable to NCI (25% × 280)	70
	120

Task 9.5

(a) Goodwill

£	594,000

	£000	£000
Consideration		3,510
Non-controlling interest at acquisition (W2)		1,900
Net assets acquired (2,000 + 1,000 + 1,350 + 400)		(4,750)
		660
Less impairment		(66)
		594

Workings

1   *Group structure*

$$\frac{1,200,000}{2,000,000} \times 100 = 60\%$$

F Ltd → V Ltd

2   *NCI at acquisition*

	£000
Share capital – attributable to NCI (40% × 2,000)	800
Share premium – attributable to NCI (40% × 1,000)	400
Retained earnings – attributable to NCI (40% × 1,350)	540
Fair value adjustment – attributable to NCI (40% × 400)	160
	1,900

(b) **Non-controlling interest**

£ | 2,068,000

	£000
Share capital – attributable to NCI (40% × 2,000)	800
Share premium – attributable to NCI (40% × 1,000)	400
Retained earnings – attributable to NCI (40% × 1,770)	708
Fair value adjustment – attributable to NCI (40% × 400)	160
	2,068

(c) **Consolidated retained earnings reserve**

£ | 5,796,000

	£000	£000
Fertwrangler Ltd		5,610
Voncarryon Ltd:		
At 31 March 20X3	1,770	
At acquisition	(1,350)	
	420	
Attributable to parent (60%)		252
Impairment of goodwill		(66)
		5,796

Task 9.6

Dumyat plc

Consolidated statement of financial position as at 31 October 20X7

	£000
ASSETS	
Non-current assets	
Goodwill (W)	2,711
Property, plant and equipment (65,388 + 31,887 + 3,000)	100,275
	102,986
Current assets	
Inventories (28,273 + 5,566)	33,839
Trade and other receivables (11,508 + 5,154)	16,662
Cash and cash equivalents (2,146 + 68)	2,214
	52,715
Total assets	155,701
EQUITY AND LIABILITIES	
Equity	
Share capital	25,000
Share premium	12,000
Retained earnings (W)	59,401
	96,401
Non-controlling interest (W)	9,023
Total equity	105,424

	£000
Non-current liabilities	
Long-term loans (25,000 + 4,000)	29,000
Current liabilities	
Trade and other payables (13,554 + 1,475)	15,029
Tax payable (6,140 + 108)	6,248
	21,277
Total liabilities	50,277
Total equity and liabilities	155,701

Workings

Note. Group structure

Dumyat plc owns 75% of Devon Ltd (9,000,000/12,000,000).

Goodwill	£000
Consideration	26,000
Non-controlling interest at acquisition	7,763
Net assets acquired (12,000 + 4,000 + 12,052 + 3,000)	(31,052)
	2,711

Retained earnings	£000
Dumyat plc	55,621
Devon Ltd – attributable to Dumyat plc (75% × (17,092 – 12,052))	3,780
	59,401

Non-controlling interest (NCI) at acquisition	£000
Share capital – attributable to NCI (25% × 12,000)	3,000
Share premium – attributable to NCI (25% × 4,000)	1,000
Retained earnings – attributable to NCI (25% × 12,052)	3,013
Revaluation reserve – attributable to NCI (25% × 3,000)	750
	7,763

Non-controlling interest (NCI) at year end	£000
Share capital – attributable to NCI (25% × 12,000)	3,000
Share premium – attributable to NCI (25% × 4,000)	1,000
Retained earnings – attributable to NCI (25% × 17,092)	4,273
Revaluation reserve – attributable to NCI (25% × 3,000)	750
	9,023

Task 9.7

Tolsta plc

Consolidated statement of financial position as at 31 October 20X8

	£000
ASSETS	
Non-current assets	
Intangible assets: goodwill (W)	8,400
Property, plant and equipment (47,875 + 31,913 + 4,500)	84,288
	92,688
Current assets	
Inventories	30,509
Trade and other receivables (14,343 + 3,656 – 2,000)	15,999
Cash and cash equivalents	2,003
	48,511
Total assets	141,199

	£000
EQUITY AND LIABILITIES	
Equity	
Share capital	45,000
Share premium	12,000
Retained earnings (W)	25,120
	82,120
Non-controlling interest (W)	11,280
Total equity	93,400
Non-current liabilities	
Long-term loan	27,000
Current liabilities	
Trade and other payables (14,454 + 3,685 – 2,000)	16,139
Tax liabilities	4,660
	20,799
Total liabilities	47,799
Total equity and liabilities	141,199

Workings

Note. Group structure

Tolsta plc owns $\frac{2}{3}$ of Balallan Ltd ($\frac{8,000,000}{12,000,000}$).

Goodwill	£000
Price paid	32,000
Non-controlling interests at acquisition	10,750
Net assets acquired (12,000 + 6,000 + 9,750 + 4,500)	(32,250)
Impairment	(2,100)
	8,400

Retained earnings	£000
Tolsta plc	26,160
Balallan Ltd – attributable to Tolsta plc ($\frac{2}{3}$% × (11,340 – 9,750))	1,060
Impairment	(2,100)
	25,120

Non-controlling interest (NCI) at acquisition	£000
Share capital – attributable to NCI ($\frac{1}{3}$ × 12,000)	4,000
Share premium – attributable to NCI ($\frac{1}{3}$ × 6,000)	2,000
Retained earnings – attributable to NCI ($\frac{1}{3}$ × 9,750)	3,250
Revaluation reserve – attributable to NCI ($\frac{1}{3}$ × 4,500)	1,500
	10,750

Non-controlling interest (NCI) at year end	£000
Share capital – attributable to NCI ($\frac{1}{3}$ × 12,000)	4,000
Share premium – attributable to NCI ($\frac{1}{3}$ × 6,000)	2,000
Retained earnings – attributable to NCI ($\frac{1}{3}$ × 11,340)	3,780
Revaluation reserve – attributable to NCI ($\frac{1}{3}$ × 4,500)	1,500
	11,280

Task 9.8

Ard plc

Consolidated statement of financial position as at 31 March 20X9

	£000
ASSETS	
Non-current assets	
Intangible assets: goodwill (W)	4,816
Property, plant and equipment	72,690
Current assets (32,782 + 10,835 – 3,000)	40,617
Total assets	118,123
EQUITY AND LIABILITIES	
Equity	
Share capital	50,000
Retained earnings (W)	21,186
Non-controlling interest (W)	11,896
Total equity	83,082
Non-current liabilities	18,000
Current liabilities (15,466 + 4,575 – 3,000)	17,041
Total liabilities	35,041
Total equity and liabilities	118,123

Workings

Note. Group structure

Ard plc owns 60% of Ledi Ltd (12,000,000/20,000,000).

Goodwill	£000
Price paid	23,000
Non-controlling interest at acquisition	11,056
Net assets acquired (20,000 + 7,640)	(27,640)
Impairment	(1,600)
	4,816

Retained earnings	£000
Ard plc	21,526
Ledi Ltd – attributable to Ard plc (60% × (9,740 – 7,640))	1,260
Impairment	(1,600)
	21,186

Non-controlling interest (NCI) at acquisition	£000
Share capital – attributable to NCI (40% × 20,000)	8,000
Retained earnings – attributable to NCI (40% × 7,640)	3,056
	11,056

Non-controlling interest (NCI) at year end	£000
Share capital – attributable to NCI (40% × 20,000)	8,000
Retained earnings – attributable to NCI (40% × 9,740)	3,896
	11,896

Task 9.9

Glebe plc

Consolidated statement of financial position as at 31 March 20X1

	£000
ASSETS	
Non-current assets	
Intangible assets – goodwill (W)	842
Property, plant and equipment (36,890 + 25,600 + 2,400)	64,890
Current assets	30,199
Total assets	95,931
EQUITY AND LIABILITIES	
Equity	
Share capital	40,000
Retained earnings (W)	15,426
Non-controlling interest (W)	8,715
Total equity	64,141
Non-current liabilities	18,000
Current liabilities	13,790
Total liabilities	31,790
Total equity and liabilities	95,931

Workings

Goodwill	£000
Price paid	18,000
Non-controlling interests at acquisition	7,182
Net assets acquired (10,000 + 11,540 + 2,400)	(23,940)
Impairment	(400)
	842

Retained earnings	£000
Glebe plc	12,249
Starks Ltd – attributable to Glebe plc (70% × (16,650 – 11,540))	3,577
Impairment	(400)
	15,426

Non-controlling interest (NCI) at acquisition	£000
Share capital – attributable to NCI (30% × 10,000)	3,000
Retained earnings – attributable to NCI (30% × 11,540)	3,462
Revaluation reserve – attributable to NCI (30% × 2,400)	720
	7,182

Non-controlling interest (NCI) at year end	£000
Share capital – attributable to NCI (30% × 10,000)	3,000
Retained earnings – attributable to NCI (30% × 16,650)	4,995
Revaluation reserve – attributable to NCI (30% × 2,400)	720
	8,715

Chapter 10

Task 10.1

P plc

Consolidated statement of profit or loss for the year ended 31 March 20X2

	£000
Continuing operations	
Revenue	6,810
Cost of sales	4,020
Gross profit	2,790
Other income	0
Operating expenses	1,300
Profit before tax	1,490
Tax	420
Profit for the period from continuing operations	1,070
Attributable to:	
Equity holders of the parent	968
Non-controlling interests (30% × 340)	102
	1,070

Task 10.2

C plc

Consolidated statement of profit or loss for the year ended 31 December 20X1

	£000
Continuing operations	
Revenue (W)	48,300
Cost of sales (W)	30,500
Gross profit	17,800
Other income	0
Operating expenses	10,600
Profit before tax	7,200
Tax	2,200
Profit for the period from continuing operations	5,000
Attributable to:	
Equity holders of the parent	4,320
Non-controlling interests (1,700 × 40%)	680
	5,000

Working

Revenue	£000
C plc	38,600
D Ltd	14,700
Total inter-company adjustment	(5,000)
	48,300

Cost of sales	£000
C plc	25,000
D Ltd	9,500
Total inter-company adjustment (5,000 − 1,000 unrealised profit)	(4,000)
	30,500

Task 10.3

Aswall plc

Consolidated statement of profit or loss for the year ended 31 March 20X4

	£000
Continuing operations	
Revenue (W)	43,515
Cost of sales (W)	(18,968)
Gross profit	24,547
Other income	0
Distribution costs	(6,756)
Administrative expenses	(4,008)
Profit from operations	13,783
Finance costs	(2,940)
Profit before tax	10,843
Tax	(3,686)
Profit for the period from continuing operations	7,157
Attributable to:	
Equity holders of the parent	6,523
Non-controlling interest (W)	634
	7,157

Workings

Revenue	£000
Aswall plc	32,412
Unsafey Ltd	12,963
Total inter-company adjustment	(1,860)
	43,515

Cost of sales	£000
Aswall plc	14,592
Unsafey Ltd	5,576
Total inter-company adjustment (1,860 – 660 unrealised profit)	(1,200)
	18,968

Non-controlling interest (NCI)	£000
Profit for the period attributable to NCI (25% × 3,196)	799
Unrealised profit attributable to NCI (25% × 660)	(165)
	634

Task 10.4

Danube plc

Consolidated statement of profit or loss for the year ended 31 March 20X2

	£000
Continuing operations	
Revenue	20,200
Cost of sales	(10,500)
Gross profit	9,700
Other income	0
Operating expenses	(4,530)
Profit from operations	5,170

Workings

Revenue	£000
Danube plc	15,800
Inn Ltd	5,400
Total inter-company adjustment	(1,000)
	20,200

Cost of sales	£000
Danube plc	8,500
Inn Ltd	2,800
Total inter-company adjustment (1,000 – 200)	(800)
	10,500

Task 10.5

Wewill plc

Consolidated statement of profit or loss for the year ended 31 March 20X4

	£000
Continuing operations	
Revenue (W)	49,600
Cost of sales (W)	(25,955)
Gross profit	23,645
Other income	0
Distribution costs	(9,910)
Administrative expenses	(5,902)
Profit from operations	7,833
Finance costs	(829)
Profit before tax	7,004
Tax	(1,913)
Profit for the period from continuing operations	5,091
Attributable to:	
Equity holders of the parent	4,729
Non-controlling interest (20% × 1,810)	362
	5,091

Workings

Revenue	£000
Wewill plc	36,400
Rokyu Ltd	14,600
Total inter-company adjustment	(1,400)
	49,600

Cost of sales	£000
Wewill plc	20,020
Rokyu Ltd	6,935
Total inter-company adjustment (1,400 – 400)	(1,000)
	25,955

Task 10.6

£144,000	
£150,000	
£156,000	✓
£160,000	

	£
Consolidated cost of sales	200,000
Less intra-group sales	(50,000)
Unrealised profit (50,000 – 40,000 × 60%)	6,000
	156,000

Chapter 11

Calculating ratios

Task 11.1

(a)	Gross profit percentage $\dfrac{522}{989} \times 100$	52.8	%
(b)	Operating profit percentage $\dfrac{214}{989} \times 100$	21.6	%
(c)	Return on capital employed $\dfrac{214}{1,400} \times 100$	15.3	%
(d)	Asset turnover (net assets) $\dfrac{989}{1,400}$	0.7	times
(e)	Interest cover $\dfrac{214}{34}$	6.3	times

Task 11.2

(a)	Current ratio $\dfrac{58,600 + 98,400}{86,200 + 6,300}$	1.7	:1
(b)	Quick (acid test) ratio $\dfrac{98,400}{86,200 + 6,300}$	1.1	:1
(c)	Trade receivables collection period $\dfrac{98,400}{772,400} \times 365$	46.5	days
(d)	Inventory turnover $\dfrac{507,400}{58,600}$	8.7	times
(e)	Inventory holding period $\dfrac{58,600}{507,400} \times 365$	42.1	days

Task 11.3

(a) Formulae

(i)	Return on capital employed	$\dfrac{\text{Profit from operations}}{\text{Total equity} + \text{Non-current liabilities}} \times 100\%$
(ii)	Operating profit percentage	$\dfrac{\text{Profit from operations}}{\text{Revenue}} \times 100\%$
(iii)	Gross profit percentage	$\dfrac{\text{Gross profit}}{\text{Revenue}} \times 100\%$
(iv)	Asset turnover (net assets)	$\dfrac{\text{Revenue}}{\text{Total assets} - \text{Current liabilities}}$
(v)	Gearing	$\dfrac{\text{Non-current liabilities}}{\text{Total equity} + \text{Non-current liabilities}} \times 100\%$

(b) Calculations

(i)	Return on capital employed $\dfrac{2,189}{17,541} \times 100$	12.5	%
(ii)	Operating profit percentage $\dfrac{2,189}{8,420} \times 100$	26.0	%
(iii)	Gross profit percentage $\dfrac{4,884}{8,420} \times 100$	58.0	%
(iv)	Asset turnover (net assets) $\dfrac{8,420}{17,541}$	0.5	times
(v)	Gearing $\dfrac{5,000}{17,541} \times 100$	28.5	%

Task 11.4

(a) Formulae

(i)	Gross profit percentage	$\dfrac{\text{Gross profit}}{\text{Revenue}} \times 100\%$
(ii)	Operating profit percentage	$\dfrac{\text{Profit from operations}}{\text{Revenue}} \times 100\%$
(iii)	Current ratio	$\dfrac{\text{Current assets}}{\text{Current liabilities}}$
(iv)	Quick (acid test) ratio	$\dfrac{\text{Current assets} - \text{Inventories}}{\text{Current liabilities}}$
(v)	Inventory holding period	$\dfrac{\text{Inventories}}{\text{Cost of sales}} \times 365$

(b) Calculations

(i)	Gross profit percentage $\dfrac{11,595}{21,473} \times 100$	54.0	%
(ii)	Operating profit percentage $\dfrac{4,080}{21,473} \times 100$	19.0	%
(iii)	Current ratio $\dfrac{4,875}{2,093}$	2.3	:1
(iv)	Quick (acid test) ratio $\dfrac{4,875 - 1,813}{2,093}$	1.5	:1
(v)	Inventory holding period $\dfrac{1,813}{9,878} \times 365$	67.0	days

Task 11.5

(a) Formulae

(i)	Operating expenses/revenue percentage	$\dfrac{\text{Dist. costs} + \text{Admin. expenses}}{\text{Revenue}} \times 100\%$
(ii)	Current ratio	$\dfrac{\text{Current assets}}{\text{Current liabilities}}$
(iii)	Quick (acid test) ratio	$\dfrac{\text{Current assets} - \text{Inventories}}{\text{Current liabilities}}$
(iv)	Gearing ratio	$\dfrac{\text{Non-current liabilities}}{\text{Total equity} + \text{Non-current liabilities}} \times 100\%$
(v)	Interest cover	$\dfrac{\text{Profit from operations}}{\text{Finance costs}}$

(b) Calculations

(i)	Operating expenses/Revenue percentage $\dfrac{4{,}841 + 3{,}007}{20{,}562} \times 100$	38.2	%
(ii)	Current ratio $\dfrac{6{,}337}{2{,}906}$	2.2	:1
(iii)	Quick (acid test) ratio $\dfrac{2{,}325}{2{,}906}$	0.8	:1
(iv)	Gearing ratio $\dfrac{14{,}000}{27{,}413}$	51.1	%
(v)	Interest cover $\dfrac{1{,}405}{800}$	1.8	times

Task 11.6

(a) Formulae

(i)	Return on shareholders' funds	$\dfrac{\text{Profit after tax}}{\text{Total equity}} \times 100\%$
(ii)	Inventory holding period	$\dfrac{\text{Inventories}}{\text{Cost of sales}} \times 365$
(iii)	Trade receivables collection period	$\dfrac{\text{Trade receivables}}{\text{Revenue}} \times 365$
(iv)	Trade payables payment period	$\dfrac{\text{Trade payables}}{\text{Cost of sales}} \times 365$
(v)	Working capital cycle	Inventory days + Receivable days – Payable days

(b) Calculations

(i)	Return on shareholders' funds $\dfrac{363}{6,241} \times 100$	5.8	%
(ii)	Inventory holding period $\dfrac{649}{2,597} \times 365$	91.2	days
(iii)	Trade receivables collection period $\dfrac{392}{4,900} \times 365$	29.2	days
(iv)	Trade payables payment period $\dfrac{286}{2,597} \times 365$	40.2	days
(v)	Working capital cycle 91.2 + 29.2 – 40.2	80.2	days

Task 11.7

(a) Formulae

(i)	Gearing	$\dfrac{\text{Non-current liabilities}}{\text{Total equity + Non-current liabilities}} \times 100\%$
(ii)	Interest cover	$\dfrac{\text{Profit from operations}}{\text{Finance costs}}$
(iii)	Current ratio	$\dfrac{\text{Current assets}}{\text{Current liabilities}}$
(iv)	Trade receivables collection period	$\dfrac{\text{Trade receivables}}{\text{Revenue}} \times 365$
(v)	Trade payables payment period	$\dfrac{\text{Trade payables}}{\text{Cost of sales}} \times 365$

(b) Calculations

(i)	Gearing $\dfrac{12,000}{13,537+12,000} \times 100$	47.0	%
(ii)	Interest cover $\dfrac{2,780}{840}$	3.3	times
(iii)	Current ratio $\dfrac{5,207}{2,686}$	1.9	:1
(iv)	Trade receivables collection period $\dfrac{1,946}{27,800} \times 365$	25.6	days
(v)	Trade payables payment period $\dfrac{1,276}{14,178} \times 365$	32.8	days

Task 11.8

(a) Formulae used to calculate the ratios

(i)	Gross profit percentage	$\dfrac{\text{Gross profit}}{\text{Revenue}} \times 100\%$
(ii)	Operating profit percentage	$\dfrac{\text{Profit from operations}}{\text{Revenue}} \times 100\%$
(iii)	Return on shareholders' funds	$\dfrac{\text{Profit after tax}}{\text{Total equity}} \times 100\%$
(iv)	Quick (acid test) ratio	$\dfrac{\text{Current assets} - \text{Inventories}}{\text{Current liabilities}}$
(v)	Operating expenses/revenue percentage	$\dfrac{\text{Dist. costs} + \text{Admin. expenses}}{\text{Revenue}} \times 100\%$

(b) Calculation of the ratios

(i) Gross profit percentage $\dfrac{16,200}{36,000} \times 100$	45.0	%
(ii) Operating profit percentage $\dfrac{3,240}{36,000} \times 100$	9.0	%
(iii) Return on shareholders' funds $\dfrac{866}{26,155} \times 100$	3.3	%
(iv) Quick (acid test) ratio $\dfrac{7,123 - 2,376}{3,876}$	1.2	:1
(v) Operating expenses/revenue percentage $\dfrac{6,840 + 6,120}{36,000} \times 100$	36.0	%

Interpreting financial statements

Note. Based on the information available at the time this book was written, we anticipate that the tasks in this section would be human marked in the real assessment.

Task 11.9

(a) Rigby Ltd is operating on a high gross profit percentage, relatively high operating profit percentage but a fairly low asset turnover. This indicates a low volume, high margin type of business. The ROCE is the same as that of Rialto Ltd but Rialto Ltd has low gross and operating profit percentages but high asset turnover indicating a high volume, low margin business.

In terms of working capital Rialto Ltd has a reasonable current ratio but low quick ratio indicating fairly large inventory levels although with inventory turnover of 10.3 times this inventory is being turned over much more rapidly than in Rigby Ltd. Rialto Ltd has virtually no receivables and both companies take a reasonable amount of credit from suppliers.

Rialto Ltd is more highly geared than Rigby Ltd but with interest cover of 5 times this would not appear to be a major problem.

(b) From the ratios given it would appear that Rigby Ltd is the jeweller with relatively low revenue, high profit margins and slower inventory turnover. Rialto Ltd with higher, low margin revenue and almost no receivables would appear to be the supermarket.

Task 11.10

To: **Duncan Tweedy**

From: **A Technician**

Date: **October 20X3**

Subject: **Comparison of profitability of Byrne Ltd and May Ltd**

The purpose of this report is to assess the relative profitability of the two companies, Byrne Ltd and May Ltd, in order to determine which company is likely to be the better investment. This will be done by using a number of key financial ratios in order to assess the performance of each company.

(a)   **Comparative profitability**

May Ltd's return on capital is significantly higher than that of Byrne Ltd. The return on capital employed for May Ltd shows that the overall return for all the providers of capital (shareholders and long term lenders) is 32.1% compared to only 21.5% for the providers of capital in Byrne Ltd. Therefore from a potential shareholder's viewpoint May provides a better overall return.

May Ltd's gross profit percentage and operating profit percentage are both also significantly higher than those of Byrne Ltd. This indicates that both May Ltd's profit after cost of sales from trading activities and its overall profit after deducting other operating expenses are a higher proportion of its sales revenue than those of Byrne Ltd. For each £1 of sales made during the reported period, May Ltd is generating more profit.

(b)   **Conclusion**

The profitability ratios show us that May Ltd is using its capital base more efficiently and making more profit from each £1 of sales than Byrne Ltd. May Ltd is definitely the more profitable company (in relative terms).

Task 11.11

Notes for meeting

(a) Comments on the changes in the ratios

Current ratio

This seems to show that the company is in a very healthy position; the ratio has improved during the year. The company's current liabilities are covered almost three times by its current assets. Most people would regard this as more than adequate.

However, a very high current ratio can also mean that working capital is not being managed very efficiently and this is borne out by the other ratios.

Quick ratio

This has deteriorated from a satisfactory 1.1 to a slightly worrying 0.6 over the year. The fact that the fall has been so sharp is probably a cause for concern.

The fall in the quick ratio suggests that the improvement in the current ratio is mainly due to an increase in inventory levels. In addition, the high current ratio coupled with the relatively low quick ratio suggests that most of the company's current assets are in the form of inventory. These factors indicate that the company may be carrying too much inventory, which means that cash is being 'tied up' unnecessarily.

Trade receivables collection period

This has risen from 32 days to 48 days during the year, which means that customers are taking longer to pay. If sales have remained at a constant level during the year, this suggests that there may be credit control problems (customers being granted too much credit or staff failing to chase debts).

The ratio should be interpreted with caution. It is possible that this apparent increase in the collection period is due to increased sales towards the year end (as receivables at the year end would be high in relation to revenue for the year).

Trade payables payment period

This has fallen slightly during the year. If the ratio is considered in isolation there does not appear to be cause for concern (most suppliers grant a credit period of around 30 days and so 27 days appears reasonable).

However, note that at the end of the year the time taken to collect receivables is considerably longer than the time taken to pay suppliers (at the start of the year the payment period and the collection period were about the same). This may reflect poor management and could lead to cash flow problems.

Inventory holding period

This has risen significantly during the year. This increase appears to confirm what was suggested by the movements in the current ratio and quick ratio: inventory levels are very high and rising and the company is probably carrying too much inventory. Given that the quick ratio has fallen during the year, this situation may lead to cash flow problems.

The increase in inventory may not necessarily be a result of poor management. For example, the company may have received several big orders shortly before the year end and management may have deliberately purchased extra inventories in order to meet them.

(b) Conclusion

The overall picture given by these five ratios seems to suggest poor working capital management. The apparent increase in the level of inventory is a particular cause for concern and the company also appears to be having problems in collecting cash from customers.

Task 11.12

Sender's address

Ms Madge Keygone

Address

December 20X4

Dear Ms Keygone,

Asbee Ltd

As requested, I am writing to explain the significance of the ratios mentioned by the shareholder in your recent meeting.

(a) Comparison with industry averages

- The current ratio for Asbee Ltd is higher than the industry average, which suggests that the company has more current assets in relation to its current liabilities than is normal for the industry. On the face of it, this is a good sign as it indicates that Asbee Ltd has better liquidity than other companies in the same industry. On the other hand, the low quick ratio (see below) suggests that the company's current assets may largely consist of inventories and receivables, which are often difficult to convert into cash quickly. This could mean that Asbee Ltd may not be able to meet its current liabilities as they fall due and that therefore it is in a worse position than other similar companies.

- The quick ratio is slightly lower than the industry average. This suggests that Asbee Ltd has less cash and receivables in relation to its current liabilities than other companies in the industry. This means that the company's liquidity position appears to be worse than that of the rest of the industry. Asbee Ltd may have very little or no actual cash, with all or most of its quick assets made up of trade receivables.

- The inventory holding period is almost twice as long as the industry average and indicates that other companies in the industry sell inventory almost twice as quickly as Asbee Ltd. This is almost certainly one of the reasons why the current ratio is high compared to other companies. The current ratio and the inventories holding period taken together suggest that inventory levels are abnormally high. There are a number of possible reasons for this: a large number of old or obsolete items which should be written down to net realisable value; or lack of control over inventories.

- The trade receivables collection period is also longer than the industry average, suggesting that Asbee Ltd takes longer to collect amounts receivable from customers than other companies in the industry. This indicates that there are problems with the management of receivables. These may include poor credit control, failure to chase overdue amounts or an increase in the level of irrecoverable debts.

(b) Conclusion

The low quick ratio is probably the main reason why the shareholder is concerned. As stated above, Asbee Ltd's true liquidity could be rather worse than the quick ratio suggests. If the company has a bank overdraft rather than a positive cash balance, this would be worrying.

The shareholder is also probably concerned that too much cash has been absorbed by inventories. In addition he or she may believe that there are inventory control problems that are not being addressed.

In combination with the low quick ratio the receivables collection period suggests that the company has potential liquidity problems. Its liquidity appears to be worse than that of the rest of the industry and the shareholder will view this as a cause for concern.

I hope that this explanation has been helpful. Please do not hesitate to contact me if you have any further queries or if you require any further explanations.

Yours sincerely,

Task 11.13

To: **Leopold Scratchy**

From: **Accounting Technician**

Subject: **Financial statements of Partridge Ltd and Carington Ltd**

Date: **June 20X5**

As requested, I have considered the risk and return of two potential investments. My analysis is based on the latest financial statements of the two companies. I have calculated four key ratios for each of the two companies.

(a) The relative risk and return of the two companies

Gross profit percentage

The two companies have approximately the same gross profit percentage and therefore equally profitable trading operations. A gross profit percentage of 59% appears to be reasonably healthy.

Operating profit percentage

Partridge Ltd has a much higher operating profit percentage than Carington Ltd which means that it is the more profitable of the two companies overall. As both companies have the same gross profit percentage, this indicates that Carington Ltd has higher operating expenses relative to its sales than Partridge Ltd.

Return on shareholders' funds

The return on the shareholders' funds of Partridge Ltd is considerably higher than that of Carington Ltd. This shows that Partridge Ltd would provide a much higher return to an investor relative to its total equity (capital 'owned' by equity shareholders) than Carington Ltd.

Gearing

Partridge Ltd has a high gearing ratio while Carington Ltd has a very low gearing ratio. This shows that Partridge Ltd is financed by loans (borrowings) as well as by equity capital (ordinary shares) and that loans make up quite a high percentage of its total capital employed. This contrasts with Carington Ltd, which has almost no loan finance. Partridge Ltd is a riskier investment than Carington Ltd. Interest on its loans must be paid regardless of the level of profit and this reduces the amount available for distribution to ordinary shareholders. This means that in a poor year, dividends to ordinary shareholders may be reduced or there may be no dividend at all.

(b) Conclusion

On the basis of the ratios calculated, an investment in Partridge Ltd would provide you with a much better return on the amount that you invest than an investment in Carington Ltd, assuming both companies maintain their current levels of profitability.

However, Partridge Ltd is much more highly geared than Carington Ltd and so Carington Ltd would be the safer investment of the two. Both companies are profitable, and while Carington Ltd appears to be less profitable overall, its return on shareholders' funds still appears to be acceptable. You may need to decide on the level of risk that you are prepared to accept, relative to the return on your investment.

I hope that these comments are helpful. Please do not hesitate to contact me if you need any further assistance.

....

Task 11.14

REPORT

To: **Peter Stewart**

From: **Accounting Technician**

Subject: **Review of financial statements of Hillhead Ltd**

Date: **DD/MM/YY**

As requested, I have analysed the efficiency and effectiveness of the management of Hillhead Ltd, based on four key ratios.

(a) The relative performance of the company for the past two years

Gross profit percentage

The gross profit margin has fallen. This means that on average the business is making less gross profit for each sale made. There could be many reasons for this fall in gross profit margin, for example, raw material prices may have increased and Hillhead Ltd has been unable to pass on these price increases to customers. Alternatively, the increase in sales suggests that management may have cut prices to try and attract new customers.

Operating profit percentage

The operating profit percentage has improved. As sales have risen and the gross profit percentage has fallen, the increase in the operating profit percentage must be as a result of lower overhead costs. Hillhead Ltd has obviously had strong control of costs during the year.

Inventory holding period

Hillhead Ltd's inventory holding period has worsened significantly. The company is taking longer to convert its inventory into cash by selling it. This suggests that it has been less efficient in managing inventory in the current year.

Trade receivables collection period

The trade receivables collection period has also worsened significantly. It could be that management allowed more credit to its customers or it may be a sign of worsening credit control or the possibility of irrecoverable debts.

(b) Suggestions for improvement of the ratios

Gross profit percentage

The gross profit percentage could be improved if selling prices could be increased without a corresponding increase in costs. Alternatively, raw materials or goods for resale could be sourced for lower prices.

Operating profit percentage

This ratio will improve if cost savings can be made and revenue remains stable. If operating expenses have reduced in the current year, there may be little scope for reducing them any further.

Inventory holding period

The long inventory holding period may indicate old or obsolete inventory, so this may need to be written off. Management needs to improve inventory ordering and purchasing/manufacture so that high levels of inventory do not build up and 'tie up' cash.

Trade receivables collection period

As the trade receivables collection period has increased, management should assess the recoverability of receivables. Credit control procedures should be tightened so that cash can be collected on a timely basis.

Task 11.15

To: Nancy Charlton

From: Accounting Technician

Subject: Performance of Limden Ltd

Date: 18 June 20X1

As requested, I have analysed the financial performance of Limden Ltd, based on the ratios provided.

(a) The relative performance of the company for the last two years

Gross profit percentage

The gross profit percentage has improved over the two years. There are several possible reasons for this: the company may have increased its sales prices or been able to reduce its direct costs or both. Alternatively it may have changed the type of product that it sells (the sales mix), so that individual sales are more profitable than before.

Operating profit percentage

The operating profit percentage has fallen significantly. Because the gross profit percentage has improved, this suggests that selling and administrative expenses have increased during 20X1.

Return on shareholders' funds

Return on shareholders' funds has also fallen significantly. This is not surprising, given that operating profit percentage has also fallen. Less profit is being generated relative to the shareholders' investment in the company. This means that less profit will be available to pay dividends to shareholders.

Gearing

Gearing (the proportion of the company's finance obtained from borrowings) has increased. The company has probably taken out significant new loans during the year. The company has become a riskier investment as the increased interest payments will reduce profits available to shareholders still further.

Interest cover

Interest cover has fallen very sharply in 20X1. This is consistent with the increase in gearing and the fall in the operating profit percentage: the additional borrowings have increased finance costs and at the same time less profit is available to cover these costs. This fall in interest cover is another indication that the company has become a riskier investment.

(b) **Advice**

On the basis of the information provided, I advise you not to invest in this company. The company's trading operations appear to be profitable, but operating profit has decreased and the additional debt suggests that Limden Ltd would be a risky investment.

....

Task 11.16

REPORT

To: Susan Smith

From: Accounting Technician

Subject: Performance of River Ltd and Mountain Ltd

Date: 15 November 20X6

As requested, I have analysed and compared the financial performance and position of River Ltd and Mountain Ltd, based on the ratios provided.

(a)   Comment on the relative performance of the two companies

The **gross profit percentage** is high for both companies. **Mountain**, which has a higher sales figure in absolute terms, also has a **higher** gross profit percentage. It is possible that its marginally greater sales volume enables it to take advantage of **discounts**. As the two companies operate in the same market, it is possibly geographical location that makes the difference in the profit margin Mountain can make.

The picture is different when it comes to **operating profit percentage**. At 21.5%, that of River is significantly higher than that of Mountain (15.4%). A likely reason for this is that **expenses are higher for Mountain**. The **asset turnover** ratios show that **River is making more efficient use of assets** than Mountain, as it is generating proportionally more sales from the assets. As discussed below, the inefficiency of Mountain may be partly because **working capital is tied up in inventory**.

The **current ratios** of both companies are **greater than one**, with Mountain having the edge slightly. These ratios indicate that the companies have sufficient current assets to meet their current liabilities. However, the quick ratios are more worrying.

Both companies have **quick ratios of less than one**, indicating potential liquidity problems. In the case of **Mountain, the quick ratio is very low** at 0.3:1. The quick ratio excludes inventory, suggesting that much of Mountain's working capital is tied up in inventory, and that inventory is not selling. Mountain, with its **lack of liquidity**, may have problems paying debts as they fall due.

The **receivables collection period is high** for both companies, but for Mountain, at 89.8 days it is considerably higher than that of River, which has 59.1 days. **Mountain needs to pay attention to credit control**. The longer a debt remains unpaid, the less likely it is to be paid.

(b)   Advice to Susan

In conclusion, although Mountain has a higher gross profit margin, it has liquidity problems, is less efficient and has ineffective credit control. **River is therefore a better investment prospect**.

Task 11.17

Tutorial note. Our answer is more detailed than you would be able to produce in your assessment. You only need to make five points.

Ratio analysis is not foolproof. There are many problems in trying to identify trends and make comparisons. Below are just a few.

(a)   Information problems

(i)   The base information is often out of date, so timeliness of information leads to problems of interpretation.

(ii)   Historical cost information may not be the most appropriate information for the decision for which the analysis is being undertaken

(iii)   Information in published accounts is generally summarised information and detailed information may be needed.

(iv)   Analysis of accounting information only identifies symptoms not causes and thus is of limited use.

(b)   Comparison problems: inter-temporal

(i)   Effects of price changes make comparisons difficult unless adjustments are made

(ii)   Impacts of changes in technology on the price of assets, the likely return and the future markets

(iii)   Impacts of a changing environment on the results reflected in the accounting information

(iv)   Potential effects of changes in accounting policies on the reported results

(v)   Problems associated with establishing a normal base year to compare other years with

(c)   **Comparison problems: inter-firm**

(i)   Selection of industry norms and the usefulness of norms based on averages

(ii)   Different firms having different financial and business risk profiles and the impact on analysis

(iii)   Different firms using different accounting policies

(iv)   Impacts of different environments on results, eg different countries or home-based versus multinational firms

Task 11.18

REPORT

To: The Directors of Knole Ltd

From: Accounting technician

Subject: The company's liquidity and cash flow

Date:

As requested, I have examined the company's financial statements for the years ended 31 October 20X7 and 20X8 and I set out my comments below.

(a)   The change in net cash from operating activities

Profit from operations has increased by approximately 20% in the year. However, the net cash from operating activities has decreased from £7,110,000 in 20X7 to £5,973,000 in 20X8. This means that the company has generated less cash from its operations than in the previous year, despite the increase in profit.

During the year the company took out additional bank loans and this has resulted in an increase of £175,000 in interest paid. Tax paid has increased by £59,000, presumably as a result of the increase in operating profit. Both these increases are relatively modest.

The main reason for the decrease in cash is the movement in working capital in the year, which has reduced cash by £9,900,000. Inventories have increased by £4,840,000, compared with an increase of

£3,606,000 in 20X7. If sales have increased, the increase in inventories is probably needed to meet customer demand. However, it could also have been caused by slow moving items or other problems. Trade receivables have increased by £2,640,000 in the period. Again, this could be because sales have increased towards the end of the year. An alternative explanation might be that customers are being allowed more credit or taking longer to pay. Trade payables have decreased by £2,420,000 in the year. This suggests that either the company is paying its suppliers too quickly or that the suppliers have changed their credit terms.

The changes in working capital mean that the cash generated by the company's operations is 'tied up' in inventories and trade receivables. This reduces the amount of cash available for paying interest on the bank loan and tax on profits. It also reduces the cash available for investing in property, plant and equipment and other non-current assets. It is almost certainly the reason why the company moved from a positive cash balance to a bank overdraft during the year. This is particularly surprising and worrying given the significant increase in profit from operations.

(b) The liquidity and financial position of the company

The current ratio and the quick (or acid test) ratio have both increased significantly during the year. The current ratio is very high and shows that in theory the company can comfortably meet its current liabilities. Similarly, the quick ratio shows that despite the cash outflow during the year, in theory the company should have no problems in meeting its day to day liabilities as they fall due. (The quick ratio is used as a measure of short term liquidity because it excludes inventories, which cannot be quickly converted into cash).

Most people would consider that a current ratio of 3.6 is far too high. The ratio confirms that the company almost certainly has too much inventory. This is one of the main reasons why the company has moved from a positive cash balance to an overdraft during the year. Again, the high quick ratio and the increase in the year show that the company is almost certainly not managing its trade receivables well. Like inventories, these need to be converted into cash much more quickly. Better working capital management would probably solve the company's cash flow problems.

The gearing ratio measures the extent to which the company is financed by debt rather than equity. The gearing ratio has increased during the year, which reflects the increase in bank loans. However, it is still very low. This suggests that the company should not have any problems in raising more finance in the longer term, should it need to. Knole Ltd is profitable and the low gearing means that investors will see it as a relatively safe investment.

If you have any questions, or require any further information, please do not hesitate to contact me.

••

AAT AQ2016 SAMPLE ASSESSMENT 1 FINANCIAL STATEMENTS OF LIMITED COMPANIES

Time allowed: 2 hours and 30 minutes

The AAT may call the assessments on their website, under study support resources, either a 'practice assessment' or 'sample assessment'.

Financial Statements of Limited Companies (FSLC) AAT sample assessment 1

Task 1 (32 marks)

You have been asked to prepare the statement of cash flows and statement of changes in equity for Chicago Ltd for the year ended 31 December 20X1.

The most recent statement of profit or loss and statement of financial position (with comparatives for the previous year) of Chicago Ltd can be viewed by clicking on the buttons below.

Chicago Ltd – Statement of profit or loss for the year ended 31 December 20X1

	£000
Continuing operations	
Revenue	160,240
Cost of sales	(113,292)
Gross profit	46,948
Profit on disposal of PPE	139
	47,087
Distribution costs	(8,675)
Administrative expenses	(18,812)
Profit from operations	19,600
Finance costs	(3,200)
Profit before tax	16,400
Tax	(3,546)
Profit for the period from continuing operations	12,854
Other comprehensive income	7,000
Total comprehensive income	19,854

BPP LEARNING MEDIA

Further information:

- The total depreciation charge for the year was £4,992,000.

- Property, plant and equipment with a carrying amount of £543,000 was sold in the year.

- Land was revalued upwards during the year by £7,000,000.

- All sales and purchases were on credit. Other expenses were paid for in cash.

- A dividend of £4,000,000 was paid during the year.

Chicago Ltd – Statement of financial position as at 31 December 20X1

	20X1 £000	20X0 £000
ASSETS		
Non-current assets		
Property, plant and equipment	77,736	31,962
Current assets		
Inventories	22,732	18,608
Trade receivables	18,251	15,162
Cash and cash equivalents	–	372
	40,983	34,142
Total assets	118,719	66,104
EQUITY AND LIABILITIES		
Equity		
Share capital	30,000	20,000
Share premium	9,340	6,270
Revaluation surplus	7,000	–
Retained earnings	14,252	5,398
Total equity	60,592	31,668

	20X1 £000	20X0 £000
Non-current liabilities		
Bank loans	40,000	18,000
Current liabilities		
Trade payables	14,712	12,316
Tax liabilities	3,270	4,120
Bank overdraft	145	–
	18,127	16,436
Total liabilities	58,127	34,436
Total equity and liabilities	118,719	66,104

(a) **Draft a reconciliation of profit before tax to net cash from operating activities for Chicago Ltd for the year ended 31 December 20X1.** **(13 marks)**

(b) **Draft the statement of cash flows for Chicago Ltd for the year ended 31 December 20X1.** **(19 marks)**

Please note:

- You don't have to use the workings tables to achieve full marks on the task. However, any data that you enter into the workings tables will be taken into consideration if you make errors in the main pro forma.

- You must enter a figure into the main pro forma in order for your workings for that figure to be taken into account.

- Show any items that need to be deducted as negative figures.

(You will be asked to draft a statement of changes in equity in Task 2 using the same data. You will be able to view the data again in Task 2.)

Chicago Ltd

Reconciliation of profit before tax to net cash from operating activities

	£000
▼	
Adjustments for:	
▼	
▼	
▼	
▼	
▼	
▼	
Cash generated by operations	
▼	
▼	
Net cash from operating activities	

Drop-down list:

Adjustment in respect of inventories
Adjustment in respect of trade payables
Adjustment in respect of trade receivables
Bank loans
Depreciation
Finance costs
Interest paid
Proceeds on disposal of PPE
Profits after tax
Profit before tax
Profit on disposal of PPE
Purchases of PPE
Revaluation surplus
Tax paid

Chicago Ltd

Statement of cash flows for the year ended 31 December 20X1

	£000
Net cash from operating activities	
Investing activities	
▼	
▼	
Net cash from investing activities	
Financing activities	
▼	
▼	
▼	
Net cash used in financing activities	
Net increase/(decrease) in cash and cash equivalents	
Cash and cash equivalents at beginning of year	
Cash and cash equivalents at end of year	

Drop-down list:

Adjustment in respect of inventories
Adjustment in respect of trade payables
Adjustment in respect of trade receivables
Bank loans
Dividends paid
Proceeds of share issue
Proceeds on disposal of PPE
Purchases of PPE
Revaluation

Workings

Proceeds on disposal of PPE	£000
▼	
▼	
Total disposal proceeds	

Purchases of PPE	£000
PPE at start of year	
▼	
▼	
▼	
▼	
Total PPE additions	

Drop-down list:

Carrying amount of PPE sold
Depreciation charge
PPE at end of year
PPE at start of year
Profit on disposal of PPE
Revaluation

Task 2 (8 marks)

This task is a continuation of the scenario in Task 1 and uses the same data.

You have been asked to prepare the statement of cash flows and statement of changes in equity for Chicago Ltd for the year ended 31 December 20X1.

The most recent statement of profit or loss and statement of financial position (with comparatives for the previous year) of Chicago Ltd can be viewed by clicking on the buttons below.

Chicago Ltd – Statement of profit or loss for the year ended 31 December 20X1

	£000
Continuing operations	
Revenue	160,240
Cost of sales	(113,292)
Gross profit	46,948
Profit on disposal of PPE	139
	47,087
Distribution costs	(8,675)
Administrative expenses	(18,812)
Profit from operations	19,600
Finance costs	(3,200)
Profit before tax	16,400
Tax	(3,546)
Profit for the period from continuing operations	12,854
Other comprehensive income	7,000
Total comprehensive income	19,854

Further information:

- The total depreciation charge for the year was £4,992,000.

- Property, plant and equipment with a carrying amount of £543,000 was sold in the year.

- Land was revalued upwards during the year by £7,000,000.

- All sales and purchases were on credit. Other expenses were paid for in cash.

- A divided of £4,000,000 was paid during the year.

Chicago Ltd – Statement of financial position as at 31 December 20X1

	20X1 £000	20X0 £000
Assets		
Non-current assets		
Property, plant and equipment	77,736	31,962
Current assets		
Inventories	22,732	18,608
Trade receivables	18,251	15,162
Cash and cash equivalents	–	372
	40,983	34,142
Total assets	118,719	66,104
Equity and liabilities		
Equity		
Share capital	30,000	20,000
Share premium	9,340	6,270
Revaluation surplus	7,000	–
Retained earnings	14,252	5,398
Total equity	60,592	31,668
Non-current liabilities		
Bank loans	40,000	18,000

	20X1 £000	20X0 £000
Current liabilities		
Trade payables	14,712	12,316
Tax liabilities	3,270	4,120
Bank overdraft	145	–
	18,127	16,436
Total liabilities	58,127	34,436
Total equity and liabilities	118,719	66,104

Draft the statement of changes in equity for Chicago Ltd for the year ended 31 December 20X1. **(8 marks)**

Please note:

Show any items that need to be deducted as negative figures.

Chicago Ltd – Statement of changes in equity for the year ended 31 December 20X1

	Share capital £000	Share premium £000	Revaluation surplus £000	Retained earnings £000	Total equity £000
Balance at 1 January 20X1					
Changes in equity					
Total comprehensive income					
Dividends					
Issue of share capital					
Balance at 31 December 20X1					

Task 3 (10 marks)

You are an AAT student working for Austin Accountants. You have been asked to prepare the financial statements of Kansas Ltd, a manufacturer of computer components, for the year ended 31 December 20X1.

Enter your answers regarding the following matters in the box provided.

Matter 1

At 31 December 20X1, Kansas Ltd held inventories which had cost £100,000. However, due to a change in the marketplace in which Kansas Ltd operates, the selling prices of some of these inventories have fallen.

- **Explain to the directors why inventories should be recognised as an asset in the statement of financial position.** **(4 marks)**

- **Identify the TWO measurement bases which should be used to determine the amount at which the inventories should be recognised in the financial statements.** **(2 marks)**

Matter 2

At a golf business event, you are approached by a supplier to Kansas Ltd. The supplier is aware that you are associated with Kansas Ltd and has asked you why the company is taking longer than usual to pay them.

Identify and explain the relevant fundamental principle in accordance with the AAT Code of Professional Ethics. (4 marks)

Task 4 (12 marks)

Fitnflexi Ltd operates a chain of gyms. The company's finance director is working on the financial statements for the year ended 31 December 20X1, and has brought the following matters to your attention:

(a) On 18 September 20X1, a claim was made against Fitnflexi Ltd by a customer in respect of a chest injury he had suffered while lifting weights in one of the company's gyms. The customer argues that he had received inadequate instructions in the use of weights from the gym's personal trainer.

Fitnflexi Ltd's legal advisers have confirmed that it is highly likely that the customer will win the case. Based upon their experience of similar cases of this nature, they have estimated that damages of approximately £20,000 will have to be paid. **(6 marks)**

(b) On 1 November 20X1, Fitnflexi Ltd entered into a six month lease for some gym equipment. Under the terms of the lease, Fitnflexi Ltd had to make a payment of £1,500 on 31 January 20X2 and a further payment of £1,500 on 30 April 20X2. The equipment has used life of five years and would have cost £20,000 had it been purchased outright on 1 November 20X1. **(6 marks)**

Explain, WITH REASONS, how each of the items above should be treated in Fitnflexi Ltd's financial statements for the year ended 31 December 20X1, using the figures from above to illustrate your answer where possible.

Task 5 (15 marks)

Diego Ltd is preparing its financial statements for the year ended 31 December 20X1. The tax charge based upon the profits of the current year has been estimated at £42,000. The company had under-estimated its tax liability for the previous year by £8,000.

(a) **What amounts should be shown in the financial statements for the year ended 31 December 20X1 in respect of the tax charge and tax liability?** **(3 marks)**

The tax charge should be [▼]

The tax liability should be [▼]

Drop-down list:

£34,000
£42,000
£50,000

Dallas Ltd purchased a motor vehicle on 1 January 20X1 for £36,000. The vehicle is expected to have a useful life of four years and a scrap value of £4,000 It is depreciated using the straight-line method. The company prepares its financial statements to 31 December each year.

(b) **How much depreciation should be recognised in the statement of profit or loss for the year ended 31 December 20X2?**

(3 marks)

£ [   ]

A machine owned by Memphis Ltd has suffered physical damage and might have become impaired.

The following information is relevant:

	£
Carrying amount	20,000
Fair value	8,000
Costs of disposal	(200)
Value in use	9,000

(c) **At what amount should the machine be recognised in the statement of financial position?** **(3 marks)**

£ [   ]

Denver Ltd sold goods for £40,000 plus VAT at 20%. The company also issued 10,000 £1 ordinary shares at par.

(d) **How much revenue in total should be recognised in the statement of profit or loss in respect of these transactions?**

(3 marks)

	✓
£40,000	
£48,000	
£50,000	
£58,000	

(e) **Which of the following costs, if any, should be included in the cost of inventories of a finished product held in a distribution warehouse at the end of the year?** **(3 marks)**

(1) Storage costs
(2) Transport costs to the warehouse

	✓
(1) only	
(2) only	
Both of them	
Neither of them	

Task 6 (30 marks)

The summarised statements of financial position of Texas plc and Houston Ltd as at 31 December 20X1, as well as further information, are shown below.

Statements of financial position

	Texas Plc £000	Houston Ltd £000
Assets		
Non-current assets		
Investment in Houston Ltd	420	
Property, plant and equipment	1,520	241
	1,940	241
Current assets		
Inventories	238	64
Trade receivables	126	30
Cash and cash equivalents	39	18
	403	112
Total assets	2,343	353
Equity and liabilities		
Equity		
Share capital	1,800	240
Retained earnings	172	60
Total equity	1,972	300
Non-current liabilities	234	19
Current liabilities		
Trade payables	103	26
Taxation	34	8
	137	34
Total liabilities	371	53
Total equity and liabilities	2,343	353

Further information:

- On 1 January 20X1, Texas plc acquired 80% of the issued share capital and voting rights of Houston Ltd for £420,000. At that date, Houston Ltd had issued share capital of £240,000, and retained earnings of £20,000. The fair value of the non-current assets of Houston Ltd on that date was £100,000 more than the carrying amount. This revaluation has not been recorded in the books of Houston Ltd (ignore any effect on the depreciation for the year).

- The directors of Texas plc have concluded that goodwill arising on the acquisition of Houston Ltd has been impaired by £25,000 during the year.

- Included in the trade receivables of Texas plc and in the trade payables of Houston Ltd at 31 December 20X1 is an inter-company balance of £6,000.

- Texas plc has decided non-controlling interest will be valued at their proportionate share of net assets.

Draft the consolidated statement of financial position for Texas plc and its subsidiary undertaking as at 31 December 20X1.

Note.

- You don't have to use the workings tables to achieve full marks on the task. However, any data that you enter into the workings tables will be taken into consideration if you make errors in the main pro forma.

- Show any items that need to be deducted as negative figures.

Texas plc – Consolidated statement of financial position as at 31 December 20X1

	£000
ASSETS	
Non-current assets	
Goodwill	
Property, plant and equipment	
Current assets	
Inventories	
Trade receivables	
Cash and cash equivalents	
Total assets	

	£000
EQUITY AND LIABILITIES	
Equity	
Share capital	
Retained earnings	
Non-controlling interest	
Total equity	
Non-current liabilities	
Current liabilities	
Trade payables	
Taxation	
Total liabilities	
Total equity and liabilities	

Workings

Goodwill		£000
	▼	
	▼	
	▼	
	▼	

Drop-down list:

Consideration
Impairment of goodwill
Inter-company transaction
Net assets acquired
Non-controlling interest at acquisition

Property, plant and equipment	£000
▽	
▽	

Drop-down list:

Adjustment to fair value
Consolidated PPE prior to fair value adjustment

Retained earnings	£000
▽	
▽	
▽	

Drop-down list:

Houston Ltd – attributable to Texas plc
Impairment of goodwill
Inter-company adjustment
Texas plc

Additional BPP Workings

Non-controlling interest at acquisition	£000
▽	
▽	
▽	

Drop-down list:

Current assets – attributable to NCI
Impairment
Non-current assets – attributable to NCI
Price paid
Retained earnings – attributable to NCI
Share capital – attributable to NCI

Non-controlling interest at year end	£000
▼	
▼	
▼	

Drop-down list:

Current assets – attributable to NCI
Impairment
Non-current assets – attributable to NCI
Price paid
Retained earnings – attributable to NCI
Share capital – attributable to NCI

Task 7 (20 marks)

You have been given the financial statements of Phoenix Ltd for the year ended 31 December 20X1. You are now required to prepare financial ratios to assist your manager in his analysis of the company.

Phoenix Ltd's statement of profit or loss and statement of financial position can be viewed by clicking on the buttons below.

Phoenix Ltd

Statement of profit or loss for the year ended 31 December 20X1

	£000
Continuing operations	
Revenue	86,482
Cost of sales	(47,875)
Gross profit	38,607
Distribution costs	(8,724)
Administrative expenses	(15,226)
Profit from operations	14,657
Finance costs	(2,962)
Profit before tax	11,695
Tax	(2,267)
Profit for the period from continuing operations	9,428

BPP
LEARNING MEDIA

Phoenix Ltd

Statement of financial position as at 31 December 20X1

	£000
ASSETS	
Non-current assets	
Property, plant and equipment	73,358
Current assets	
Inventories	4,620
Trade receivables	11,639
Cash and cash equivalents	–
	16,259
Total assets	89,617
EQUITY AND LIABILITIES	
Equity	
Ordinary share capital (£1 shares)	34,000
Retained earnings	13,624
Total equity	47,624
Non-current liabilities	
Bank loans	32,755
Current liabilities	
Trade payables	6,979
Bank overdraft	276
Tax liabilities	1,983
	9,238
Total liabilities	41,993
Total equity and liabilities	89,617

(a) **Identify the formulas that are used to calculate each of the following ratios.** **(10 marks)**

Inventory holding period (days) [▼]

Drop-down list:

Inventories/Cost of sales × 365 days
Inventories/Revenue × 365 days
Cost of sales/Inventories × 365 days
Revenue/Inventories × 365 days

Current ratio [▼]

Drop-down list:

(Current assets – Trade receivables)/Current liabilities
(Current assets – Inventories)/Current liabilities
Total assets/Total liabilities
Current assets/Current liabilities

Gearing [▼]

Drop-down list:

Revenue/(Total assets – Current liabilities) × 100%
Total debt/(Total debt + Equity) × 100%
Profit from operations/(Total equity + Non-current liabilities) × 100%
Trade receivables/Revenue × 100%

Asset turnover (net assets) [▼]

Drop-down list:

Revenue/(Total assets – Total liabilities)
Revenue/Total assets
Revenue/(Total assets – Current liabilities)
Revenue/Non-current assets

Return on capital employed [▼]

Drop-down list:

Profit from operations/Total equity × 100%
Profit from operations/(Total equity + Non-current liabilities) × 100%
Profit after tax/Total equity × 100%
Profit after tax/(Total equity + Non-current liabilities) × 100%

(b)   Calculate the above ratios to ONE decimal place.

(i)	Inventory holding period (days)		days
(ii)	Current ratio		:1
(iii)	Gearing		%
(iv)	Asset turnover (net assets)		times
(v)	Return on capital employed		%

Task 8 (23 marks)

Lisa Brady, a potential investor, has asked for your assistance in analysing Arizona Ltd, to help her determine whether or not she should buy shares in the company.

Lisa has recently received a large cash sum from a pension plan and is keen to invest in Arizona Ltd after reading a report in a newspaper that the industry sector in which Arizona Ltd operates is performing well.

You have calculated the following ratios in respect of Arizona Ltd's most recent financial statements and have obtained an industry average for each for comparative purposes.

	Arizona Ltd	Industry average
Return on capital employed	11.5%	14.3%
Working capital cycle	18 days	29 days
Quick/Acid test ratio	0.9:1	1.5:1
Interest cover	2.2 times	3.5 times

Prepare notes for Lisa that include the following:

* **Comments on whether each of Arizona Ltd's ratios is better or worse as compared to its industry average and what this may tell you about the company.** **(20 marks)**

* **Advice, with reasons, as to whether or not she should buy shares in the company, based solely on your analysis of the ratios in (a) above.** **(3 marks)**

AAT AQ2016 SAMPLE ASSESSMENT 1 FINANCIAL STATEMENTS OF LIMITED COMPANIES

ANSWERS

Financial Statements of Limited Companies (FSLC) AAT sample assessment 1

Task 1 (32 marks)

(a) Draft a reconciliation of profit before tax to net cash from operating activities for Chicago Ltd for the year ended 31 December 20X1.

(b) Draft the statement of cash flows for Chicago Ltd for the year ended 31 December 20X1.

Chicago Ltd

Reconciliation of profit before tax to net cash from operating activities

	£000
Profit before tax	16,400
Adjustments for:	
Depreciation	4,992
Profit on disposal of PPE	-139
Finance costs	3,200
Adjustment in respect of inventories	-4,124
Adjustment in respect of trade receivables	-3,089
Adjustment in respect of trade payables	2,396
Cash generated by operations	19,636
Tax paid	-4,396
Interest paid	-3,200
Net cash from operating activities	12,040

Chicago Ltd

Statement of cash flows for the year ended 31 December 20X1

	£000
Net cash from operating activities	12,040
Investing activities	
Proceeds on disposal of PPE	682
Purchases of PPE	-44,309
Net cash from investing activities	-43,627
Financing activities	
Bank loans	22,000
Dividends paid	-4,000
Proceeds of share issue	13,070
Net cash used in financing activities	31,070
Net increase/(decrease) in cash and cash equivalents	-517
Cash and cash equivalents at beginning of year	372
Cash and cash equivalents at end of year	-145

Workings

Proceeds on disposal of PPE	£000
Carrying amount of PPE sold	543
Profit on disposal of PPE	139
Total disposal proceeds	682

Purchases of PPE	£000
PPE at start of year	31,962
Depreciation charge	-4,992
Carrying amount of PPE sold	-543
Revaluation	7,000
PPE at end of year	-77,736
Total PPE additions	-44,309

Task 2 (8 marks)

Draft the statement of changes in equity for Chicago Ltd for the year ended 31 December 20X1.

Please note:

Show any items that need to be deducted as negative figures.

Chicago Ltd – Statement of changes in equity for the year ended 31 December 20X1

	Share capital £000	Share premium £000	Revaluation surplus £000	Retained earnings £000	Total equity £000
Balance at 1 January 20X1	20,000	6,270		5,398	31,668
Changes in equity					
Total comprehensive income			7,000	12,854	19,854
Dividends				-4,000	-4,000
Issue of share capital	10,000	3,070			13,070
Balance 31 December 20X1	30,000	9,340	7,000	14,252	60,592

319

Task 3 (10 marks)

Matter 1

Explain to the directors why inventories should be recognised as an asset in the statement of financial position:

Inventories are recognised as an asset in the statement of financial position because:

- They meet the definition of an asset – they are resources controlled by the entity as a result of past events and from which future economic benefits (cash flows, inflows, revenue, profits, income) are expected to flow to the entity; and

- They satisfy the recognition criteria – it is probable that future economic benefits will flow to Kansas Ltd and the inventories have a cost or value that can be measured reliably.

Identify the TWO measurement bases which should be used to determine the amount at which the inventories should be recognised in the financial statements:

Historical cost and (net) realisable value.

Matter 2

Identify and explain the relevant fundamental principle in accordance with the AAT Code of Professional Ethics:

The relevant fundamental principle is confidentiality.

A professional accountant must:

- Not disclose information to third parties without proper specific authority unless there is a legal or professional right or duty to disclose.

- Not use confidential information to their personal advantage or to the advantage of third parties.

Task 4 (12 marks)

(a) A provision of £20,000 should be recognised as a liability in the statement of financial position, with a corresponding expense shown in the statement of profit or loss.

This is because Sandown Ltd has a present obligation as a result of a past event.

It is probable that an outflow of resources embodying economic benefits will be required to settle the obligation; and a reliable estimate can be made of the amount of the obligation.

(b)   The lease is an operating lease because:

- the lease term is not for a major part of the economic life of the asset;

- at the inception of the lease, the present value of the minimum lease payments does not amount to at least substantially all of the fair value of the leased asset.

The lease payments should be recognised as an expense on a straight-line basis over the lease term.

Lease payments of £1,000 (£1,500 × 2 × 2/6) should therefore be recognised in the statement of profit or loss for the year ended 31 December 20X1.

....

Task 5 (15 marks)

(a)   What amounts should be shown in the financial statements for the year ended 31 December 20X1 in respect of the tax change and tax liability?

The tax charge should be	£50,000.
The tax liability should be	£42,000.

Dallas Ltd purchased a motor vehicle on 1 January 20X1 for £36,000. The vehicle is expected to have a useful life of four years and a scrap value of £4,000. It is depreciated using the straight-line method. The company prepares its financial statements to 31 December each year.

(b)   How much depreciation should be recognised in the statement of profit or loss for the year ended 31 December 20X2?

£	8,000

(c)   At what amount should the machine be recognised in the statement of financial position?

£	9,000

(d)   How much revenue in total should be recognised in the statement of profit or loss in respect of these transactions?

	✓
£40,000	✓
£48,000	
£50,000	
£58,000	

(e) **Which of the following costs, if any, should be included in the cost of inventories of a finished product held in a distribution warehouse at the end of the year?**

(1) Storage costs
(2) Transport costs to the warehouse

	✓
(1) only	
(2) only	✓
Both of them	
Neither of them	

Task 6 (30 marks)

Texas plc – Consolidated statement of financial position as at 31 December 20X1

	£000
ASSETS	
Non-current assets	
Goodwill	107
Property, plant and equipment	1,861
	1,968
Current assets	
Inventories	302
Trade receivables	150
Cash and cash equivalents	57
	509
Total assets	2,477

	£000
EQUITY AND LIABILITIES	
Equity	
Share capital	1,800
Retained earnings	179
Non-controlling interest	80
Total equity	2,059
Non-current liabilities	253
Current liabilities	
Trade payables	123
Taxation	42
	165
Total liabilities	418
Total equity and liabilities	2,477

Workings

Goodwill	£000
Consideration	420
Non-controlling interest at acquisition	72
Net assets acquired	-360
Impairment of goodwill	-25
	107

Property, plant and equipment	£000
Consolidated PPE prior to fair value adjustment	1,761
Adjustment to fair value	100
	1,861

Retained earnings	£000
Texas plc	172
Houston Ltd – attributable to Texas plc	32
Impairment of goodwill	–25
	179

Additional BPP Workings

Non-controlling interest at acquisition	£000
Share capital attributable to NCI: 20% × 240,000	48
Retained earnings attributable to NCI: 20% × 20,000	4
Revaluation reserve attributable to NCI: 20% × 100,000	20
	72

Non-controlling interest at year end	£000
Share capital attributable to NCI: 20% ×240,000	48
Retained earnings attributable to NCI: 20% × 60,000	12
Revaluation reserve attributable to NCI: 20% × 100,000	20
	80

Task 7 (20 marks)

(a) **Identify the formulas that are used to calculate each of the following ratios.**

Inventory holding period (days)	Inventories / Cost of sales × 365 days
Current ratio	Current assets / Current liabilities
Gearing	Total debt / (Total debt + Equity) × 100%
Asset turnover (net assets)	Revenue / (Total assets – Current liabilities)
Return on capital employed	Profit from operations / (Total equity + Non-current liabilities) × 100%

(b) **Calculate the above ratios to ONE decimal place**

(i)	Inventory holding period (days)	35.2	days
(ii)	Current ratio	1.8	: 1
(iii)	Gearing	40.8	%
(iv)	Asset turnover (net assets)	1.1	times
(v)	Return on capital employed	18.2	%

Task 8 (23 marks)

Prepare notes for Lisa that include the following:

- **Comments on whether each of Arizona Ltd's ratios is better or worse as compared to its industry average and what this may tell you about the company.**

- **Advice, with reasons, as to whether or not she should buy shares in the company, based solely on your analysis of the ratios in (a) above.**

Comments

Return on capital employed is worse.

Capital is working less efficiently in terms of generating profits (less profit being generated by capital employed).

This could be due to...

- lower profits

- higher equity (higher share capital / higher retained earnings / revaluation surplus)

- also higher non-current liabilities

...which is consistent with the worsening of the interest cover ratio.

Working capital cycle is better.

Working capital / cash is tied up for a shorter period / circulating at a faster rate / good for cash flow.

Inventories may be turning over at a quicker rate (better / shorter inventory holding period / sold sooner / holding less inventories), collecting debts sooner (trade receivables collection period may be better / shorter), or paying its creditors later (longer trade payables payment period).

Quick ratio/Acid test ratio is worse.

More risky / less solvent / liquidity issues.

Unable to cover short term debts (current assets less inventories are less than current liabilities).

This could be due to...

- lower trade receivables or cash and cash equivalents

- higher current liabilities (also allow trade payables, bank overdraft, tax liability)

...which would be consistent with the shortening of the working capital cycle.

Interest cover is worse.

Less profit is available to meet interest payments / more risky.

May be caused by lower operating profits.

May be caused by higher interest payments / higher interest rates.

May have more debt / loans / gearing ratio may be higher.

Could be more difficult to obtain finance in the future.

Advice

Advice is not to buy shares

Only the working capital cycle is better, but this could be due to taking longer to pay suppliers.

Return on capital employed is worse (capital working less efficiently in terms of generating profits).

Quick/Acid test ratio is worse (less solvent / less able to cover short-term debts / liquidity could be a concern).

Interest cover is worse (more risky).

AAT AQ2016 SAMPLE ASSESSMENT 2 FINANCIAL STATEMENTS OF LIMITED COMPANIES

You are advised to attempt sample assessment 2 online from the AAT website. This will ensure you are prepared for how the assessment will be presented on the AAT's system when you attempt the real assessment. Please access the assessment using the address below:

www.aat.org.uk/training/study-support/search

The AAT may call the assessments on their website, under study support resources, either a 'practice assessment' or 'sample assessment'.

AAT AQ2016
SAMPLE ASSESSMENT 2

BPP PRACTICE ASSESSMENT 1
FINANCIAL STATEMENTS OF
LIMITED COMPANIES

Time allowed: 2 hours and 30 minutes

Financial Statements of Limited Companies
BPP practice assessment 1

The following information is relevant to Task 1 and Task 2

You have been asked to help prepare the financial statements of Ricschtein Ltd for the year ended 31 March 20X7. The company's trial balance as at 31 March 20X7 is shown below.

Ricschtein Ltd
Trial balance as at 31 March 20X7

	Debit £000	Credit £000
Share capital		7,000
Trade payables		2,236
Property, plant and equipment – cost	39,371	
Property, plant and equipment – accumulated depreciation at 31 March 20X7		13,892
Trade receivables	4,590	
Accruals		207
7% bank loan repayable 20Y2		14,000
Cash at bank	423	
Retained earnings at 1 April 20X6		9,552
Interest	490	
Sales		36,724
Purchases	21,749	
Distribution costs	5,517	
Administrative expenses	4,251	
Inventories as at 1 April 20X6	6,120	
Dividends paid	1,100	
	83,611	83,611

331

Further information:

- The share capital of the company consists of ordinary shares with a nominal value of £1.

- At the beginning of the year the issued share capital was 7,000,000 ordinary shares. At the end of the year another 3,000,000 ordinary shares were issued at a price of £3.00 per share. Due to a misunderstanding about the date of the share issue, this has not been accounted for in the ledger accounts in the trial balance.

- The inventories at the close of business on 31 March 20X7 cost £7,304,000.

- Administrative expenses of £87,000 relating to February 20X7 have not been included in the trial balance.

- The company paid £36,000 insurance costs in June 20X6, which covered the period from 1 July 20X6 to 30 June 20X7. This was included in the administrative expenses in the trial balance.

- Interest on the bank loan for the last six months of the year has not been included in the accounts in the trial balance.

- The tax charge for the year has been calculated as £1,170,000.

- All of the operations are continuing operations.

Task 1 (24 marks)

(a) **Draft the statement of profit or loss and other comprehensive income for Ricschtein Ltd for the year ended 31 March 20X7.**

(18 marks)

Ricschtein Ltd
Statement of profit or loss and other comprehensive income for the year ended 31 March 20X7

	£000
Revenue	
Cost of sales	
Gross profit	
Distribution costs	
Administrative expenses	
Profit from operations	
Finance costs	
Profit before tax	
Tax	
Profit for the period from continuing operations	

Workings

(Complete the left hand column by writing in the correct narrative from the list provided.)

Cost of sales	£000
▼	
▼	
▼	

Picklist:

Accruals
Closing inventories
Opening inventories
Prepayments
Purchases

Administrative expenses	£000
▼	
▼	
▼	

Picklist:

Accruals
Administrative expenses
Prepayments

(b) **Draft the statement of changes in equity for Ricschtein Ltd for the year ended 31 March 20X7.** **(6 marks)**

Ricschtein Ltd
Statement of changes in equity for the year ended 31 March 20X7

	Share capital £000	Share premium £000	Retained earnings £000	Total equity £000
Balance at 1 April 20X6				
Changes in equity				
Total comprehensive income				
Dividends				
Issue of share capital				
Balance at 31 March 20X7				

Task 2 (16 marks)

Draft the statement of financial position for Ricschtein Ltd as at 31 March 20X7. **(16 marks)**

(Complete the left hand column by writing in the correct line item from the list.)

Ricschtein Ltd
Statement of financial position as at 31 March 20X7

	£000
ASSETS	
Non-current assets	
▼	
Current assets	
▼	
▼	
▼	
Total assets	
EQUITY AND LIABILITIES	
Equity	
▼	
▼	
▼	
Total equity	
Non-current liabilities	
▼	
Current liabilities	
▼	
▼	
Total liabilities	
Total equity and liabilities	

Picklist:

Bank loan
Cash and cash equivalents
Inventories
Property, plant and equipment
Retained earnings
Share capital
Share premium
Tax liability
Trade and other payables
Trade and other receivables

Workings

(Complete the left hand column by writing in the correct narrative from the list provided.)

Trade and other receivables		£000
	▼	
	▼	

Picklist:

Accruals: trial balance
Additional administrative expenses accrual
Additional administrative expenses prepaid
Additional finance costs accrual
Additional finance costs prepaid
Trade and other payables
Trade and other receivables

Retained earnings		£000
	▼	
	▼	
	▼	

Picklist:

Dividends paid
Premium paid on share issue
Profit/(loss) for the period from continuing operations
Retained earnings at 1 April 20X6
Total profit for the year

Trade and other payables		£000
	▼	
	▼	
	▼	
	▼	

Picklist:

Accruals: trial balance
Additional administrative expenses accrual
Additional administrative expenses prepaid
Additional finance costs accrual
Additional finance costs prepaid
Dividends
Tax liability
Trade and other payables
Trade and other receivables

Task 3 (10 marks)

The IASB's *Conceptual Framework for Financial Reporting* states that there is one important assumption that underlies the preparation of general purpose financial statements. The *Conceptual Framework* also identifies and describes four qualitative characteristics that enhance the usefulness of financial information that is relevant and faithfully represented.

(a) Identify and briefly explain the 'underlying assumption'.

(3 marks)

(b) List the FOUR ENHANCING qualitative characteristics of useful financial information. **(4 marks)**

(c) Briefly explain ONE of these qualitative characteristics.

(3 marks)

Task 4 (12 marks)

Oaktree Ltd publishes specialist magazines and technical manuals. The company prepares its financial statements to 31 March each year.

During the year ended 31 March 20X7, a customer took out a 12 month subscription for one of the company's monthly specialist magazines, starting on 1 July 20X6. Under the terms of the subscription, Oaktree Ltd supplied 12 copies of the magazine at the beginning of each month over the 12 month period. The price of the subscription was £1,500.

Oaktree Ltd also sold an old printing press for £5,000 during the year.

Prepare brief notes for a meeting with the directors of Oaktree Ltd to cover the following, in accordance with IFRS 15 *Revenue from Contracts with Customers*:

(a) **What is the definition of revenue? What is excluded from revenue?** **(3 marks)**

(b) **State the process for recognising revenue associated with the sale of goods in the financial statements.** **(5 marks)**

(c) **Calculate the amount of revenue, if any, that should be recognised in the financial statements of Oaktree Ltd for the year ending 31 March 20X7 in respect of the subscription and the sale of the printing press.** **(4 marks)**

....

Task 5 (15 marks)

(a) At the beginning of the year, Broad Ltd had the following balance:

Accrued interest payable £12,000 credit

During the year, Broad Ltd charged interest payable of £41,000 to profit or loss. The closing balance on accrued interest payable account at the end of the year was £15,000 credit.

How much interest paid should Broad Ltd show in its statement of cash flows for the year? **(3 marks)**

£38,000	
£41,000	
£44,000	
£53,000	

(b) Monty, an accountant in practice, performs bookkeeping services for both Stumpy Ltd and Grind Ltd. The companies are in dispute about a series of sales that Stumpy Ltd made to Grind Ltd.

Complete the following statement by selecting the pair of ethical principles which are threatened. **(3 marks)**

'For Monty, this situation threatens the fundamental principles of...'

Objectivity and integrity	
Objectivity and professional behaviour	
Objectivity and confidentiality	
Professional competence and due care and confidentiality	

(c) A company leases some plant on 1 January 20X4. The fair value of the plant is £9,000, and the company leases it for four years, paying four annual instalments of £3,000 beginning on 31 December 20X4.

The company uses the sum of the digits method to allocate interest.

What is the interest charge for the year ended 31 December 20X5? **(3 marks)**

£600	
£750	
£900	
£1,000	

(d) **Which of the following events after the reporting period would normally be classified as a *non-adjusting event*, according to IAS 10 *Events After the Reporting Period*?** **(3 marks)**

1   The company announced a plan to discontinue an operation.
2   A customer was discovered to be insolvent.

1 only	
2 only	
Both 1 and 2	
Neither 1 nor 2	

BPP LEARNING MEDIA

(e) Narrow Ltd is being sued by a customer and will have to pay an estimated £100,000 sum in compensation if it loses the case. At its accounting year end lawyers advise the company that it is possible (ie less than a 50% likelihood of occurrence) that it may lose the case. **(3 marks)**

In accordance with IAS 37 *Provisions, Contingent Liabilities and Contingent Assets* the possible future outflow should be:

Recognised in the statement of financial position as a provision	
Recognised in the statement of financial position as a contingent liability	
Only disclosed as a note to the financial statements	
Neither recognised in the statement of financial position nor included in the notes	

Task 6 (30 marks)

The Managing Director of Wells plc has asked you to prepare the statement of financial position for the group.

Wells plc has one subsidiary, Wilkie Ltd.

The statements of financial position of the two companies as at 31 October 20X9 are set out below.

Statements of financial position as at 31 October 20X9

	Wells plc £000	Wilkie Ltd £000
ASSETS		
Non-current assets		
Property, plant and equipment	44,352	19,884
Investment in Wilkie Ltd	19,000	
	63,352	19,884
Current assets		
Inventories	14,670	3,432
Trade and other receivables	6,756	2,249

	Wells plc £000	Wilkie Ltd £000
Cash and cash equivalents	1,245	342
	22,671	6,023
Total assets	86,023	25,907
EQUITY AND LIABILITIES		
Equity		
Share capital	35,000	12,000
Retained earnings	26,036	8,332
Total equity	61,036	20,332
Non-current liabilities		
Long-term loans	14,000	4,000
Current liabilities		
Trade and other payables	8,877	1,445
Tax liabilities	2,110	130
	10,987	1,575
Total liabilities	24,987	5,575
Total equity and liabilities	86,023	25,907

Additional data

- The share capital of Wilkie Ltd consists of ordinary shares of £1 each. Ownership of these shares carries voting rights in Wilkie Ltd.

- Wells plc acquired 9,000,000 shares in Wilkie Ltd on 1 November 20X8.

- At 1 November 20X8 the balance of retained earnings of Wilkie Ltd was £5,344,000.

- Included in trade and other receivables for Wells plc and in trade and other payables for Wilkie Ltd is an inter-company transaction for £1,250,000 that took place in early October 20X9.

- The directors of Wells plc have concluded that goodwill has been impaired by £1,500,000 during the year.

- Wells plc has decided non-controlling interests will be valued at their proportionate share of net assets.

Draft a consolidated statement of financial position for Wells plc and its subsidiary as at 31 October 20X9. (30 marks)

Wells plc
Consolidated statement of financial position as at 31 October 20X9

	£000
ASSETS	
Non-current assets	
Intangible assets: goodwill	
Property, plant and equipment	
Current assets	
Inventories	
Trade and other receivables	
Cash and cash equivalents	
Total assets	
EQUITY AND LIABILITIES	
Equity	
Share capital	
Retained earnings	
Non-controlling interest	
Total equity	

	£000
Non-current liabilities	
Long-term loans	
Current liabilities	
Trade and other payables	
Tax liabilities	
Total liabilities	
Total equity and liabilities	

Workings

(Complete the left hand column by writing in the correct narrative from the list provided.)

Goodwill	£000

▼	
▼	
▼	
▼	

Picklist:

Impairment
Consideration
Non-controlling interests at acquisition
Net assets acquired

Retained earnings	£000
▼	
▼	
▼	

Picklist:

Impairment
Wells plc
Wilkie Ltd – attributable to Wells plc

Non-controlling interest (NCI) at acquisition	£000
▼	
▼	

Picklist:

Current assets – attributable to NCI
Impairment
Non-current assets – attributable to NCI
Price paid
Retained earnings – attributable to NCI
Share capital – attributable to NCI

Non-controlling interest (NCI) at year end	£000
▼	
▼	

Picklist:

Current assets – attributable to NCI
Impairment
Non-current assets – attributable to NCI
Price paid
Retained earnings – attributable to NCI
Share capital – attributable to NCI

Task 7 (20 marks)

David Alexander is a shareholder in Cairngorm Ltd. He has asked you to assist him by calculating ratios in respect of the financial statements for the year ended 31 March 20X9. The financial statements of Cairngorm Ltd are set out below:

Cairngorm Ltd

Statement of profit or loss for the year ended 31 March 20X9

	£000
Continuing operations	
Revenue	14,800
Cost of sales	(7,770)
Gross profit	7,030
Distribution costs	(3,700)
Administrative expenses	(2,072)
Profit from operations	1,258
Finance costs	(630)
Profit before tax	628
Tax	(294)
Profit for the period from continuing operations	334

Cairngorm Ltd
Statement of financial position as at 31 March 20X9

	£000
ASSETS	
Non-current assets	
Property, plant and equipment	18,916
Current assets	
Inventories	1,632
Trade and other receivables	1,776
Cash and cash equivalents	0
	3,408
Total assets	22,324
EQUITY AND LIABILITIES	
Equity	
Share capital	6,500
Retained earnings	5,138
Total equity	11,638
Non-current liabilities	
Bank loans	9,000

	£000
Current liabilities	
Trade payables	855
Tax liabilities	294
Bank overdraft	537
	1,686
Total liabilities	10,686
Total equity and liabilities	22,324

(a) **State the formulae that are used to calculate the following ratios:** **(10 marks)**

(Write in the correct formula from the list provided)

(i) Inventory holding period	▼
Formulae: Inventories/Cost of sales × 365 Inventories/Revenue × 365 Cost of sales/Inventories × 365 Revenue/Inventories × 365	
(ii) Trade receivables collection period	▼
Formulae: Trade payables/Cost of sales × 365 Trade receivables/Cost of sales × 365 Revenue/Trade receivables × 365 Trade receivables/Revenue × 365	

(iii)	Trade payables payment period	▼

Formulae:

Trade payables/Revenue × 365

Trade payables/Cost of sales × 365

Revenue/Trade payables × 365

Cost of sales/Trade payables × 365

(iv)	Working capital cycle	▼

Formulae:

Current assets/Current liabilities

Current assets – Inventories/Current liabilities

Inventory days + Receivables days – Payables days

Inventory days + Receivables days + Payables days

(v)	Gearing Ratio	▼

Formulae:

Current assets/Current liabilities

Revenue/Total assets – Current liabilities

Non-current liabilities/Total equity + Non-current liabilities

Profit after tax/Number of issued ordinary shares

(b) **Calculate the following ratios to the nearest ONE DECIMAL PLACE.** **(10 marks)**

(i)	Inventory holding period (days)		days
(ii)	Trade receivables collection period		days
(iii)	Trade payables payment period		days
(iv)	Working capital cycle		days
(v)	Gearing ratio		%

Task 8 (23 marks)

John Brams is a shareholder of Ma Leer Ltd. He has obtained some ratios that are based on the financial statements of the company for the last two years (to December 20X4 and 20X5). He is interested in how the directors have managed the business in the past year and in the company's financial performance. You have been asked to analyse the financial performance of the company using the ratios computed. The ratios John has obtained are set out below. Sales revenue has remained relatively stable throughout 20X4 and 20X5.

Ratio	20X5	20X4
Return on capital employed	15%	19%
Gross profit percentage	46%	42%
Operating profit percentage	20%	22%
Expense/revenue percentage	26%	24%
Asset turnover (based on net assets)	0.75	0.86

Prepare a report for John Brams that includes the following.

(a) Your comments on the financial performance of Ma Leer Ltd for the two years based on your analysis of the ratios and what this tells you about the company.   (20 marks)

(b) Your opinion, with reasons based on your analysis of the ratios above, as to how well the company has been managed during the year.   (3 marks)

Task 8 (25 marks).

John Evans is a shareholder of Mo Leer Ltd. He has obtained some ratios that the based on the financial statements of the company for the last two years (to December 20X4 and 20X5). He is interested in how the directors have managed the business in the past year and in the company's financial performance. You have been asked to analyse the financial performance of the company using the ratios computed. The ratios John has obtained are set out below. Sales revenue has remained profitable throughout 20X4 and 20X5.

	20X5	20X4
Return on capital employed	15%	18%
Gross profit percentage	46%	43%
Operating profit percentage	20%	22%
Expense/revenue percentage	26%	24%
Asset turnover (based on net assets)	0.75	0.86

Prepare a report for John Evans that includes the following

(a) Your comments on the financial performance of Mo Leer Ltd for the two years based on your analysis of the ratios and what this tells you about the company. (20 marks)

(b) Your opinion, with reasons based on your analysis of the ratios above, as to how well the company has been managed during the year. (5 marks)

BPP PRACTICE ASSESSMENT 1 FINANCIAL STATEMENTS OF LIMITED COMPANIES

ANSWERS

Financial Statements of Limited Companies
BPP practice assessment 1

Task 1

(a) **Ricschtein Ltd**
Statement of profit or loss and other comprehensive income for the year ended 31 March 20X7

	£000
Revenue	36,724
Cost of sales (W)	(20,565)
Gross profit	16,159
Distribution costs	(5,517)
Administrative expenses (W)	(4,329)
Profit from operations	6,313
Finance costs (490 + 490)	(980)
Profit before tax	5,333
Tax	(1,170)
Profit for the period from continuing operations	4,163

Workings

Cost of sales	£000
Opening inventories	6,120
Purchases	21,749
Closing inventories	(7,304)
	20,565

Administrative expenses	£000
Administrative expenses	4,251
Accruals	87
Prepayments (36 × 3/12)	(9)
	4,329

(b) **Ricschtein Ltd**
Statement of changes in equity for the year ended 31 March 20X7

	Share capital £000	Share premium £000	Retained earnings £000	Total equity £000
Balance at 1 April 20X6	7,000		9,552	16,552
Changes in equity				
Total comprehensive income			4,163	4,163
Dividends			(1,100)	(1,100)
Issue of share capital	3,000	6,000	0	9,000
Balance at 31 March 20X7	10,000	6,000	12,615	28,615

Task 2

Ricschtein Ltd
Statement of financial position as at 31 March 20X7

	£000
ASSETS	
Non-current assets	
Property, plant and equipment (39,371 – 13,892)	25,479
Current assets	
Inventories	7,304
Trade and other receivables (W)	4,599
Cash and cash equivalents (423 + 9,000)	9,423
	21,326
Total assets	46,805
EQUITY AND LIABILITIES	
Equity	
Share capital (7,000 + 3,000)	10,000
Share premium	6,000
Retained earnings (W)	12,615
Total equity	28,615
Non-current liabilities	
Bank loan	14,000
Current liabilities	
Trade and other payables (W)	3,020
Tax liability	1,170
	4,190
Total liabilities	18,190
Total equity and liabilities	46,805

Workings

Trade and other receivables	£000
Trade and other receivables	4,590
Additional administrative expenses prepaid	9
	4,599

Retained earnings	£000
Retained earnings at 1 April 20X6	9,552
Total profit for the year	4,163
Dividends paid	(1,100)
	12,615

Trade and other payables	£000
Trade and other payables	2,236
Accruals: trial balance	207
Additional administrative expenses accrual	87
Additional finance costs accrual	490
	3,020

Task 3

Note. Based on the information available at the time this book was written, we anticipate that this task would be human marked in the real assessment.

(a) The underlying assumption is going concern.

Financial statements are normally prepared on the assumption that the entity will continue to operate for the foreseeable future. This means that its management does not intend or need to liquidate or curtail the scale of its operations materially. For example, if an entity is a going concern there should be no need to sell off any significant part of the business or restrict any of its normal trading activities.

(b) The four enhancing qualitative characteristics of useful financial information are:

- Comparability
- Verifiability
- Timeliness
- Understandability

(c) **Comparability**

Users need to be able to compare information about a reporting entity with similar information about other entities and with information about the same entity for a different period or another date.

Consistency helps to achieve comparability. Consistency is the use of the same methods for the same items from one period to the next and in a single period, the use of the same methods across entities.

Comparability does not mean uniformity. For information to be comparable, like things must look alike and different things must look different.

Verifiability

If information is verifiable, it means that different knowledgeable and independent observers could reach a consensus (broad agreement but not necessarily complete agreement) that a particular way of presenting an item is a faithful representation.

Verification can be direct (for example, through an observation, such as counting cash). It can also be indirect (for example, through checking the quantities and costs used in calculating the value of closing inventories and checking the calculation itself).

Timeliness

To be useful, information must be available to decision makers in time to be capable of influencing their decisions.

Generally, the older the information is, the less useful it is. For example, the latest set of financial statements is normally the most relevant for decision-making. However, older financial information may still be useful for identifying and assessing trends (for example, growth in profits over a number of years).

Understandability

Classifying, characterising and presenting information clearly and concisely makes it understandable.

However, some information is complex and cannot be made easier to understand. Excluding this information from the financial statements would make them more understandable, but they would also be incomplete and potentially misleading.

BPP
LEARNING MEDIA

Financial reports are prepared for users who have a reasonable knowledge of business and economic activities and who review and analyse the information diligently. Users may sometimes need help from an adviser in order to understand complex financial information.

Note. Candidates only needed to explain ONE of the enhancing qualitative characteristics.

....

Task 4

Note. Based on the information available at the time this book was written, we anticipate that this task would be human marked in the real assessment.

(a) IFRS 15 *Revenue from Contracts with Customers* defines revenue as the 'income arising in the course of an entity's ordinary activities'. In the case of a publisher, this would be income arising from the sale of magazines. Revenue does not include sales taxes, value added taxes or goods and service taxes which are only collected for third parties, because these do not represent economic benefits flowing to the entity. The same is true for revenues collected by an agent on behalf of a principal. Revenue for the agent is only the commission received for acting as agent.

(b) Revenue from the sale of goods should be recognised when the performance obligation(s) in the contract is/are satisfied. There is a five-step process for deciding the amount of revenue to recognise, and when it should be recognised:

(i)   Identify the contract(s) with a customer.

(ii)   Identify the performance obligations in the contract.

(iii) Determine the transaction price.

(iv)   Allocate the transaction price to the performance obligations in the contract

(v)   Recognise revenue when (or as) the entity satisfies a performance obligation.

(c) The subscription is effectively 12 separate purchases paid for in advance. At the year-end, the company has transferred 9 of the 12 monthly issues to the customer, so it should recognise £1,125 (1,500 × 9/12).

The sale of the printing press does not arise in the course of the ordinary activities of the company, so the sale proceeds cannot be recognised as revenue.

....

Task 5

(a)

£38,000	✓
£41,000	
£44,000	
£53,000	

	£
Opening balance	12,000
Profit or loss	41,000
Closing balance	(15,000)
	38,000

(b)

Objectivity and integrity	
Objectivity and professional behaviour	
Objectivity and confidentiality	✓
Professional competence and due care and confidentiality	

(c)

£600	
£750	
£900	✓
£1,000	

The interest charge is 3/10 × £3,000

(d)

1 only	✓
2 only	
Both 1 and 2	
Neither 1 nor 2	

(e)

Recognised in the statement of financial position as a provision	
Recognised in the statement of financial position as a contingent liability	
Only disclosed as a note to the financial statements	✓
Neither recognised in the statement of financial position nor included in the notes	

This is a contingent liability because the outflow of economic benefit is only possible, rather than probable. Contingent liabilities are only disclosed and are not recognised in the statement of financial position.

Task 6

Wells plc
Consolidated statement of financial position as at 31 October 20X9

	£000
ASSETS	
Non-current assets	
Intangible assets: goodwill (W)	4,492
Property, plant and equipment	64,236
	68,728
Current assets	
Inventories	18,102
Trade and other receivables (6,756 + 2,249 – 1,250)	7,755
Cash and cash equivalents	1,587
	27,444
Total assets	96,172
EQUITY AND LIABILITIES	
Equity	
Share capital	35,000
Retained earnings (W)	26,777
	61,777
Non-controlling interest (W)	5,083
Total equity	66,860
Non-current liabilities	
Long-term loans	18,000
Current liabilities	
Trade and other payables (8,877 + 1,445 – 1,250)	9,072
Tax liabilities	2,240
	11,312
Total liabilities	29,312
Total equity and liabilities	96,172

Workings

Note. Group structure

Wells plc owns 75% of Wilkie Ltd (9,000,000/12,000,000)

Goodwill	£000
Consideration	19,000
Non-controlling interest at acquisition	4,336
Net assets acquired (12,000 + 5,344)	(17,344)
Impairment	(1,500)
	4,492

Retained earnings	£000
Wells plc	26,036
Wilkie Ltd – attributable to Wells plc (75% × (8,332 – 5,344))	2,241
Impairment	(1,500)
	26,777

Non-controlling interest (NCI) at acquisition	£000
Share capital – attributable to NCI (25% × 12,000)	3,000
Retained earnings – attributable to NCI (25% × 5,344)	1,336
	4,336

Non-controlling interest (NCI) at year end	£000
Share capital – attributable to NCI (25% × 12,000)	3,000
Retained earnings – attributable to NCI (25% × 8,332)	2,083
	5,083

Task 7

(a) Formulae used to calculate the ratios

(i)	Inventory holding period	$\dfrac{\text{Inventories}}{\text{Cost of sales}} \times 365$
(ii)	Trade receivables collection period	$\dfrac{\text{Trade receivables}}{\text{Revenue}} \times 365$
(iii)	Trade payables payment period	$\dfrac{\text{Trade payables}}{\text{Cost of sales}} \times 365$
(iv)	Working capital cycle	Inventory days + Receivables days – Payables days
(v)	Gearing ratio	$\dfrac{\text{Non - current liabilities}}{\text{Total equity + Non - current liabilities}} \times 100\%$

(b) Calculation of the ratios

(i)	**Inventory holding period (days)** $\dfrac{1{,}632}{7{,}770} \times 365$	76.7	days
(ii)	**Trade receivables collection period** $\dfrac{1{,}776}{14{,}800} \times 365$	43.8	days
(iii)	**Trade payables payment period** $\dfrac{855}{7{,}770} \times 365$	40.2	days
(iv)	**Working capital cycle** 76.7 + 43.8 – 40.2	80.3	days
(v)	**Gearing ratio** $\dfrac{9{,}000}{11{,}638+9{,}000} \times 100$	43.6	%

Task 8

REPORT

To: John Brams

From: Accounting Technician

Subject: Financial performance of Ma Leer Ltd

Date: 10 January 20X6

As requested, I have analysed the financial performance of Ma Leer Ltd, based on the ratios provided.

(a)   The financial performance of the company

Return on capital employed

Return on capital employed has deteriorated significantly during the year. This suggests that investors are not obtaining as a good a return on the capital that they have invested as in previous years. There are two reasons for this. The company is slightly less profitable in 20X5 than it was in 20X4. In addition the company is not generating as much profit (or return) from its capital (assets) as in the previous year.

Gross profit percentage

This has improved significantly during the year. There could be several reasons for this. One reason is costs of sales may have fallen. Alternatively the company may have changed its 'sales mix', so that, although the overall sales revenue has remained stable, it has sold a greater proportion of products with a higher gross margin.

Operating profit percentage and expense/revenue percentage

There has been a slight fall in the company's operating profit percentage. This has occurred despite the improvement in the gross profit percentage during the year. There must have been a significant rise in operating expenses (such as administrative expenses). This is confirmed by the expenses/revenue percentage, which has risen slightly. This suggests that 'non-trading' expenses have risen fairly sharply compared with sales. Alternatively there may have been a large unusual expense of some kind during the year.

Asset turnover

Asset turnover has fallen during the year. The company appears to be operating less efficiently than in the previous year and is therefore generating less sales revenue relative to the capital invested in the business (represented by its net assets). There are a number of possible reasons for this, including investment in new assets towards the end of the year. However, the other ratios suggest that the most likely reason for the fall is either that sales have been disappointing following increased investment (an expected rise in sales has not materialised) or that the company now has a higher proportion of assets that are not being used to generate sales.

(b) How well the company has been managed

The overall picture is of a company which is probably not being managed as well as in previous years. Operating expenses seem to be disproportionately high compared with sales, suggesting poor control, and the company appears to be operating less efficiently than before, failing to turn increased investment in assets into additional profit. The fact that the company's gross profit percentage has increased despite this indicates that there is nothing fundamentally wrong with the business and that with better management there could be considerable scope for improvement in return on capital employed and overall performance.

BPP PRACTICE ASSESSMENT 2 FINANCIAL STATEMENTS OF LIMITED COMPANIES

Time allowed: 2 hours and 30 minutes

PRACTICE ASSESSMENT 2

Financial Statements of Limited Companies
BPP practice assessment 2

The following information is relevant to Task 1 and Task 2

You have been asked to prepare a statement of cash flows and a statement of changes in equity for Kenadie Ltd for the year ended 30 September 20X6. The statement of profit or loss and statement of financial position (with comparatives for the previous year) of Kenadie Ltd are set out below.

Kenadie Ltd
Statement of profit or loss for the year ended 30 September 20X6

	£000
Continuing operations	
Revenue	31,461
Cost of sales	(16,304)
Gross profit	15,157
Loss on disposal of property, plant and equipment	(183)
Distribution costs	(5,663)
Administrative expenses	(3,681)
Profit from operations	5,630
Finance costs – interest on loan	(800)
Profit before tax	4,830
Tax	(919)
Profit for the period from continuing operations	3,911

Kenadie Ltd
Statement of financial position as at 30 September 20X6

	20X6 £000	20X5 £000
ASSETS		
Non-current assets		
Property, plant and equipment	29,882	19,100
Current assets		
Inventories	4,837	4,502
Trade receivables	5,244	4,978
Cash and cash equivalents	64	587
	10,145	10,067
Total assets	40,027	29,167
EQUITY AND LIABILITIES		
Equity		
Share capital	8,000	5,000
Share premium account	2,500	1,000
Retained earnings	15,570	12,359
Total equity	26,070	18,359
Non-current liabilities		
Bank loan	10,000	7,000
Current liabilities		
Trade payables	3,038	2,954
Tax liabilities	919	854
	3,957	3,808
Total liabilities	13,957	10,808
Total equity plus liabilities	40,027	29,167

Further information:

- The total depreciation charge for the year was £2,172,000.

- Property, plant and equipment costing £1,103,000, with accumulated depreciation of £411,000, was sold in the year.

- All sales and purchases were on credit. Other expenses were paid for in cash.

- A dividend of £700,000 was paid during the year.

Task 1 (32 marks)

(a) **Prepare a reconciliation of profit before tax to net cash from operating activities for Kenadie Ltd for the year ended 30 September 20X6.** **(13 marks)**

(Complete the left hand column by writing in the correct line item from the list provided.)

Reconciliation of profit before tax to net cash from operating activities

		£000
▼		
Adjustments for:		
▼		
▼		
▼		
▼		
▼		
▼		
Cash generated by operations		
▼		
▼		
Net cash from operating activities		

Picklist:

Adjustment in respect of inventories
Adjustment in respect of trade payables
Adjustment in respect of trade receivables
Depreciation
Finance costs
Interest paid
Loss on disposal of property, plant and equipment
New bank loans
Proceeds on disposal of property, plant and equipment
Profit after tax
Profit before tax
Profit from operations
Purchases of property, plant and equipment
Tax paid

(b) Prepare the statement of cash flows for Kenadie Ltd for the year ended 30 September 20X6.   (19 marks)

(Complete the left hand column by writing in the correct line item from the list provided.)

Kenadie Ltd
Statement of cash flows for the year ended 30 September 20X6

	£000
Net cash from operating activities	
Investing activities	
▼	
▼	
Net cash used in investing activities	
Financing activities	
▼	
▼	
▼	
Net cash from financing activities	
Net increase/(decrease) in cash and cash equivalents	
Cash and cash equivalents at the beginning of the year	
Cash and cash equivalents at the end of the year	

Picklist:

Adjustment in respect of inventories
Adjustment in respect of trade payables
Adjustment in respect of trade receivables
Dividends paid
New bank loans
Proceeds of share issue
Proceeds on disposal of property, plant and equipment
Purchases of property, plant and equipment

Workings

(Complete the left hand column by writing in the correct narrative from the list provided.)

Proceeds on disposal of property, plant and equipment (PPE)	£000
▼	
▼	

Picklist:

Carrying amount of PPE sold
Depreciation charge
Loss on disposal
PPE at end of year
PPE at start of year

Purchases of property, plant and equipment (PPE)	£000
PPE at start of year	
▼	
▼	
▼	
Total PPE additions	

Picklist:

Carrying amount of PPE sold
Depreciation charge
Loss on disposal of PPE
PPE at end of year

Task 2 (8 marks)

Draft the statement of changes in equity for Kenadie Ltd for the year ended 30 September 20X6. **(8 marks)**

Kenadie Ltd
Statement of changes in equity for the year ended 30 September 20X6

	Share capital £000	Share premium £000	Retained earnings £000	Total equity £000
Balance at 1 October 20X5				
Changes in equity				
Profit for the year				
Dividends				
Issue of share capital				
Balance at 30 September 20X6				

Task 3 (10 marks)

(a) What is the objective of general purpose financial reporting according to the IASB *Conceptual Framework for Financial Reporting?* **(3 marks)**

(b) Give **ONE** example of a **PRIMARY** user of general purpose financial reports (financial statements) and explain their need for the information in financial statements. **(4 marks)**

(c) Briefly explain **ONE** limitation of general purpose financial reports. **(3 marks)**

Task 4 (12 marks)

You work for a firm of Chartered Accountants. Otto Line is the managing director of Morel Ltd. He would like you to advise him on the accounting treatment of some matters that have arisen during the financial year as follows.

Matter 1

(a) During the year an incident at one of the company's factories resulted in poisonous waste material being discharged into a river, causing serious damage to the environment. In an interview with the local newspaper, the managing director accepted responsibility for the damage and promised that the company would clean up the discharge and restore the river to its previous condition, even though it is not legally obliged to do so. The board of directors has a reliable estimate that the cost of cleaning up the damage would be £850,000.

(b) During the year three people were seriously injured as a result of food poisoning. It was claimed that the food poisoning came from products sold by Morel Ltd. Legal proceedings have started seeking damages from the company of £2,000,000. Lawyers working for Morel Ltd have advised that it is probable that the company will not be found liable.

Prepare notes for a meeting with the directors, explaining how Morel Ltd should treat the two matters set out in the data above in its financial statements. **(8 marks)**

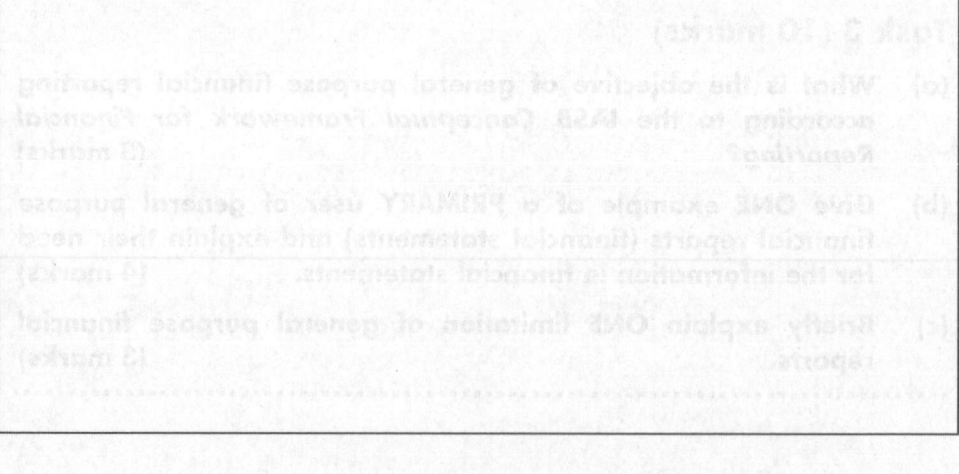

Matter 2

In order to thank you for your help in this matter and for other advice you have given during the year, you and your partner have been offered an all-expenses paid week in the company villa in Portugal.

Explain, with reference to the AAT Code of Professional Ethics, whether you should accept or reject this offer. **(4 marks)**

Task 5 (15 marks)

(a) The following measures relate to a non-current asset:

(i) Carrying amount £20,000
(ii) Fair value less costs of disposal £18,000
(iii) Value in use £22,000
(iv) Replacement cost £50,000

What is the recoverable amount of the asset, according to IAS 36 *Impairment of Assets*? **(4 marks)**

£18,000	
£20,000	
£22,000	
£50,000	

(b) A company purchased a machine at a cost of £24,000. Delivery costs totalled £1,000, the cost of installing the machine was £2,000 and there were also general administrative expenses of £3,500 in connection with the purchase.

What amount should be recognised as the cost of the machine, according to IAS 16 *Property, Plant and Equipment*? (3 marks)

£24,000	
£25,000	
£27,000	
£30,500	

(c) Goodwill arising on a business combination is never amortised.

Is this statement True or False? **(2 marks)**

True	
False	

(d) A business sells three products and at the year-end details of the inventories of these products are:

	Cost £	Selling price £	Selling costs £
Basic	14,300	15,700	2,400
Standard	21,600	21,300	1,000
Premium	17,500	28,600	1,800

At what value should closing inventories be recognised in the statement of financial position? **(3 marks)**

£51,100	
£53,100	
£53,400	
£65,600	

(e) The tax charge of Roamer Ltd based upon its profits for the current year is £48,000. The company had under-estimated its tax liability for the previous year by £9,000.

What will be the tax charge and tax liability recognised in the financial statements of Roamer Ltd at the end of the current accounting period? (3 marks)

Tax charge	Tax liability	
£39,000	£39,000	
£39,000	£48,000	
£57,000	£48,000	
£57,000	£57,000	

Task 6 (30 marks)

The Managing Director of Wraymand plc has asked you to prepare the statement of profit or loss. The company has one subsidiary, Blonk Ltd. The statements of profit or loss of the two companies for the year ended 31 March 20X7 are set out below.

Statements of profit or loss for the year ended 31 March 20X7

	Wraymand plc £000	Blonk Ltd £000
Continuing operations		
Revenue	38,462	12,544
Cost of sales	(22,693)	(5,268)
Gross profit	15,769	7,276
Other income – dividend from Blonk Ltd	580	–
Distribution costs	(6,403)	(2,851)
Administrative expenses	(3,987)	(2,466)
Profit from operations	5,959	1,959
Finance costs	(562)	(180)
Profit before tax	5,397	1,779
Tax	(1,511)	(623)
Profit for the period from continuing operations	3,886	1,156

Further information:

- Wraymand plc acquired 75% of the ordinary share capital of Blonk Ltd on 1 April 20X6.

- During the year Wraymand plc sold goods which had cost £1,100,000 to Blonk Ltd for £1,600,000. Three quarters of the goods had been sold by Blonk Ltd by the end of the year.

Draft a consolidated statement of profit or loss for Wraymand plc and its subsidiary for the year ended 31 March 20X7.   (30 marks)

Wraymand plc
Consolidated statement of profit or loss for the year ended 31 March 20X7

	£000
Continuing operations	
Revenue	
Cost of sales	
Gross profit	
Other income	
Distribution costs	
Administrative expenses	
Profit from operations	
Finance costs	
Profit before tax	
Tax	
Profit for the period from continuing operations	
Attributable to:	
Equity holders of the parent	
Non-controlling interest	

380

Workings

Revenue	£000
Wraymand plc	
Blonk Ltd	
Total inter-company adjustment	

Cost of sales	£000
Wraymand plc	
Blonk Ltd	
Total inter-company adjustment	

Task 7 (20 marks)

You have been asked to assist a shareholder in Forth Ltd. She has asked you to calculate ratios in respect of the financial statements of the company for the year ending 31 October 20X7. The financial statements of Forth Ltd are set out below:

Forth Ltd
Statement of profit or loss for the year ended 31 October 20X7

	£000
Continuing operations	
Revenue	2,400
Cost of sales	(1,392)
Gross profit	1,008
Distribution costs	(540)
Administrative expenses	(240)
Profit from operations	228
Finance costs	(91)

	£000
Profit before tax	137
Tax	(44)
Profit for the period from continuing operations	93

Forth Ltd
Statement of financial position as at 31 October 20X7

	£000
ASSETS	
Non-current assets	
Property, plant and equipment	4,750
Current assets	
Inventories	320
Trade receivables	360
Cash and cash equivalents	0
	680
Total assets	5,430
EQUITY AND LIABILITIES	
Equity	
Share capital	2,500
Retained earnings	1,239
Total equity	3,739
Non-current liabilities	
Bank loans	1,300
Current liabilities	
Trade payables	195

	£000
Tax liabilities	44
Bank overdraft	152
	391
Total liabilities	1,691
Total equity and liabilities	5,430

(a) **State the formulae that are used to calculate each of the following ratios:** **(10 marks)**

(Write in the correct formula from the list provided)

(i) Gross profit percentage		▼
Formulae:		
Gross profit/Total equity × 100		
Gross profit/Revenue × 100		
Gross profit/Total assets × 100		
Gross profit/Total assets – Current liabilities		
(ii) Operating profit percentage		▼
Formulae:		
Profit from operations/Revenue × 100		
Profit from operations/Total assets × 100		
Profit from operations/Total equity + Non-current liabilities × 100		
Profit from operations/Finance costs × 100		
(iii) Administrative expenses/revenue percentage		▼
Formulae:		
Administrative expenses/Revenue × 100		
Distribution costs + Administrative expenses/Revenue × 100		
Administrative expenses/Cost of sales × 100		
Revenue/Administrative expenses × 100		

(iv)	Current ratio		▼

Formulae:

Total assets/Total liabilities

Current assets – Inventories/Current liabilities

Current assets/Current liabilities

Total assets – Inventories/Total liabilities

(v)	Inventory holding period		▼

Formulae:

Inventories/cost of sales × 365

Inventories/revenue × 365

Cost of sales/inventories × 365

Revenue/inventories × 365

(b) Calculate the ratios to the nearest ONE DECIMAL PLACE.

(10 marks)

(i)	Gross profit percentage		%
(ii)	Operating profit percentage		%
(iii)	Administrative expenses/revenue percentage		%
(iv)	Current ratio		:1
(v)	Inventory holding period		days

Task 8 (23 marks)

You have been asked by the Managing Director of Gariroads Ltd to advise the company on the feasibility of raising a loan to finance the expansion of its activities.

A meeting has already been held with the bank and they have been sent a copy of the financial statements of the company for the past two years. The Managing Director wants you to comment on the likelihood of the bank lending the company money on the basis of the financial position revealed in the financial statements alone.

You have calculated the following ratios in respect of Gariroads Ltd's financial statements for the last two years to assist you in your analysis.

		20X7	20X6
(i)	Current ratio	2.2	2.1
(ii)	Quick ratio	0.8	1.3
(iii)	Gearing ratio	51.1%	31.2%
(iv)	Interest cover	1.8 times	4.5 times

Prepare a letter for the Managing Director of Gariroads that includes the following:

(a) **Comments on how the liquidity and financial position of Gariroads Ltd has changed over the two years based solely on the ratios calculated, suggesting possible reasons for the changes.** **(20 marks)**

(b) **A conclusion, with reasons, as to whether it is likely that the bank will lend the company money based solely on the ratios calculated and their analysis.** **(3 marks)**

••

BPP
LEARNING MEDIA

BPP PRACTICE ASSESSMENT 2
FINANCIAL STATEMENTS OF LIMITED COMPANIES

ANSWERS

Financial Statements of Limited Companies
BPP practice assessment 2

Task 1

(a) **Reconciliation of profit before tax to net cash from operating activities**

	£000
Profit before tax	4,830
Adjustments for:	
Depreciation	2,172
Loss on disposal of property, plant and equipment	183
Finance costs	800
Adjustment in respect of inventories (4,837 – 4,502)	(335)
Adjustment in respect of trade receivables (5,244 – 4,978)	(266)
Adjustment in respect of trade payables (3,038 – 2,954)	84
Cash generated by operations	7,468
Tax paid	(854)
Interest paid	(800)
Net cash from operating activities	5,814

BPP LEARNING MEDIA

(b) **Kenadie Ltd**
Statement of cash flows for the year ended 30 September 20X6

	£000
Net cash from operating activities	5,814
Investing activities	
Purchases of property, plant and equipment (W)	(13,646)
Proceeds on disposal of property, plant and equipment (W)	509
Net cash used in investing activities	(13,137)
Financing activities	
Proceeds of share issue (10,500 – 6,000)	4,500
New bank loans (10,000 – 7,000)	3,000
Dividends paid	(700)
Net cash from financing activities	6,800
Net increase/(decrease) in cash and cash equivalents	(523)
Cash and cash equivalents at the beginning of the year	587
Cash and cash equivalents at the end of the year	64

Workings

Proceeds on disposal of property, plant and equipment (PPE)	£000
Carrying amount of PPE sold	692
Loss on disposal	(183)
	509

Purchases of property, plant and equipment (PPE)	£000
PPE at start of year	19,100
Depreciation charge	(2,172)
Carrying amount of PPE sold	(692)
PPE at end of year	(29,882)
Total PPE additions	(13,646)

Task 2

Kenadie Ltd

Statement of changes in equity for the year ended 30 September 20X6

	Share capital £000	Share premium £000	Retained earnings £000	Total equity £000
Balance at 1 October 20X5	5,000	1,000	12,359	18,359
Changes in equity				
Profit for the year			3,911	3,911
Dividends			(700)	(700)
Issue of share capital	3,000	1,500		4,500
Balance at 30 September 20X6	8,000	2,500	15,570	26,070

Task 3

Note. Based on the information available at the time this book was written, we anticipate that this task would be human marked in the real assessment.

(a) The IASB *Conceptual Framework for Financial Reporting* states that the objective of general purpose financial reporting is to provide financial information about the reporting entity that is useful to existing and potential investors, lenders and other creditors in making decisions about providing resources to the entity.

BPP
LEARNING MEDIA

(b) Examples of primary users of financial information and their information needs:

Existing and potential investors

Investors and potential investors need information to help them determine whether they should buy, hold or sell their investment. They need information which helps them to assess the ability of the entity to pay dividends and to assess the potential changes in the market price of their investment.

Existing and potential lenders and other creditors

Lenders need information that helps them to make decisions about providing or settling loans. They need information which helps them to assess whether their loans and the interest attaching to them will be paid when due.

Tutorial note. Candidates only needed to write about ONE example of a PRIMARY user. According to the IASB *Conceptual Framework*, the primary users are the providers of capital (ie, those given in the answer to part (a) above). Although there may be other users of financial statements, eg, employees, the government, the public, general purpose financial statements are not primarily prepared for them.

(c) Limitations of general purpose financial reports (according to the IASB *Conceptual Framework*):

- **They are not designed to show the value of a reporting entity** (the market value of the company's shares). However, they provide information that may help users to estimate its value.

- **They may not meet the needs of every individual user**. Individual investors, lenders and other creditors (primary users) may have different information needs, which may conflict.

- **They are prepared primarily for existing and potential investors, lenders and other creditors**. Other groups of people, such as regulators and members of the public, may be interested in financial information about an entity. These groups may find general purpose financial reports useful, but they are **not primarily directed towards these other groups**.

- **They are based on estimates, judgements and models rather than exact depictions.** The *Conceptual Framework* establishes the concepts that underlie those estimates, judgements and models.

Tutorial note. Candidates only needed to write about ONE limitation.

Task 4

Matter 1

(a) Clean up costs

Morel Ltd has a constructive obligation because it has publicly accepted responsibility for the damage to the environment and has created a valid expectation that it will restore the river to its previous condition. As the incident and the interview appear to have taken place before the year end the company has a present obligation as the result of a past event. It is probable that there will be an outflow of resources embodying economic benefits: the company will incur costs as a result of cleaning up the discharge. A reliable estimate has been made of the costs. Therefore, in accordance with IAS 37 *Provisions, Contingent Liabilities and Contingent Assets,* the company should recognise a provision of £850,000 at its year end.

(b) Legal proceedings

Because the company will probably not be liable it is unlikely that there is a present obligation or that there will be an outflow of resources embodying economic benefits (IAS 37). Therefore no provision should be made. However, the company does have a contingent liability (unless the chances of its being found liable for damages are remote). Details of the claim should be disclosed in the notes to the financial statements.

Matter 2

This offer of a free holiday should not be accepted due to the principles of professional behaviour and objectivity. The offer looks disreputable and is of significant value. Such a gift, if accepted, could be seen from an observer's point of view as payment in kind for special favours, or may indicate that you may be biased towards that client in future.

Task 5

(a)

£18,000	
£20,000	
£22,000	✓
£50,000	

Recoverable amount is the higher of value in use and fair value less costs of disposal.

(b)

£24,000	
£25,000	
£27,000	✓
£30,500	

The cost of property, plant and equipment is the cost of bringing it into working condition for its intended use. Therefore the cost includes delivery and installation costs but does not include the administrative expenses.

	£
Cost	
Purchase price	24,000
Delivery costs	1,000
Installation costs	2,000
	27,000

(c)

True	✓
False	

Goodwill arising on a business combination is recognised at cost in the statement of financial position and reviewed for impairment each year.

(d)

£51,100	✓
£53,100	
£53,400	
£65,600	

	Inventory value £
Basic – NRV (15,700 – 2,400)	13,300
Standard – NRV (21,300 – 1,000)	20,300
Premium – cost	17,500
	51,100

(e)

Tax charge	Tax liability	
£39,000	£39,000	
£39,000	£48,000	
£57,000	£48,000	✓
£57,000	£57,000	

Tax charge:

	£
Tax on profits for the year	48,000
Adjustments relating to previous years	9,000
	57,000

Task 6

Wraymand plc
Consolidated statement of profit or loss for the year ended 31 March 20X7

	£000
Continuing operations	
Revenue (W)	49,406
Cost of sales (W)	(26,486)
Gross profit	22,920
Other income	–
Distribution costs (6,403 + 2,851)	(9,254)
Administrative expenses (3,987 + 2,466)	(6,453)
Profit from operations	7,213
Finance costs (562 + 180)	(742)
Profit before tax	6,471
Tax (1,511 + 623)	(2,134)
Profit for the period from continuing operations	4,337
Attributable to:	
Equity holders of the parent	4,048
Non-controlling interest (25% × 1,156)	289
	4,337

Workings

Revenue	£000
Wraymand plc	38,462
Blonk Ltd	12,544
Total inter-company adjustment	(1,600)
	49,406

Cost of sales	£000
Wraymand plc	22,693
Blonk Ltd	5,268
Total inter-company adjustment (1,600 – (1/4 × 500))	(1,475)
	26,486

Task 7

(a) Formulae used to calculate the ratios

(i)	Gross profit percentage	$\dfrac{\text{Gross profit}}{\text{Revenue}} \times 100\%$
(ii)	Operating profit percentage	$\dfrac{\text{Profit from operations}}{\text{Revenue}} \times 100\%$
(iii)	Administrative expenses/revenue percentage	$\dfrac{\text{Administrative expenses}}{\text{Revenue}} \times 100\%$
(iv)	Current ratio	$\dfrac{\text{Current assets}}{\text{Current liabilities}}$
(v)	Inventory holding period	$\dfrac{\text{Inventories}}{\text{Cost of sales}} \times 365$

(b) Calculation of ratios

(i)	Gross profit percentage $\dfrac{1,008}{2,400} \times 100$	42.0	%
(ii)	Operating profit percentage $\dfrac{228}{2,400} \times 100$	9.5	%
(iii)	Administrative expenses/revenue percentage $\dfrac{240}{2,400} \times 100$	10.0	%

(iv)	Current ratio $\dfrac{680}{391}$	1.7	:1
(v)	Inventory holding period $\dfrac{320}{1,392} \times 365$	83.9	days

Task 8

Note. Based on the information available at the time this book was written, we anticipate that this task would be human marked in the real assessment.

Accounting Technician

20 High Street

Anytown

20 June 20X7

Dear Sir,

As requested, I have reviewed the key ratios calculated from the financial statements of Gariroads Ltd to establish whether further finance could be obtained for expansion.

(a) Commentary on liquidity and financial position

There has been a slight increase in the current ratio in the year which is positive and the overall ratio is at a comfortable level above 2. The company's current assets have increased relative to its current liabilities.

However, the quick ratio shows a worsening position as it has fallen from 1.3 to 0.8 showing that Gariroads may struggle to meet its obligations from assets that are quickly convertible into cash. The fact that the current ratio has risen while the quick ratio has fallen suggests that it is the level of inventories that has risen, rather than trade receivables or cash. It is quite likely that the level of cash has fallen during the year, possibly even that a positive cash balance has become an overdraft.

The gearing ratio has increased in the year from a relatively safe 31% to a high 51%. New loans have been taken out during the year and the company is likely to be seen as risky by future lenders. The sharp increase in the gearing ratio suggests that total borrowings may have more than doubled compared with the previous year.

Interest cover has decreased from 4.5 times to 1.8 times which again would be seen as a risk factor by lenders. The most obvious reason for the worrying fall in interest cover is the sharp increase in the amount that the company has borrowed. Other reasons for this could include a fall in profit from operations and/or higher interest rates on the additional loan. Because there are less profits available to cover the interest payments, future lenders would be very cautious about lending money to Gariroads Ltd.

(b) **Conclusion**

Overall, Gariroads has a worsening liquidity position and increased gearing in 20X7 compared to 20X6. While the company is still able to meet its interest payments, the ability to do so has decreased. If the fall in interest cover is partly the result of falling profits, this is a very worrying sign.

Gariroads is already very highly geared. A potential lender would view the company as a risky and unattractive prospect. On the basis of these four ratios, it is unlikely that the bank would lend further cash to the business at the moment, unless there is a very strong possibility of increased profits and much better interest cover in the near future.

Yours faithfully

Accounting Technician

BPP PRACTICE ASSESSMENT 3 FINANCIAL STATEMENTS OF LIMITED COMPANIES

Time allowed: 2 hours and 30 minutes

PRACTICE ASSESSMENT 3

Financial Statements of Limited Companies
BPP practice assessment 3

The following information is relevant to Task 1 and Task 2

You have been asked to help prepare the financial statements of Nevis Ltd for the year ended 31 March 20X9. The company's trial balance as at 31 March 20X9 is shown below.

Nevis Ltd

Trial balance as at 31 March 20X9

	Debit £000	Credit £000
Share capital		12,000
Share premium		2,000
Trade and other payables		2,642
Motor vehicles – cost	21,840	
Motor vehicles – acc depreciation at 1 April 20X8		4,675
Plant and equipment – cost	32,800	
Plant and equipment – acc depreciation at 1 April 20X8		16,000
Trade and other receivables	4,567	
Accruals		239
6% bank loan repayable 20Y6		12,000
Cash at bank	3,519	
Retained earnings at 1 April 20X8		6,590
Interest	360	
Sales		65,113

	Debit £000	Credit £000
Purchases	44,000	
Distribution costs	2,905	
Administrative expenses	4,098	
Inventories as at 1 April 20X8	5,640	
Dividends paid	1,530	
	121,259	121,259

Further information:

- The inventories at the close of business on 31 March 20X9 were valued at £6,806,000.

- The company hired some temporary office space for the period 1 March to 31 May 20X9. The contract price for the three months was £144,000 and this was paid in full on 8 March. Office rental is included in administrative expenses.

- Depreciation is to be provided for the year to 31 March 20X9 as follows:

  | Motor vehicles | 25% per annum | Straight line basis |
  | Plant and equipment | 20% per annum | Diminishing balance basis |

  Depreciation is apportioned as follows:

	%
Cost of sales	50
Distribution costs	20
Administrative expenses	30

- Interest on the bank loan for the last six months of the year has not been included in the accounts in the trial balance.

- The tax charge for the year has been calculated as £2,540,000.

- The company issued 2,000,000 new ordinary shares during the year. They had a nominal value of £1 but were sold for £1.50 per share. This transaction is included in the trial balance above.

- All of the operations are continuing operations.

Task 1 (24 marks)

(a) **Draft the statement of profit or loss and other comprehensive income for Nevis Ltd for the year ended 31 March 20X9.**

(18 marks)

Nevis Ltd
Statement of profit or loss and other comprehensive income for the year ended 31 March 20X9

	£000
Revenue	
Cost of sales	
Gross profit	
Distribution costs	
Administrative expenses	
Profit from operations	
Finance costs	
Profit before tax	
Tax	
Profit for the period from continuing operations	

Workings

(Complete the left hand column by writing in the correct narrative from the list provided.)

Cost of sales	£000
▼	
▼	
▼	
▼	

Picklist:

Accruals
Closing inventories
Depreciation
Opening inventories
Prepayments
Purchases

Distribution costs		£000
	▼	
	▼	

Picklist:

Accruals
Depreciation
Distribution costs
Prepayments

Administrative expenses		£000
	▼	
	▼	
	▼	

Picklist:

Accruals
Administrative expenses
Depreciation
Prepayment

(b) **Draft the statement of changes in equity for Nevis Ltd for the year ended 31 March 20X9.** **(6 marks)**

Nevis Ltd
Statement of changes in equity for the year ended 31 March 20X9

	Share capital £000	Share premium £000	Retained earnings £000	Total equity £000
Balance at 1 April 20X8				
Changes in equity				
Total comprehensive income				
Dividends				
Issue of share capital				
Balance at 31 March 20X9				

Task 2 (16 marks)

Draft the statement of financial position for Nevis Ltd as at 31 March 20X9. **(16 marks)**

(Complete the left hand column by writing in the correct line item from the list provided.)

Nevis Ltd
Statement of financial position as at 31 March 20X9

	£000
ASSETS	
Non-current assets	
▼	
Current assets	
▼	
▼	
▼	
Total assets	

	£000
EQUITY AND LIABILITIES	
Equity	
▼	
▼	
▼	
Total equity	
Non-current liabilities	
▼	
Current liabilities	
▼	
▼	
Total liabilities	
Total equity and liabilities	

Picklist:

Bank loan
Cash and cash equivalents
Inventories
Property, plant and equipment
Retained earnings
Share capital
Share premium
Tax liabilities
Trade and other payables
Trade and other receivables

Workings

(Complete the left hand column by writing in the correct narrative from the list provided.)

Property, plant and equipment	£000
▼	
▼	
▼	
▼	

Picklist:

Accumulated depreciation – motor vehicles
Accumulated depreciation – plant and equipment
Motor vehicles – cost
Plant and equipment – cost

Trade and other receivables	£000
▼	
▼	

Picklist:

Accruals: trial balance
Additional administrative expenses accrual
Additional administrative expenses prepaid
Additional finance costs accrued
Additional finance costs prepaid
Prepayments
Trade and other payables
Trade and other receivables

Retained earnings	£000

Picklist:

Dividends paid
Other comprehensive income for the year
Retained earnings at 1 April 20X8
Total comprehensive income for the year
Total profit for the year

Trade and other payables	£000

Picklist:

Accruals: trial balance
Additional administrative expenses accrual
Additional administrative expenses prepaid
Additional finance costs accrual
Additional finance costs prepaid
Dividends
Prepayments
Tax liabilities
Trade and other payables
Trade and other receivables

••

BPP
LEARNING MEDIA

Task 3 (10 marks)

In accordance with the IASB *Conceptual Framework for Financial Reporting*

(a) **Explain what is meant by 'measurement'.** **(3 marks)**

(b) **Identify the FOUR possible measurement bases.** **(4 marks)**

(c) **Explain how assets are measured under ONE measurement base.** **(3 marks)**

Task 4 (12 marks)

The directors of Munro Ltd believe that one of the company's machines may have become impaired. The machine has a carrying amount of £45,000 and the directors estimate that it will generate cash flows with a net present value of £38,000 over the remainder of its useful life. It could be sold for £42,000 and disposal costs would be £1,000.

Prepare brief notes to answer the following points for the directors:

(a) **State how, according to IAS 36 *Impairment of Assets*, an impairment loss is calculated and which two figures are needed to calculate it.** **(4 marks)**

(b) **Explain what is meant by each of these figures.** **(4 marks)**

(c) **Calculate the impairment loss relating to the machine and state how this should be treated in the financial statements.** **(4 marks)**

Task 5 (15 marks)

(a) You have strong views in support of a client who is being threatened with legal action by a supplier who is alleging late payment of invoices. You have offered to state publicly your views on the matter, in defence of your client.

Identify the type of threat to objectivity described above. **(3 marks)**

Familiarity	
Self-review	
Advocacy	
Intimidation	

(b) A company sold some plant which had cost £100,000 for £20,000. At the time of sale the carrying amount of the plant was £18,000.

Which of the following correctly states the treatment of the transaction in the company's statement of cash flows for the period? **(3 marks)**

Proceeds of sale	Profit on sale	
Cash inflow under financing activities	Deducted from profit in calculating net cash from operating activities	
Cash inflow under investing activities	Added to profit in calculating net cash from operating activities.	
Cash inflow under financing activities	Added to profit in calculating net cash from operating activities	
Cash inflow under investing activities	Deducted from profit in calculating net cash from operating activities	

(c) A company has three different products in its inventories. The following information applies:

Product	Costs incurred to date £	Estimated selling costs £	Selling price £
(i)	738	208	915
(ii)	800	294	1,120
(iii)	640	220	900

At what value should the inventories be stated in the company's financial statements in accordance with IAS 2 *Inventories*? **(3 marks)**

£2,147	
£2,178	
£2,900	
£2,935	

(d) **According to IAS 38 *Intangible Assets*, which of the following statements are true?** **(3 marks)**

(i) Internally generated brands should never be capitalised

(ii) Intangible assets can be revalued upwards

(i) only	
(ii) only	
Both (i) and (ii)	
Neither (i) nor (ii)	

(e) On 1 January 20X1 Stockbridge Ltd purchased a machine for £560,000. The residual value was estimated as £80,000 and the useful life was expected to be 10 years Stockbridge Ltd depreciates plant on a straight line basis.

At 1 January 20X6 the machine's remaining useful life was reassessed to be 4 years and the residual value was still considered to be £80,000.

What is the depreciation charge for the item of plant for the current year to 31 December 20X6? **(3 marks)**

£32,000	
£56,000	
£60,000	
£80,000	

413

Task 6 (30 marks)

Data

Teal plc acquired 80% of the issued share capital of Amber Ltd on 1 January 20X9 for £4,600,000. At that date Amber Ltd had issued share capital of £3,000,000 and retained earnings of £840,000.

The summarised statements of financial position for the two companies one year later at 31 December 20X9 are as follows:

	Teal plc £000	Amber Ltd £000
ASSETS		
Investment in Amber Ltd	4,600	
Non-current assets	7,500	4,590
Current assets	3,800	1,570
Total assets	15,900	6,160
EQUITY AND LIABILITIES		
Equity		
Share capital	5,000	3,000
Retained earnings	7,800	1,510
Total equity	12,800	4,510
Non-current liabilities	1,000	750
Current liabilities	2,100	900
Total liabilities	3,100	1,650
Total equity and liabilities	15,900	6,160

Additional data

- The fair value of the non-current assets of Amber Ltd at 1 January 20X9 was £4,200,000. The book value of the non-current assets at 1 January 20X9 was £3,900,000. The revaluation has not been recorded in the books of Amber Ltd (ignore any effect on the depreciation for the year).

- The directors of Teal plc have decided that non-controlling interest will be valued at the proportionate share of Amber Ltd's net assets.

(a) **Draft the consolidated statement of financial position for Teal plc and its subsidiary as at 31 December 20X9.** (20 marks)

Teal plc
Consolidated statement of financial position as at 31 December 20X9

	£000
ASSETS	
Non-current assets	
Intangible assets: goodwill	
Property, plant and equipment	
Current assets	
Total assets	
EQUITY AND LIABILITIES	
Equity	
Share capital	
Retained earnings	
Non-controlling interest	
Total equity	
Non-current liabilities	
Current liabilities	
Total liabilities	
Total equity and liabilities	

Workings

(Complete the left hand column by writing in the correct narrative from the list provided.)

Goodwill		£000
	▼	
	▼	
	▼	

Picklist:

Consideration
Non-controlling interest at acquisition
Net assets acquired

Retained earnings		£000
	▼	
	▼	

Picklist:

Amber Ltd – attributable to Teal plc
Revaluation
Teal plc

Non-controlling interest (NCI) at acquisition		£000
	▼	
	▼	
	▼	

Picklist:

Current assets – attributable to NCI
Non-current assets – attributable to NCI
Price paid
Retained earnings – attributable to NCI
Revaluation reserve – attributable to NCI
Share capital – attributable to NCI

Non-controlling interest (NCI) at year end	£000
▼	
▼	
▼	

Picklist:

Consideration
Current assets – attributable to NCI
Non-current assets – attributable to NCI
Retained earnings – attributable to NCI
Revaluation reserve – attributable to NCI
Share capital – attributable to NCI

Data

Blue plc acquired 75% of the issued share capital of Brown Ltd on 1 January 20X9.

Summarised statements of profit or loss for the year ended 31 December 20X9 are shown below:

	Blue plc £000	Brown Ltd £000
Continuing operations		
Revenue	61,200	22,300
Cost of sales	(29,100)	(8,600)
Gross profit	32,100	13,700
Other income – dividend from Brown Ltd	2,500	–
Operating expenses	(3,750)	(1,900)
Profit from operations	30,850	11,800

Additional data

- During the year Blue plc sold goods which had cost £600,000 to Brown Ltd for £1,000,000. None of these goods remain in inventory at the end of the year.

- Goodwill of £900,000 arose on the acquisition. The directors of Blue plc have concluded that goodwill has been impaired by 10% during the year.

(b) Draft the consolidated statement of profit or loss for Blue plc and its subsidiary up to and including the profit from operations line for the year ended 31 December 20X9.

(10 marks)

Blue plc

Consolidated statement of profit or loss for the year ended 31 December 20X9

	£000
Continuing operations	
Revenue	
Cost of sales	
Gross profit	
Other income	
Operating expenses	
Profit from operations	

Workings

Revenue	£000
Blue plc	
Brown Ltd	
Total inter-company adjustment	

Cost of sales	£000
Blue plc	
Brown Ltd	
Total inter-company adjustment	

Task 7 (20 marks)

Lucy Carmichael is considering buying shares in Tweed Ltd. She wishes to assess the level of profitability and risk of the company. She has asked you to assist her by calculating ratios in respect of the financial statements of the company for the year ended 31 March 20X8. The financial statements of Tweed Ltd are set out below.

Tweed Ltd

Statement of profit or loss for the year ended 31 March 20X8

	£000
Continuing operations	
Revenue	16,000
Cost of sales	(8,640)
Gross profit	7,360
Distribution costs	(3,600)
Administrative expenses	(2,880)
Profit from operations	880
Finance costs	(308)
Profit before tax	572
Tax	(117)
Profit for the period from continuing operations	455

Tweed Ltd
Statement of financial position as at 31 March 20X8

	£000
ASSETS	
Non-current assets	
Property, plant and equipment	9,800
Current assets	
Inventories	1,728
Trade receivables	1,600
Cash and cash equivalents	0
	3,328
Total assets	13,128
EQUITY AND LIABILITIES	
Share capital	3,000
Retained earnings	4,372
Total equity	7,372
Non-current liabilities	
Bank loans	4,400
Current liabilities	
Trade payables	1,210
Tax liabilities	117
Bank overdraft	29
	1,356
Total liabilities	5,756
Total equity and liabilities	13,128

(a) **State the formulae that are used to calculate each of the following ratios:** **(10 marks)**

(Write in the correct formula from the list provided)

(i) Return on capital employed		▼

Formulae:

Profit after tax/Total equity × 100

Profit from operations/Total equity × 100

Profit after tax/Total equity + Non-current liabilities × 100

Profit from operations/Total equity + Non-current liabilities × 100

(ii) Return on shareholders' funds		▼

Formulae:

Profit after tax/Total equity × 100

Profit before tax/Total equity × 100

Profit from operations/Total equity × 100

Profit from operations/Total equity + Non-current liabilities × 100

(iii) Gross profit percentage		▼

Formulae:

Gross profit/Total equity × 100

Gross profit/Revenue × 100

Gross profit/Total assets × 100

Gross profit/Total assets – Current liabilities

(iv) Quick (acid test) ratio		▼

Formulae:

Current assets/Current liabilities

Total assets – Inventories/Total liabilities

Total assets/Total liabilities

Current assets – Inventories/Current liabilities

(v)	Interest cover	▼

Formulae:

Finance costs/Profit from operations

Finance costs/Revenue

Profit from operations/Finance costs

Revenue/Finance costs

(b) **Calculate the following ratios to the nearest ONE DECIMAL PLACE.** **(10 marks)**

(i)	Return on capital employed		%
(ii)	Return on shareholders' funds		%
(iii)	Gross profit percentage		%
(iv)	Quick (acid test) ratio		:1
(v)	Interest cover		times

Task 8 (23 marks)

Clare Miller, a shareholder in Selston plc, is debating whether to keep or sell her shares in the company. Her main concern is the level of return she is receiving from Selston plc, but she also wishes to ensure that her shareholding is safe.

She has asked you to analyse the company's most recent financial statements with a view to assisting her in her decision.

You have calculated the following three accounting ratios for Selston plc, for years 20X8 and 20X7, and an extract from the company's statement of cash flows is also provided below.

	20X8	20X7
Return on shareholders' funds	7.2%	12.8%
Asset turnover (non-current assets)	2.5 times	3.6 times
Interest cover	1.7 times	4.1 times

Selston plc: Statement of cash flows (extract) for year 20X8

	£000
Operating activities	140
Investing activities	(220)
Financing activities	200
Increase in cash and cash equivalents	120

Prepare notes for Clare that include:

(a) **Comments on the relative performance of Selston plc in respect of the two years, giving possible reasons for any differences (the extract of the statement of cash flows may assist you in some aspects of this) based upon the ratios calculated**

(20 marks)

(b) **Advice to Clare, with ONE principal reason only to support this, as to whether or not she should keep or sell her shares in the company.** **(3 marks)**

....

BPP LEARNING MEDIA

BPP PRACTICE ASSESSMENT 3
FINANCIAL STATEMENTS OF LIMITED COMPANIES

ANSWERS

Financial Statements of Limited Companies
BPP practice assessment 3

Task 1

(a) **Nevis Ltd**
Statement of profit or loss and other comprehensive income for the year ended 31 March 20X9

	£000
Revenue	65,113
Cost of sales (W)	(47,244)
Gross profit	17,869
Distribution costs (W)	(4,669)
Administrative expenses (W)	(6,648)
Profit from operations	6,552
Finance costs (6% × 12,000)	(720)
Profit before tax	5,832
Tax	(2,540)
Profit for the period from continuing operations	3,292

Workings

Cost of sales	£000
Opening inventories	5,640
Purchases	44,000
Depreciation (50% × 8,820)	4,410
Closing inventories	(6,806)
	47,244

Distribution costs	£000
Distribution costs	2,905
Depreciation (20% × 8,820)	1,764
	4,669

Administrative expenses	£000
Administrative expenses	4,098
Depreciation (30% × 8,820)	2,646
Prepayment (144 × 2/3)	(96)
	6,648

	£000
Depreciation	
Motor vehicles (25% × 21,840)	5,460
Plant and equipment (20% × 32,800 – 16,000)	3,360
	8,820

(b) Nevis Ltd
Statement of changes in equity for the year ended 31 March 20X9

	Share capital £000	Share premium £000	Retained earnings £000	Total equity £000
Balance at 1 April 20X8	10,000	1,000	6,590	17,590
Changes in equity				
Total comprehensive income			3,292	3,292
Dividends			(1,530)	(1,530)
Issue of share capital	2,000	1,000		3,000
Balance at 31 March 20X9	12,000	2,000	8,352	22,352

Share premium

	£000
As at 31 March 20X9	2,000
On shares issued during the year (50p × 2,000)	(1,000)
As at 1 April 20X8	1,000

Task 2

Nevis Ltd

Statement of financial position as at 31 March 20X9

	£000
ASSETS	
Non-current assets	
Property, plant and equipment (W)	25,145
Current assets	
Inventories	6,806
Trade and other receivables (W)	4,663
Cash and cash equivalents	3,519
	14,988
Total assets	40,133

	£000
EQUITY AND LIABILITIES	
Equity	
Share capital	12,000
Share premium	2,000
Retained earnings (W)	8,352
Total equity	22,352
Non-current liabilities	
Bank loan	12,000
Current liabilities	
Trade and other payables (W)	3,241
Tax liabilities	2,540
	5,781
Total liabilities	17,781
Total equity and liabilities	40,133

Workings

Property, plant and equipment	£000
Motor vehicles – cost	21,840
Plant and equipment – cost	32,800
Accumulated depreciation – motor vehicles (4,675 + 5,460)	(10,135)
Accumulated depreciation – plant and equipment (16,000 + 3,360)	(19,360)
	25,145

Trade and other receivables	£000
Trade and other receivables	4,567
Additional administrative expenses prepaid	96
	4,663

Retained earnings	£000
Retained earnings at 1 April 20X8	6,590
Total profit for the year	3,292
Dividends paid	(1,530)
	8,352

Trade and other payables	£000
Trade and other payables	2,642
Accruals: trial balance	239
Additional finance costs accrual	360
	3,241

Task 3

Note. Based on the information available at the time this book was written, we anticipate that this task would be human marked in the real assessment.

(a) Measurement is the process of determining the monetary amounts at which items are recognised and carried in the financial statements.

(b) The four measurement bases are:

- Historic cost
- Current cost
- Realisable value
- Present value

(c) **Historical cost:** Assets are recorded at the amount of cash paid or the fair value of the consideration given to acquire them at the time of the acquisition.

Current cost: Assets are carried at the amount of cash that would have to be paid if the same or a similar asset was acquired currently.

Realisable value: Assets are carried at the amount of cash that could currently be obtained by selling the asset.

Present value: Assets are carried at the present discounted value of the future net cash inflows that the item is expected to generate in the normal course of business.

Note. Candidates only needed to give ONE of the above.

....

Task 4

Note. Based on the information available at the time this book was written, we anticipate that this task would be human marked in the real assessment.

(a) IAS 36 *Impairment of Assets* states that if an asset's carrying amount is greater than its recoverable amount, the asset is impaired. The impairment loss is the difference between an asset's carrying amount and its recoverable amount.

(b) The carrying amount of an asset is the amount at which it is recognised in the statement of financial position after deducting accumulated depreciation or amortisation and accumulated impairment losses.

An asset's recoverable amount is the higher of its fair value less costs of disposal and its value in use. IAS 36 defines value in use as the present value of the future cash flows expected to be derived from an asset, including any cash flows arising on its disposal.

(c) The recoverable amount of the machine is £41,000. This is its fair value less costs of disposal (42,000 – 1,000), which is higher than its value in use of £38,000.

The impairment loss is £4,000: the difference between the carrying amount and the recoverable amount (45,000 – 41,000).

The impairment loss should be recognised immediately in profit or loss.

....

Task 5

(a)

Familiarity	
Self-review	
Advocacy	✓
Intimidation	

The risk is that, since you are prepared to promote your opinion, people will have difficulty in believing that you are objective.

(b)

Proceeds of sale	Profit on sale	
Cash inflow under financing activities	Deducted from profit in calculating net cash from operating activities	
Cash inflow under investing activities	Added to profit in calculating net cash from operating activities	
Cash inflow under financing activities	Added to profit in calculating net cash from operating activities	
Cash inflow under investing activities	Deducted from profit in calculating net cash from operating activities	✓

The company has made a profit on disposal, so this amount is deducted in calculating net cash from operating activities.

(c)

£2,147	✓
£2,178	
£2,900	
£2,935	

Inventories	£000
Product I (915 – 208)	707
Product II (Cost)	800
Product III (Cost)	640
	2,147

(d)

(i) only	
(ii) only	
Both (i) and (ii)	✓
Neither (i) nor (ii)	

Although it is rare for an intangible asset to be revalued, IAS 38 allows a choice between the cost model and the revaluation model.

(e)

£32,000	
£56,000	
£60,000	✓
£80,000	

Net carrying amount at 1 January 20X6:

	£
Cost	560,000
Depreciation ((560,000 – 80,000) ÷ 10 × 5)	(240,000)
	320,000
Charge for 20X6 (320,000 – 80,000 ÷ 4)	60,000

Task 6

(a) **Teal plc**

Consolidated statement of financial position as at 31 December 20X9

	£000
ASSETS	
Non-current assets	
Intangible assets: goodwill (W)	1,288
Property, plant and equipment (7,500 + 4,590 + 300)	12,390
Current assets	5,370
Total assets	19,048
EQUITY AND LIABILITIES	
Equity	
Share capital	5,000
Retained earnings (W)	8,336
Non-controlling interest (W)	962
Total equity	14,298
Non-current liabilities	1,750
Current liabilities	3,000
Total liabilities	4,750
Total equity and liabilities	19,048

Workings

Goodwill	£000
Consideration	4,600
Non-controlling interests at acquisition	828
Net assets acquired (3,000 + 840 + 300)	(4,140)
	1,288

BPP
LEARNING MEDIA

Retained earnings	£000
Teal plc	7,800
Amber Ltd – attributable to Teal plc (80% × (1,510 – 840))	536
	8,336

Non-controlling interest (NCI) at acquisition	£000
Share capital – attributable to NCI (20% × 3,000)	600
Retained earnings – attributable to NCI (20% × 840)	168
Revaluation reserve – attributable to NCI (20% × 300)	60
	828

Non-controlling interest (NCI) at year end	£000
Share capital – attributable to NCI (20% × 3,000)	600
Retained earnings – attributable to NCI (20% × 1,510)	302
Revaluation reserve – attributable to NCI (20% × 300)	60
	962

(b) Blue plc

Consolidated statement of profit or loss for the year ended 31 December 20X9

	£000
Continuing operations	
Revenue (W)	82,500
Cost of sales (W)	(36,700)
Gross profit	45,800
Other income	0
Operating expenses (3,750 + 1,900 + 90)	(5,740)
Profit from operations	40,060

Workings

Revenue	£000
Blue plc	61,200
Brown Ltd	22,300
Total inter-company adjustment	(1,000)
	82,500

Cost of sales	£000
Blue plc	29,100
Brown Ltd	8,600
Total inter-company adjustment	(1,000)
	36,700

Task 7

(a) Formulae used to calculate the ratios

(i)	Return on capital employed	$\dfrac{\text{Profit from operations}}{\text{Total equity} + \text{non-current liabilities}} \times 100\%$
(ii)	Return on shareholders' funds	$\dfrac{\text{Profit after tax}}{\text{Total equity}} \times 100\%$
(iii)	Gross profit percentage	$\dfrac{\text{Gross profit}}{\text{Revenue}} \times 100\%$
(iv)	Quick (acid test) ratio	$\dfrac{\text{Current assets} - \text{inventories}}{\text{Current liabilities}}$
(v)	Interest cover	$\dfrac{\text{Profit from operations}}{\text{Finance costs}}$

(b) Calculation of the ratios

(i)	Return on capital employed $\dfrac{880}{7,372+4,400} \times 100$		7.5	%
(ii)	Return on shareholders' funds $\dfrac{455}{7,372} \times 100$		6.2	%
(iii)	Gross profit percentage $\dfrac{7,360}{16,000} \times 100$		46.0	%
(iv)	Quick (acid test) ratio $\dfrac{1,600}{1,356}$		1.2	:1
(v)	Interest cover $\dfrac{880}{308}$		2.9	times

Task 8

Note. Based on the information available at the time this book was written, we anticipate that this task would be human marked in the real assessment.

Notes for Clare Miller on the performance of Selston plc

(a) Return on shareholders' funds

Return on shareholders' funds has deteriorated significantly. This means that the company has made less profit than in the previous year, relative to the total shareholders' funds invested in the company.

The most obvious reason for this is that profit after tax is lower in 20X8 than it was in 20X7.

It is also possible that shareholders' funds have increased during the year, either because there has been an issue of shares, or because the company's net assets have increased, possibly as a result of purchasing non-current assets. The cash flow information suggests that either or both these things may have happened: there has been a cash outflow from investing activities and a cash inflow from financing activities.

Asset turnover

Asset turnover (based on non-current assets) has also become significantly worse. The company is generating less sales revenue from its assets than in the previous year.

Sales revenue may be lower in 20X8 than in 20X7.

Another possible reason for the fall is that the company's non-current assets have increased during the year. The assets may have been revalued upwards. Because there has been a large cash outflow in investing activities a more likely explanation is that the company has made major asset purchases during the year.

Unless the asset purchases were made early in the year they will not have generated a full year's revenue in 20X8. Therefore asset turnover (and financial performance generally) should improve in future.

Interest cover

Interest cover has fallen significantly. There is less profit available to meet interest payments and therefore less profit available for distribution to shareholders.

Operating profit may have fallen in the year.

Alternatively, interest payments may be higher than in previous years, probably because the company has taken out additional loans (possibly to purchase the new non-current assets). The cash inflow from financing activities suggests that this is the main reason for the fall.

If the company has increased its borrowings, gearing will be higher. This means that the company is now a riskier investment. Profits for ordinary shareholders may become more volatile, because a greater proportion of operating profit will be used to pay loan interest. The company may find it harder to raise additional finance if this is needed in the future.

(b) On the basis of the information provided, you are advised to sell your shares in Selston plc. The ratios suggest that you will receive a lower rate of return on your investment in future. The company has also become a riskier investment.

Note. Candidates were asked for ONE reason why Clare should keep or sell her shares in the company. Another possible answer would be that Clare should keep the shares, because the company's investment in non-current assets suggests that profits may improve in future periods.

BPP PRACTICE ASSESSMENT 4
FINANCIAL STATEMENTS OF LIMITED COMPANIES

Time allowed: 2 hours and 30 minutes

PRACTICE ASSESSMENT 4

PRACTICE ASSESSMENT 4

BPP PRACTICE ASSESSMENT 4
FINANCIAL STATEMENTS OF
LIMITED COMPANIES

Time allowed: 2 hours and 30 minutes

Financial Statements of Limited Companies
BPP practice assessment 4

The following information is relevant to Task 1 and Task 2

You have been asked to help prepare the financial statements of Martin Ltd for the year ended 31 October 20X9. The company's trial balance as at 31 October 20X9 is shown below.

Martin Ltd

Trial balance as at 31 October 20X9

	Debit £000	Credit £000
Share capital		9,000
Trade and other payables		1,347
Property, plant and equipment – cost	39,880	
Property, plant and equipment – accumulated depreciation at 31 October 20X9		21,780
Trade and other receivables	2,234	
Accruals		146
8% bank loan repayable 20Y6		14,000
Cash at bank	9,654	
Retained earnings at 1 November 20X9		3,465
Interest	560	
Sales		46,433
Purchases	32,553	
Distribution costs	2,450	
Administrative expenses	3,444	
Inventories as at 1 November 20X8	4,466	
Dividends paid	930	
	96,171	96,171

Additional data:

- The inventories at the close of business on 31 October 20X9 were valued at £4,987,000. On 4 November 20X9, goods included in this total at a value of £550,000 were found to be damaged and were sold for £300,000.

- Land, which is non-depreciable, is included in the trial balance at a value of £8,000,000. It is to be revalued at £12,000,000 and this revaluation is to be included in the financial statements for the year ended 31 October 20X9.

- The company paid £512,000 for one year's insurance on 1 February 20X9, this is due to expire on 31 January 20Y0. Insurance is included in administrative expenses.

- Distribution costs of £66,000 owing at 31 October 20X9 are to be accrued.

- Interest on the bank loan for the last six months of the year has not been included in the accounts in the trial balance.

- The tax charge for the year has been calculated as £980,000.

- All of the operations are continuing operations.

Task 1 (24 marks)

(a) **Draft the statement of profit or loss and other comprehensive income for Martin Ltd for the year ended 31 October 20X9.**

(18 marks)

Martin Ltd

Statement of profit or loss and other comprehensive Income for the year ended 31 October 20X9

	£000
Revenue	
Cost of sales	
Gross profit	
Distribution costs	
Administrative expenses	
Profit from operations	
Finance costs	
Profit before tax	
Tax	

	£000
Profit for the period from continuing operations	
Other comprehensive income	
Gain on revaluation	
Total comprehensive income for the year	

Workings

(Complete the left hand column by writing in the correct narrative from the list provided.)

Cost of sales	£000
▼	
▼	
▼	

Picklist:

Accruals
Closing inventories
Opening inventories
Prepayments
Purchases

Distribution costs	£000
▼	
▼	

Picklist:

Accruals
Distribution costs
Prepayments

Administrative expenses	£000
Profit for the period from continuing operations ▼	
Other comprehensive income ▼	

Picklist:

Accruals
Administrative expenses
Prepayment

(b) **Draft the statement of changes in equity for Martin Ltd for the year ended 31 October 20X9.** **(6 marks)**

Martin Ltd

Statement of changes in equity for the year ended 31 October 20X9

	Share capital £000	Revaluation reserve £000	Retained earnings £000	Total equity £000
Balance at 1 November 20X8				
Changes in equity				
Total comprehensive income				
Dividends				
Balance at 31 October 20X9				

Task 2 (16 marks)

Draft the statement of financial position for Martin Ltd as at 31 October 20X9. **(16 marks)**

Martin Ltd

(Complete the left hand column by writing in the correct line item from the list provided.)

Statement of financial position as at 31 October 20X9

	£000
ASSETS	
Non-current assets	
▼	
Current assets	
▼	
▼	
▼	
Total assets	

	£000
EQUITY AND LIABILITIES	
Equity	
▼	
▼	
▼	
Total equity	
Non-current liabilities	
▼	
Current liabilities	
▼	
▼	
Total liabilities	
Total equity and liabilities	

Picklist:

Bank loan
Cash and cash equivalents
Inventories
Property, plant and equipment
Retained earnings
Revaluation reserve
Share capital
Tax liabilities
Trade and other payables
Trade and other receivables

Workings

(Complete the left hand column by writing in the correct narrative from the list provided.)

Property, plant and equipment	£000
▼	
▼	
▼	

Picklist:

Property, plant and equipment – Cost
Property, plant and equipment – Accumulated depreciation
Revaluation

Trade and other receivables	£000
▼	
▼	

Picklist:

Accruals: trial balance
Additional distribution costs accrual
Additional distribution costs prepaid
Additional finance costs accrual
Additional finance costs prepaid
Administrative expenses accrual
Administrative expenses prepaid
Trade and other payables
Trade and other receivables

Retained earnings		£000
	▼	
	▼	
	▼	

Picklist:

Dividends paid
Other comprehensive income for the year
Retained earnings at 1 November 20X8
Revaluation reserve
Total comprehensive income for the year
Total profit for the year

Trade and other payables		£000
	▼	
	▼	
	▼	
	▼	

Picklist:

Accruals: trial balance
Additional distribution costs accrual
Additional distribution costs prepaid
Additional finance costs accrual
Additional finance costs prepaid
Administrative expenses accrual
Administrative expenses prepaid
Dividends
Tax payable
Trade and other payables
Trade and other receivables

Task 3 (10 marks)

(a) **List the elements that appear in financial statements according to the *Conceptual Framework for Financial Reporting*.**

(5 marks)

(b) **Define the elements that appear in the statement of financial position of a company in accordance with the definitions in the *Conceptual Framework for Financial Reporting*.** **(5 marks)**

Task 4 (12 marks)

(a) **List the fundamental ethical principles of the AAT *Code of Professional Ethics*.** **(3 marks)**

(b) **In each of the following situations, state the fundamental ethical principle that is threatened, giving a brief explanation for your answer.** **(9 marks)**

(i) A client of your company has just moved their business to another firm. Some time ago, they requested your manager to send over the client's books and records. He did not. Each time they called to chase up the request, it seems that your manager 'screened' the call and never responded.

(ii) You work for a firm of chartered accountants and are required to fill out a time sheet to record each hour worked for each client each day. Last Friday you forgot to prepare the sheet for the week, and you are now doing it on Monday morning. However you are not absolutely sure how long you worked for each client on Thursday and Friday as, due to pressure of work, you did not record it.

(iii) While at a party at the weekend, you meet a client of yours who is clearly very concerned about some VAT issues. You know enough about VAT to carry out your daily work, but you are not an expert on the areas of imports and exports on which your client is asking your opinion.

Task 5 (15 marks)

(a) Which, if any, of the following two statements are correct, according to IAS 1 *Presentation of Financial Statements*?

(3 marks)

(i) Financial statements should be prepared at least annually.

(ii) A complete set of financial statements must include notes.

(i) only	
(ii) only	
Both (i) and (ii)	
Neither (i) nor (ii)	

(b) Which of the following items would not appear as a line item in a company's statement of changes in equity, according to IAS 1 *Presentation of Financial Statements*? **(3 marks)**

Dividends paid	
Gain on revaluation of properties	
Issue of share capital	
Total comprehensive income for the year	

(c) Which one of the following would normally be classified as a cash flow arising from operating activities, according to IAS 7 *Statement of Cash Flows*? **(3 marks)**

Cash paid to a supplier	
Cash received from a share issue	
Cash paid to purchase property	
Cash received from the sale of an investment	

(d) The directors of Worcester Ltd consider that a machine with a carrying amount of £15,000 may have become impaired. At present it could be sold for £12,000 and disposal costs would be £400. The directors estimate that the machine will generate cash flows with a net present value of £11,500 over the remainder of its useful life.

What is the amount of the impairment loss that will be recognised in the statement of profit or loss, in accordance with IAS 36 *Impairment of Assets*? **(3 marks)**

£Nil	
£3,000	
£3,400	
£3,500	

(e) On 15 March 20X7, Yare Ltd received an order for goods with a sales value of £900,000. The customer paid a deposit of £90,000.

At 31 March 20X7 the goods had not yet been despatched.

According to IFRS 15 *Revenue from Contracts with Customers*, how should Yare Ltd report this transaction in its financial statements for the year ended 31 March 20X7? **(3 marks)**

Revenue £900,000; trade receivable £810,000	
Revenue £90,000; trade receivable £nil	
Revenue £nil; trade payable £90,000	
Revenue £90,000; trade payable £90,000; trade receivable £90,000	

Task 6 (30 marks)

The Managing Director of Harris plc has asked you to prepare the statement of financial position for the group. Harris plc has one subsidiary, Skye Ltd. The statements of financial position of the two companies as at 31 March 20X8 are set out below.

Statements of financial position as at 31 March 20X8

	Harris plc £000	Skye Ltd £000
ASSETS		
Non-current assets		
Property, plant and equipment	47,875	31,913
Investment in Skye Ltd	32,000	
	79,875	31,913
Current assets		
Inventories	25,954	4,555
Trade and other receivables	14,343	3,656
Cash and cash equivalents	1,956	47
	42,253	8,258
Total assets	122,128	40,171
EQUITY AND LIABILITIES		
Equity		
Share capital	57,000	15,000
Retained earnings	26,160	14,340
Total equity	83,160	29,340
Non-current liabilities		
Long-term loans	20,000	7,000
Current liabilities		
Trade and other payables	14,454	3,685
Tax liabilities	4,514	146
	18,968	3,831
Total liabilities	38,968	10,831
Total equity and liabilities	122,128	40,171

Further information:

- The share capital of Skye Ltd consists of ordinary shares of £1 each. Ownership of these shares carries voting rights in Skye Ltd.

- Harris plc acquired 9,000,000 shares in Skye Ltd on 1 April 20X7.

- At 1 April 20X7 the balance of retained earnings of Skye Ltd was £11,260,000.

- The directors of Harris plc have concluded that goodwill has been impaired by £4,000,000 during the year.

- Non-controlling interest is measured as the proportionate share of the fair value of Skye Ltd's net assets.

Draft a consolidated statement of financial position for Harris plc and its subsidiary as at 31 March 20X8. (30 marks)

Harris plc
Consolidated statement of financial position as at 31 March 20X8

	£000
ASSETS	
Non-current assets	
Intangible assets: goodwill	
Property, plant and equipment	
Current assets	
Inventories	
Trade and other receivables	
Cash and cash equivalents	
Total assets	

	£000
EQUITY AND LIABILITIES	
Equity	
Share capital	
Retained earnings	
Non-controlling interest	
Total equity	
Non-current liabilities	
Long-term loans	
Current liabilities	
Trade and other payables	
Tax liabilities	
Total liabilities	
Total equity and liabilities	

Workings

(Complete the left hand column by writing in the correct narrative from the list provided.)

Goodwill		£000

	▼	
	▼	
	▼	

Picklist:

Impairment
Consideration
Net assets acquired
Non-controlling interests at acquisition

Retained earnings	£000
▼	
▼	
▼	

Picklist:

Harris plc
Impairment
Skye Ltd – attributable to Harris plc

Non-controlling interest (NCI) at acquisition	£000
▼	
▼	

Picklist:

Current assets – attributable to NCI
Impairment
Non-current assets – attributable to NCI
Price paid
Retained earnings – attributable to NCI
Share capital – attributable to NCI

Non-controlling interest (NCI) at year end	£000
▼	
▼	

Picklist:

Current assets – attributable to NCI
Impairment
Non-current assets – attributable to NCI
Price paid
Retained earnings – attributable to NCI
Share capital – attributable to NCI

Task 7 (20 marks)

You have been asked to calculate ratios for Sienna Ltd in respect of its financial statements for the year ending 31 October 20X9 to assist your manager in his analysis of the company.

Sienna Ltd's statement of profit or loss and statement of financial position are set out below.

Sienna Ltd
Statement of profit or loss for the year ended 31 October 20X9

	£000
Continuing operations	
Revenue	37,384
Cost of sales	(21,458)
Gross profit	15,926
Distribution costs	(6,142)
Administrative expenses	(6,158)
Profit from operations	3,626
Finance costs	(639)
Profit before tax	2,987
Tax	(687)
Profit for the period from continuing operations	2,300

Sienna Ltd

Statement of financial position as at 31 October 20X9

	£000
ASSETS	
Non-current assets	
Property, plant and equipment	23,366
Current assets	
Inventories	4,461
Trade receivables	3,115
Cash and cash equivalents	213
	7,789
Total assets	31,155
EQUITY AND LIABILITIES	
Equity	
Share capital	3,000
Retained earnings	16,679
Total equity	19,679
Non-current liabilities	
Bank loans	8,000
Current liabilities	
Trade and other payables	2,789
Tax liabilities	687
	3,476
Total liabilities	11,476
Total equity and liabilities	31,155

459

(a) **State the formulae that are used to calculate each of the following ratios:** **(10 marks)**

(Write in the correct formula from the list provided)

(i)	Operating profit percentage	▼

Formulae:

Profit from operations/Revenue × 100

Profit from operations/Total assets × 100

Profit from operations/Total equity + Non-current liabilities × 100

Profit from operations/Finance costs × 100

(ii)	Return on shareholders' funds	▼

Formulae:

Profit after tax/Total equity × 100

Profit before tax/Total equity × 100

Profit from operations/Total equity × 100

Profit from operations/Total equity + Non-current liabilities × 100

(iii)	Quick (acid test) ratio	▼

Formulae:

Current assets/Current liabilities

Total assets – Inventories/Total liabilities

Total assets/Total liabilities

Current assets – Inventories/Current liabilities

(iv)	Inventory turnover	▼

Formulae:

Cost of sales/Inventories

Inventories/Cost of sales

Inventories/Revenue

Revenue/Inventories

BPP
LEARNING MEDIA

(v)	Interest cover		▼

Formulae:

Finance costs/Profit from operations

Finance costs/Revenue

Profit from operations/Finance costs

Revenue/Finance costs

(b) **Calculate the ratios to the nearest ONE DECIMAL PLACE.**

(10 marks)

(i)	Operating profit percentage		%
(ii)	Return on shareholders' funds		%
(iii)	Quick (acid test) ratio		:1
(iv)	Inventory turnover		times
(v)	Interest cover		times

Task 8 (23 marks)

Louise Michaels is a shareholder in Hoy Ltd. She wishes to assess the effectiveness of the management in using its resources. She has asked you to assist her by analysing the financial statements of the company, which are set out below.

Louise has obtained a report from the internet that gives the industry ratio averages for the sector in which Hoy Ltd operates.

She has emailed you and asked you to explain some of the points she is unsure about. A copy of the email is shown below

From: lm1000@warmmail.com

To: aatstudent@dfsexam

Date: 27 November 20X9

Subject: Accounting ratios

Hi

I found these sector ratios on the internet. This is the same sector as the company I have invested in. The profit figures are straightforward but I'm a bit lost about the rest. Can you help?

Many thanks

Louise

	Industry averages	Hoy Ltd
Gearing	65.00%	88.65%
Current ratio	1.6:1	1.9:1
Acid test ratio	0.9:1	0.7:1
Trade receivables collection period	33 days	25.6 days
Trade payables payment period	36 days	32.9 days

Prepare an email reply for Louise that includes:

(a)   Comments on whether the company has performed better or worse, based on the ratios calculated compared to the industry averages and what this tells you about the company.
                                                                    (20 marks)

(b)   Advice, with reasons, to Louise as to whether or not to continue with her investment.   (3 marks)

· ·

BPP PRACTICE ASSESSMENT 4
FINANCIAL STATEMENTS OF LIMITED COMPANIES

ANSWERS

Financial Statements of Limited Companies
BPP practice assessment 4

Task 1

(a)   Martin Ltd

Statement of profit or loss and other comprehensive income
For the year ended 31 October 20X9

	£000
Revenue	46,433
Cost of sales (W)	(32,282)
Gross profit	14,151
Distribution costs (W)	(2,516)
Administrative expenses (W)	(3,316)
Profit from operations	8,319
Finance costs (8% × 14,000)	(1,120)
Profit before tax	7,199
Tax	(980)
Profit for the period from continuing operations	6,219
Other comprehensive income	
Gain on revaluation (12,000 – 8,000)	4,000
Total comprehensive income for the year	10,219

Workings

Cost of sales	£000
Opening inventories	4,466
Purchases	32,553
Closing inventories (4,987 – 250)	(4,737)
	32,282

465

Distribution costs	£000
Distribution costs	2,450
Accruals	66
	2,516

Administrative expenses	£000
Administrative expenses	3,444
Prepayment (512 × 3/12)	(128)
	3,316

(b) **Martin Ltd**

Statement of changes in equity for the year ended 31 October 20X9

	Share capital £000	Revaluation reserve £000	Retained earnings £000	Total equity £000
Balance at 1 November 20X8	9,000		3,465	12,465
Changes in equity				
Total comprehensive income		4,000	6,219	10,219
Dividends			(930)	(930)
Balance at 31 October 20X9	9,000	4,000	8,754	21,754

Task 2

Martin Ltd

Statement of financial position as at 31 October 20X9

	£000
ASSETS	
Non-current assets	
Property, plant and equipment (W)	22,100
Current assets	
Inventories (4,987 – 250)	4,737
Trade and other receivables (W)	2,362
Cash and cash equivalents	9,654
	16,753
Total assets	38,853
EQUITY AND LIABILITIES	
Equity	
Share capital	9,000
Revaluation reserve	4,000
Retained earnings (W)	8,754
Total equity	21,754
Non-current liabilities	
Bank loan	14,000
Current liabilities	
Trade and other payables (W)	2,119
Tax liabilities	980
	3,099
Total liabilities	17,099
Total equity and liabilities	38,853

Workings

Property, plant and equipment	£000
Property, plant and equipment – Cost	39,880
Property, plant and equipment – Accumulated depreciation	(21,780)
Revaluation	4,000
	22,100

Trade and other receivables	£000
Trade and other receivables	2,234
Administrative expenses prepaid	128
	2,362

Retained earnings	£000
Retained earnings at 1 November 20X8	3,465
Total profit for the year	6,219
Dividends paid	(930)
	8,754

Trade and other payables	£000
Trade and other payables	1,347
Accruals: trial balance	146
Additional distribution costs accrual	66
Additional finance costs accrual	560
	2,119

Task 3

Note. Based on the information available at the time this book was written, we anticipate that this task would be human marked in the real assessment.

(a) The elements that appear in financial statements are:

- Assets
- Liabilities
- Equity
- Income
- Expenses

(b) Assets, liabilities and equity appear in the statement of financial position of a company. The *Conceptual Framework for Financial Reporting* defines them as follows:

Assets are resources controlled by an entity as a result of past events and from which future economic benefits are expected to flow to the entity.

Liabilities are present obligations of an entity arising from past events, the settlement of which is expected to result in an outflow from the entity of resources embodying economic benefits.

Equity is the residual interest in the assets of an entity after deducting all its liabilities.

....

Task 4

Note. Based on the information available at the time this book was written, we anticipate that this task would be human marked in the real assessment.

(a) The fundamental ethical principles of the AAT *Code of Professional Ethics* are:

Integrity
Objectivity
Professional competence and due care
Confidentiality
Professional behaviour

(b) (i) The ethical principle is professional behaviour.

This is simply unprofessional behaviour by your manager due to him not acting on a client's instructions and screening their calls to avoid them. You may consider reporting the matter to your in-house ethics committee, if there is one.

(ii) The ethical principle is integrity.

From a personal point of view this is a matter of integrity. Your clients are charged fees on the basis of the hours that you and other members of the firm work for them, so it is important that the recording of these hours is accurate. Therefore you are right to be concerned about not knowing the precise hours, and should ensure that this situation does not happen again.

(iii) The ethical principle is professional competence and due care.

This raises issues of professional competence and due care. You know that you do not have the knowledge to answer these questions at this time and in this situation. For your own professional safety, you should make the client clearly aware of this and not be prepared to give any opinion, as this may be relied upon by the client despite the circumstances. The most appropriate form of action would be to make an appointment with the client to discuss the matter properly after you have done some research into these specific areas, or refer them to a colleague with experience in this area.

Task 5

(a)

(i) only	
(ii) only	
Both (i) and (ii)	✓
Neither (i) nor (ii)	

(b)

Dividends paid	
Gain on revaluation of properties	✓
Issue of share capital	
Total comprehensive income for the year	

A gain on revaluation of properties is reported as a line item in other comprehensive income, but in the statement of changes in equity it forms part of total comprehensive income for the year.

(c)

Cash paid to a supplier	✓
Cash received from a share issue	
Cash paid to purchase property	
Cash received from the sale of an investment	

Cash received from a share issue is a cash flow from financing activities. Cash paid to purchase property and cash received from the sale of an investment are cash flows from investing activities.

(d)

£Nil	
£3,000	
£3,400	✓
£3,500	

Recoverable amount is fair value less costs of disposal of £11,600 (12,000 – 400) as this is higher than value in use of £11,500. The recoverable amount is lower than carrying amount so the impairment loss is £3,400 (15,000 – 11,600).

(e)

Revenue £900,000; trade receivable £810,000	
Revenue £90,000; trade receivable £nil	
Revenue £nil; trade payable £90,000	✓
Revenue £90,000; trade payable £90,000; trade receivable £90,000	

No revenue should be recognised according to IFRS 15 *Revenue from Contracts with Customers*, because Yare Ltd has not yet satisfied the performance obligation in the contract by delivering the goods to the buyer.

Task 6

Harris plc

Consolidated statement of financial position as at 31 March 20X8

	£000
ASSETS	
Non-current assets	
Intangible assets: goodwill (W)	12,244
Property, plant and equipment	79,788
	92,032
Current assets	
Inventories	30,509
Trade and other receivables	17,999
Cash and cash equivalents	2,003
	50,511
Total assets	142,543
EQUITY AND LIABILITIES	
Equity	
Share capital	57,000
Retained earnings (W)	24,008
	81,008
Non-controlling interest (W)	11,736
Total equity	92,744

	£000
Non-current liabilities	
Long-term loans	27,000
Current liabilities	
Trade and other payables	18,139
Tax liabilities	4,660
	22,799
Total liabilities	49,799
Total equity and liabilities	142,543

Workings

Note. Group structure

Harris plc owns 60% of Skye Ltd (9,000,000/15,000,000)

Goodwill	£000
Consideration	32,000
Non-controlling interest at acquisition	10,504
Net assets acquired (15,000 + 11,260)	(26,260)
Impairment	(4,000)
	12,244

Retained earnings	£000
Harris plc	26,160
Skye Ltd – attributable to Harris plc (60% × (14,340 – 11,260))	1,848
Impairment	(4,000)
	24,008

Non-controlling interest (NCI) at acquisition	£000
Share capital – attributable to NCI (40% × 15,000)	6,000
Retained earnings – attributable to NCI (40% × 11,260)	4,504
	10,504

Non-controlling interest (NCI) at year end	£000
Share capital – attributable to NCI (40% × 15,000)	6,000
Retained earnings – attributable to NCI (40% × 14,340)	5,736
	11,736

Task 7

(a) Formulae used to calculate the ratios

(i)	Operating profit percentage	$\dfrac{\text{Profit from operations}}{\text{Revenue}} \times 100\%$
(ii)	Return on shareholders' funds	$\dfrac{\text{Profit after tax}}{\text{Total equity}} \times 100\%$
(iii)	Quick (acid test) ratio	$\dfrac{\text{Current assets} - \text{inventories}}{\text{Current liabilities}}$
(iv)	Inventory turnover	$\dfrac{\text{Cost of sales}}{\text{Inventories}}$
(v)	Interest cover	$\dfrac{\text{Profit from operations}}{\text{Finance costs}}$

(b) Calculation of the ratios

(i)	Operating profit percentage	$\dfrac{3,626}{37,384} \times 100$	9.7	%
(ii)	Return on shareholders' funds	$\dfrac{2,300}{19,679} \times 100$	11.7	%
(iii)	Quick (acid test) ratio	$\dfrac{7,789 - 4,461}{3,476}$	0.96	:1

(iv)	Inventory turnover	$\dfrac{21,458}{4,461}$	4.8	times
(v)	Interest cover	$\dfrac{3,626}{639}$	5.7	times

Task 8

Note. Based on the information available at the time this book was written, we anticipate that this task would be human marked in the real assessment.

From: aatstudent@dfsexam

To: lm1000@warmmail.com

Date: 2 December 20X9

Subject: Comparison of accounting ratios of Hoy Ltd with industry averages

As requested, I have compared the accounting ratios computed from the financial statements of Hoy Ltd with the industry averages. I set out my comments below.

(a) Gearing

At 88.5%, Hoy Ltd's gearing ratio is considerably higher than the industry average. This shows that Hoy Ltd has a relatively high level of long-term borrowings or debt, which means that it is a riskier investment than most other companies in the industry.

Current ratio

The current ratio is better than the industry average. Hoy Ltd's current liabilities are covered almost twice by its current assets.

Acid test (quick) ratio

This is lower than the industry average; Hoy Ltd's current liabilities are greater than its trade receivables plus its cash. This means that Hoy Ltd is less likely to be able to meet its liabilities in the short term than most other companies in the industry sector. Because the current ratio is relatively high, Hoy Ltd must have a high level of inventories.

Trade receivables collection period

At 25.6 days, this is considerably better than the industry average and suggests that Hoy Ltd is more efficient at collecting its debts than most other companies in the industry. This means that more cash will be available to pay suppliers and lenders.

Trade payables payment period

Again, this is slightly lower than the industry average. This suggests that Hoy Ltd pays its suppliers relatively quickly, possibly more quickly than is necessary. This may be one of the reasons that the company has relatively few 'quick' assets.

(b) Conclusion

On the basis of these ratios, you should not continue to invest in this company. The low acid test ratio, together with the low trade payables payment period, suggest that the company is not managing its liquid resources particularly well. The high gearing ratio is a worrying sign. The company appears to be a risky investment and probably suffers a high level of interest. This means that fewer profits will be available for shareholders.

••